WHAT PEOPLE ARE SAYING ABOUT "DREAM SLEEPS"

"DREAM SLEEPS is filled with the kind of castle hotels that make for lifelong memories. Everyone from families to single travelers will find their ideal European wish fulfilled."

Dan Hallinan, owner of Travelling with Children travel agency, Berkeley, California

"Spending a night in a *real* castle was the highlight of my trip to Germany with my granddaughter."

Lydia Henricksen, Pacific Grove, California

"Reading DREAM SLEEPS from beginning to end gave me insight into the history of castles and palaces, and an understanding of their reincarnation as some of Europe's most unique accommodations. I plan to schedule several into my next European vacation."

Renate Pore, Charleston, West Virginia

"I can't wait to sleep in one of these castles — and wake up viewing the vast morning countryside like a queen of yore."

Connie Smith, Nevada City, California

"On past car trips through Europe, we have come across many lovely castles and villas that have been converted into hotels. We always wished we had known about them in advance, so we could have made reservations. DREAM SLEEPS is going to be very useful as we plan future trips."

Jeffrey Feiffer, Washington, D.C.

"I have been photographing castles in Europe for 20 years and highly recommend DREAM SLEEPS to anyone who wants to experience nostalgic Europe."

L. Douglas Franga, photographer for the desk calendar
Castles in Europe, Gern

Dream Sleeps

Castle & Palace Hotels of Europe

Dream Sleeps

Castle & Palace Hotels of Europe

by Pamela L. Barrus

CAROUSEL PRESS

Berkeley, California

Published by: **CAROUSEL PRESS**   P.O. Box 6038 • Berkeley, CA 94706-0038 • 510.527.5849
www.carousel-press.com • info@carousel-press.com

Distributed to the book trade by Publishers Group West

Editor: Carole Terwilliger Meyers
Cover, interior, maps: Poulson/Gluck Design
Photographs: All front and back cover photos and all interior photos provided by the respective hotel
or its representative, with the exception of those by Pamela L. Barrus that appear on pages 11, 17, 25,
38, 40, 41, 45, 47, 51, 53, 61, 63, 65, 67, 69, 85, 93, 95, 103, 109, 111, 135, 157, 159, 169, 179, 187, 209,
211, 222, 227, 229, 231, 233, 235, 237, 243, 249, 255, 259, 263, 273, 274, 277, 278, 283; and those by
Carole Terwilliger Meyers that appear on pages 127, 150, 151, 217, 251. Front cover depicts Burg Hotel-
Restaurant auf Schönburg in Germany. Back cover: top, depicts Burg Hotel-Restaurant auf Schönburg
in Germany; second from top, depicts Hotel Danieli in Italy; third from top, depicts Pousada do Castelo
in Portugal; author photo by Gregory Coleman (taken at Parador de Cardona in Spain).
Researchers: Carole Terwilliger Meyers; Debbie Murray
Printer: Data Reproductions

Library of Congress Cataloging-in-Publication Data
    Barrus, Pamela L.
        Dream sleeps : castle & palace hotels of Europe / by Pamela L.
    Barrus.
            p.   cm.
        Includes bibliographical references and index.
        ISBN 0-917120-16-7
        1. Hotels—Europe—Guidebooks.   2. Castles—Europe—Guidebooks.
    3. Palaces—Europe—Guidebooks.   4. Europe—Guidebooks.   I. Title.
    TX907.5.E85B37   1998
    647.944'01—dc21   97-43138
                                                                        CIP

The information in this book was correct at press time. The author and publisher disclaim any liability
due to changes, errors, or omissions and cannot be held responsible for the experiences of readers while
traveling. Specific prices are gathered in the year before publication and are mentioned only to provide
an approximate idea of what to expect; telephone numbers are included so that the reader can call for
current rates. All establishments listed in this book are mentioned to alert the reader to their existence;
they are endorsed by neither the author nor publisher. No business has paid to be included.

Reader Feedback: Please let us know if any place listed in this book doesn't live up to your expecta-
tions. The author will look into the situation on your behalf and adjust any misinformation in the next
edition of *Dream Sleeps: Castle & Palace Hotels of Europe*. Please also alert us to any exciting discoveries.

Special Sales: Bulk purchases of Carousel Press titles are available to corporations at special discounts.
Custom editions can be produced to use as premiums and promotional items. For more information,
call 510-527-5849.

Manufactured in the United States of America
Second Edition
10 9 8 7 6 5 4 3 2

 Printed on recycled paper (20% post-consumer content)

For my mother

CONTENTS

Acknowledgments

It is impossible to write a book without a lot of help and support.

I would like to thank Elvi Taveras of Virgin Atlantic Airways for the superb service I received to and from the U.K. while I was updating the sections on Great Britain and Ireland.

The proprietors of the castle and palace hotels and their U.S. representatives have been more than generous with their time in answering my endless, picky questions, and with their resources in supplying me with some superb photos for this edition. Special thanks to Pilar Vico of Marketing Ahead, Jackie Gurney and Joan Rylett of the Landmark Trust, Joanne Joham of Schlosshotels, Brenda Homick of Relais & Châteaux, and Ylka Van Bemmel of Small Leading Hotels of the World.

James Coleman, computer genius, saved me months of tedious labor and brought me out of the dark ages of my Smith-Corona.

Encouragement and support honors go to Gregory Coleman, Evelyn Robinson, Mary Barrus, Mort Barrus, Nick Kondrats, Gwyneth Burt, and Alida Van Gores.

And many thanks to Carole Terwilliger Meyers of Carousel Press, who loves castles as much as I do.

Introduction

The genesis of *Dream Sleeps* occurred in the early 1980s, when I was traveling in India during the searing-hot pre-monsoon month of May. I stopped then at the Rambagh Palace Hotel, in Jaipur, where I heard about the Maharani Suite and its bathroom equipped with a marble pedestal from which thirteen shower heads positioned on four walls spray water all at once. Alas, I never actually got into the Maharani Suite. The richest man in India, I was told, had been staying in it for two weeks and had no intention of leaving. The experience, however, left me fascinated with palaces, and castles, that offer lodging.

Ten years have passed since I wrote the first edition of this book. After sorting through a large box I had filled diligently with saved clippings and notes about castle and palace hotels, I realized that this new edition was going to need as much renovation as a castle in ruins. Some castle hotels listed in the first edition have lowered the portcullis[1] and raised the drawbridge as a result of floods, new uses for the property, and even old age—on the part of the proprietors that is. Happily, new properties have opened to take their place.

The biggest changes in the castle hotel scene have occurred in the British Isles. More and more castles are opening their doors to guests. Those of you who believe passionately in the preservation of historic buildings will delight in the Landmark Trust—a charity devoted to giving new life to hundreds of special properties by renting them out as self-catering houses.

Lodging is one of the major expenses on any trip. With a little pre-planning, it can also be one of the highlights. When you return home from your European vacation and are asked "Where did you stay?", wouldn't you like to reply that your home away from home was a five-hundred-year-old castle or an historic royal palace?

This book is written so you can experience more on your vacation than the standard hotel room, where you return only to sleep. The romance of sleeping in Mary Queen of Scots' bedchamber or King Henry VIII's palace is undeniable. The kings and queens might be forgotten, and the cannon and catapults might have been moved to museums, but their legacy remains for us to enjoy.

Depending on your plans, the castle and palace hotels in this guide can be regarded in two ways. The hotel can be an end in itself, with your vacation revolving around the hotel, its facilities, and the surrounding area. Or, if you're touring a specific area, the hotel can provide historical atmosphere and enrich your experience.

[1] *For definitions of castle terms, please refer to the glossary.*

Among the castles and palaces in this book is something to suit everyone. If you want to be treated as visiting royalty—demanding perfect climate control, high-tech computer check-in service, and state-of-the-art plumbing—you will find the perfect hotel here. If you thrive instead on faded glory, you, too, will find plenty of suitable sleeping spots. Some hotels are modern throughout, while others have scarcely changed in centuries. Most fall somewhere in between.

You do need to bring with you an open mind and a spirit of adventure. Even when enormous renovations have updated the structures, you still might find the occasional chair that needs reupholstering or a room with tiny windows. That's part of the charm. Fortunately, decent bathrooms and central heating have become common.

There are many more outstanding castle and palace hotels deserving of a place in this book. For now, to alert you to their existence even though I have not yet been able to visit them, they are listed at the end of each chapter under "More Hotels." I hope to personally visit each so that I can include more detailed descriptions in a future edition of *Dream Sleeps*.

I have intentionally left out those hotels where management seemed indifferent or wouldn't allow me through the door to tour the premises, or where the family dogs wouldn't let me out of the car. I excluded as well those hotels that were impossible to find and those that reminded me a little *too much* of *The Rocky Horror Picture Show*.

From among the hundreds of castle and palace hotels in Europe, I chose the ones in this guide because:

- they are authentic, with interesting histories.

- they are in scenic or interesting locales within reasonable access by public transportation or rental car. (Many of the hotels are not near big cities, but instead are in areas with spectacular scenery and incredibly hospitable and friendly people. Though I visited most of these hotels using public transportation, many are much easier to reach with a car. Often it is convenient to leave your car at the hotel and take a train for excursions into nearby cities.)

- they are comfortable, clean, and friendly.

- they serve good food. (Almost every hotel in this guide has its own restaurant where you can be assured of well-prepared meals, usually with continental and regional specialties. Should you be unable to actually spend the night due to budget or time constraints, consider stopping in just for a meal. Always call ahead to confirm times and to make reservations, and note that some dining rooms are open for hotel guests only. Note, too, that some hotels host medieval banquets—usually a group dinner with hearty food and lusty entertainment.)

- they are well established and not likely to go out of business soon.
- they are fun. (You can sleep in antique canopy beds, explore secret passageways, view the countryside through arrow-slit windows, and even linger in haunted rooms and towers.)

The owners and managers of these hotels cannot be praised too highly. The pride they take in their castle or palace is evident in the attention they give to details and the effort they make to ensure that their guests have a good time. Many owners are descendants of families that have lived in the building for centuries and tell delightful stories about the hotel's history. In most cases they have inherited the property and wish to do something practical with it. Some owners have fallen in love with their castle or palace, purchased it, and spent small fortunes renovating and rebuilding. Others have opened their doors to guests as a way of fighting rising costs and taxes. Fortunately for us, they have not chosen to torch the family home to avoid paying "roof taxes" imposed by the government.

MAKING A RESERVATION

Once upon a time you could just walk into a castle or palace hotel and ask for a room. Those days are now history. Many of the hotels listed here are booked up to a year in advance, essentially wrecking any chance for spontaneity. If you're traveling at the height of the summer season, you absolutely must have a reservation. In spring and fall bookings are generally lighter, but if your heart is set on a particular place, you need to reserve as early as possible.

To make a reservation, you can:

FAX This is the most convenient option given time zone differences.

TELEPHONE This will, of course, give you the most immediate answer and is the best choice if you speak the language.

SEND A LETTER This is the least efficient option.

BOOK THROUGH THE U.S. REPRESENTATIVE (Agency telephone numbers are listed in the appendix.) This convenient option sometimes costs more than if you contact the hotel yourself.

CONTACT YOUR TRAVEL AGENT This saves you time, and your travel agent can arrange the rest of your trip, too.

Whichever method you choose, be prepared with a first and second choice of date. To avoid disappointment, specify the type of room you want. If you want a view and/or a room in the historic part of the castle, say so. I think it is well worth the additional expenditure to stay in a special room. Who wants to travel thousands of miles only to stay in an annex across the garden with just a glimpse of the castle? (Beware. Although the rooms can be lovely, this type of annex room is sometimes referred to as a "castle view" room.)

RATES

Inexpensive	$75 or less
Moderate	$75 to $150
Expensive	$150 to $250
Very Expensive	$250 and above

Because exchange rates and inflation change rapidly and regularly, it would be impossible here to list specific prices for rooms. Also, rates often depend on the season, the view, and the plumbing. However, the rates remain fixed relative to one other. For example, an inexpensive hotel always costs less than a moderate one.

Rates listed are for the lowest-priced double occupancy room. Expect to pay more during the summer high season and on holidays. An unfortunate universal rule is that a double room is always cheaper per person for two people traveling together than it is for a single person traveling alone.

Unless otherwise indicated, all hotels in this guide accept major credit cards. However, it is always wise to inquire about a hotel's policy before checking in, since this policy can change without notice.

CHILDREN

With a few indicated exceptions, hotels in this guide welcome children. You know your own child. If a castle is described as "elegant and full of antiques," and your child is jet-propelled, you might be happier in a place that is "fun to explore," or one offering plenty of on-site recreation.

Children younger than age two are almost always allowed free accommodations. Discounts for children older than two usually depend on sharing with two adults. Children's discounts are noted wherever possible; otherwise inquire at the time of booking, since the time of year and type of room available are factors. In addition, since the price of meals can be high, ask if a children's menu is offered or if plate sharing is acceptable.

With advance notice, many hotels will arrange for a baby-sitter. In Great Britain and Ireland you might come across the term "baby-listening." This is an intercom service that uses the room telephone to alert the front office when your baby awakens.

Facilities For The Disabled

European ideas of what constitutes facilities for the disabled do not conform with American standards. Keep in mind that the nature of a castle's architecture—winding stairways in turrets, narrow halls and doorways—makes access difficult. Many hotels now have elevators, but ramps are rare. If you have special needs, inquire when booking.

On the Origin of Castles and Palaces

When the great English jurist Sir Edward Coke declared back in 1623 that "a man's house is his castle," he couldn't have known what a home in a castle was actually like. By that time, castles were already useless relics left to deteriorate throughout the European countryside.

No one living knows for sure what life was really like in a castle. Poetry and fairy tales have created romantic images of valiant knights who rescue beautiful young maidens from dragons and then live happily ever after in elegant clothes and surroundings while dining at great feasts.

It's a lot of fun to think of castles in this way, but in reality they were built for military purposes: for defense, to store arms, to house troops, and to protect a strategic geographical position. Never designed for comfort, they were dark, confined, and unsanitary, especially during times of siege. (One castle in England was surrendered during a siege in 1088 because the stench inside became overpowering.) Usually the owners preferred living in nearby halls built of wood or stone, with plenty of doors for ventilation (windows weren't happening yet).

Medieval kings seldom had their own castles to live in. Instead, they traveled constantly through the country, squashing rebellions or presiding over courts while staying in whatever castle or hall was available. All costs of feeding such a retinue were borne by the host.

Life in these early days was lawless and brutal, as described in the *Anglo-Saxon Chronicles,* one of our first English-language histories of medieval times. In England during one war in 1137, a monk wrote:

> Every powerful man made his castles and held them against the King [Stephen]. They burdened the unhappy people of the country with forced labor on the castles. And when the castles were made, they filled them with devils and evil men and women, and put them to prison for their gold and silver, and tortured them with unspeakable tortures. And it lasted the nineteen winters while Stephen was King; and ever it was worse.

If a man undertook military service, he would be given protection or land. The better he was at riding a horse, the more potentially successful he could be. Of course, only the very wealthy could afford their own horses or hire cavalrymen. These knights attained a privileged status and followed a code of chivalry and brotherhood among themselves—but certainly not toward men of lesser birth or their enemies during the Crusades.

The castles fell because the nature of warfare changed with improved siege techniques brought back from the Crusades. Kings grew more powerful and governments became more centralized. Industry and trade in growing towns drew attention away from warfare, and knights were replaced by mercenary soldiers. Each country also had its own reasons for the decline of its castles, whether it was the Hundred Years' War, the Thirty Years' War, or Oliver Cromwell.

When comfort became more important than defense, medieval life came to an end, and the castles were eventually abandoned. As the nobility became increasingly civilized and stylish, they built huge and fashionable manor houses, often resembling the ancient castles with towers and crenellation. While castles had strictly a defensive function, the palaces that replaced them were royal residences designed to reflect the architectural fashion of the time.

The word "palace" comes from the Latin *palatium,* meaning the hill on which the Roman emperors built their residences. From the time of the Renaissance, every nobleman in Italy built his own private *palazzo,* and the idea soon spread throughout Europe. Architects went to Italy to learn their craft and returned to their own countries with new ideas. Conspicuous consumption became popular as royalty built bigger and more luxurious homes. The beautiful Renaissance *châteaux* in the Loire Valley began as hunting lodges, and the Baroque palace of Versailles became the ultimate model of splendid living.

The kings and knights of long ago and the nobility who followed would be envious of the comfort, warmth, and hospitality of today's castle hotels. Dungeons are now lounges or bars, and great halls have been converted into dining rooms where chefs prepare elegant cuisine for their guests. Mighty towers that once witnessed sword fights and heroic defenses now house comfortable rooms where guests can dream peacefully of long-ago times.

I invite you to indulge your adventurous soul and get the royal treatment at one of these magnificent castle or palace hotels, which successfully combine the glory of yesteryear with the creature comforts of today.

Austria

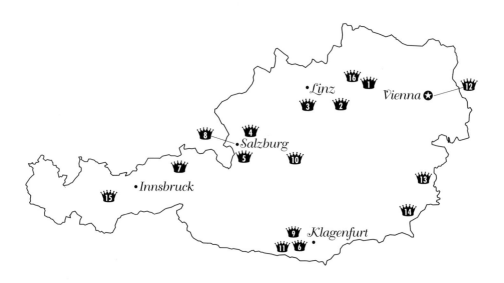

Austria was once the heart of the great Habsburg empire, which lasted for more than six hundred and forty years. Patrons of art and music and lovers of gracious living, the Habsburgs set the style for the beautiful buildings, parks, and art treasures seen in Austria today. After the final rout of the Turks in the seventeenth century, the Austrian nobles began building palaces and mansions in an Italian Baroque style that was soon modified into a national style. Many of the palace hotels described here date from that time and remain remarkably unchanged. Wealthy noblemen then often owned hunting lodges, which their descendants sometimes operate today as hotels.

The castle and palace hotels in Austria range from luxurious to simple. Some are run by a prince or baroness; others are run by warm and friendly families whose great-grandfathers bought the properties only a hundred or so years ago. In the few hotels where things have become frayed and worn, they still are spotlessly clean and comfortable.

Almost every hotel listed includes breakfast in the price of the room. Without question, an Austrian breakfast is the best on the Continent. Usually served buffet-style, it offers everything from meats, cheeses, eggs, juices, and fruits, to cereals and breads. Most hotels also offer a half-pension plan at considerable savings. If you're economy-minded, this plan allows you to eat well at breakfast, skip lunch, and return for a hearty dinner.

Even though Austria is a small country, it is impossible to see everything in one trip. The Austrian provinces differ greatly from one another, and each is worthy of exploration. Try visiting one province at a time. Pick a central location, and make day trips out.

Public transportation in Austria is excellent, with convenient and efficient trains or buses reaching even the remotest areas. All of the castle and palace hotels listed can be reached by public transportation.

As you travel in this lovely country you'll often hear the word *Gemütlichkeit*, which means a combination of charm, hospitality, and a smiling welcome—promising you a wonderful experience.

For further information on Austria, contact the Austrian National Tourist Office at: P.O. Box 1142, New York, New York 10108-1142, Tel 212-944-6880, Fax 212-730-4568; or P. O. Box 491938, Los Angeles, California 90049, Tel 310-477-3332, Fax 310-477-5141. Or visit their website at: www.austria-info.at/.

Hotel Schloss Dürnstein

A Seventeenth-Century Palace

One of the loveliest spots along the Danube River is the Wachau region, with its little town of Dürnstein. Here the steep drop of forested hills, vineyards, and charming villages nestling under ancient castles combine to create a special ambiance. To make your arrival especially memorable, travel here on one of the paddle-wheel steamers that dock directly in front of the Hotel Schloss Dürnstein.

THE PAST 🌀 The town's most illustrious—and reluctant—visitor was Richard the Lion-Hearted of England, who was held captive in the castle above the town from 1192 to 1193. It seems that during the Third Crusade, Richard and Leopold, the duke of Austria, had a terrible quarrel in the Holy Land: Leopold had captured a Muslim fort and raised his flag above it. When Richard came along, he took down the Austrian flag and raised his own. On his return voyage to England a storm destroyed Richard's boat, obliging him to travel overland through Leopold's territory. Legend has it that one night he met a man who was roasting some meat on a spit. Casting precautions aside, Richard asked if he could share the meal if he helped with the preparations. Some fat dripping from the meat flared the fire and the cook recognized his dinner companion, for he, too, had been on the Third Crusade. A bounty had been placed on Richard's head, and he was soon arrested. The English had no idea where he was being held until Richard's loyal friend, the troubadour Blondel de Nesle, began visiting castles throughout Germany and Austria, singing Richard's favorite song at nightfall in the hope of a response. At Dürnstein his song was answered, but it was nearly a year before the ransom could be raised and delivered.

Just down the hill from this historic castle, which is now a ruin, is the Renaissance-era schloss of Dürnstein. Built in 1630, it belonged for centuries to the counts of Starhemberg—one of the oldest families in Austria. In 1683 the Emperor Leopold I stayed here while the Turks were besieging Vienna. The Thiery family took over the castle nearly fifty years ago and continue to run it today.

THE PRESENT 🌀 Schloss Dürnstein is now a lovely hotel, richly furnished throughout with antiques, chandeliers, and fine art. White and green ceramic

stoves, parquet floors topped with Oriental carpets, and vaulted ceilings create an elegant atmosphere. Most guest rooms are furnished with antiques; the Princes Room and Baroque Room are exceptional.

You'll find the outside terrace an idyllic spot for lounging with a glass of local Wachau wine while gazing at the scenery. Dinner is a special event enjoyed in an intimate dining room with white vaulted ceilings, red velvet chairs, and decorations of crossed swords on the walls.

Roses and ivy-covered walls surround the secluded swimming pool. Should you wish to take a walk along the Danube, a tunnel leads down to the river.

A-3601 Dürnstein, Wachau. **Tel:** 011-43-2711-212. **Fax:** 011-43-2711-351. **Rooms:** 38, including 3 suites; all with bath. **Rates:** Very expensive; doubles from AS2500; includes breakfast, lunch or dinner, service, and tax. **Dates closed:** November 10 through March 25. **Dining facilities:** Restaurant; outside terrace; bar. **Children:** Age 5 and younger sharing with parents free. **Facilities for disabled:** None. **On-site recreation:** Outdoor and indoor swimming pools; sauna; fitness club. **Nearby diversions:** Hiking; cycling; tennis; golf; boat rides along the Danube; rock climbing. **Proprietors:** Johann and Rosemarie Thiery. **Operated as a hotel since:** 1937. **U.S. representative:** Schlosshotels; Relais & Châteaux; Euro-Connection.

Directions: Dürnstein is on the Danube River about a 1-hour drive northwest of Vienna. You can also reach the town by taking a train from Vienna's Franz Josef railroad station to Krems. Just outside the station is a bus that can take you the 5 kilometers west to Dürnstein; the hotel also provides a transfer service.

Schloss Ernegg

A Sixteenth-Century Castle

For over three hundred years the counts of Auersperg have lived in this romantic castle tucked away in the woods of the Alpine foothills. The charming and gracious proprietor, Countess Hilda Auersperg, and her daughter, Alexandra, carry on the family tradition. The countess refers to her large castle—which is in reality a manorial mansion with many castle-like features—not as a hotel, but rather as a private home with paying guests. Staying here provides you a glimpse into the traditional lifestyle of an Austrian country lord.

THE PAST The first documents on this property date back to 979, when Otto II gave the land to the bishop Wolfgang of Regensburg, who built a fortress called Ehrnegg or Ernekke in defense against the Turks. Succeeding bishops rented the property to different noblemen.

Most of the castle we see today dates from 1524, when Wolfgang von Oedt, a cupbearer (literally a man who bears the drinking cups) to Emperor Ferdinand I, bought and restored it. You can still see his family crest over the entrance to the courtyard tower. In 1656 Ferdinand's son sold the prop-

erty to Sigmund Erasmus, the first Auersperg, who then came to live at the castle. The Auersperg family crest is found over the front porch. Erasmus restored the chapel in 1675. A plaque bearing his name is found at the back of the altar.

THE PRESENT This warm, intimate castle is built in an unusual trapezoidal shape with a lovely, three-story arcaded inner courtyard. Each story rests on a series of granite columns, and the walls are painted white with a deep salmon trim. Potted plants and flowers line the corridors.

Public rooms display a fine collection of antiques, white tile ceramic stoves, and oil paintings. The large guest rooms are individually furnished and bear names such as *Roserlzimmer* (the Rose Room), *Waffenkammer* (the Arms Chamber), and *Anastasius-Gruen-Zimmer* (from the pseudonym of

Anton Auersperg—an ancestor and well-known author in Austria and Germany).

The dining room, decorated in a hunting motif, features both excellent cuisine enhanced by produce from the castle's own garden and a wine cellar with a wide selection of vintages. In good weather, you may eat outside on the terrace. The vaulted-ceilinged bar is warmed by an open fire in the evening.

A-3261 Steinakirchen am Forst, Niederösterreich. Tel: 011-43-7488-214. Fax: 011-43-7488-6771. Rooms: 21; most with bath. **Rates:** Moderate; doubles from AS1300; includes breakfast, service, and tax. The hotel does not encourage credit cards. **Dates closed:** October 1 through April 30. **Dining facilities:** Restaurant and outdoor terrace for hotel guests only. **Children:** Under age 1 free; age 1 through 5 sharing with parents AS190; age 6 through 12 sharing with parents AS290. The hotel's larger guest rooms are well-suited for children, and there is a special playroom and sandpit. **Facilities for disabled:** None. **On-site recreation:** 9- and 18-hole golf courses with special golf programs; deer stalking accompanied by the castle's game keeper; trout fishing; horseback riding. **Nearby diversions:** Tennis; swimming; bicycle tours; country walks; narrow gauge railway. **Proprietor:** Countess Hilda Maria Auersperg. **Operated as a hotel since:** 1967. **U.S. representative:** None.

Directions: Ernegg is 126 kilometers west of Vienna. From the Vienna-Salzburg autobahn, take the Ybbs exit south through Wieselburg and continue on to Steinakirchen. With prior arrangement, you can be met at the Amstetten train station.

Schloss Feyregg

A Seventeenth-Century Palace

Often overlooked by foreign tourists, Upper Austria is noted for its spas, abbeys, and beautiful scenery. Bad Hall is famous for its iodine brine springs—the most powerful in central Europe. Its eighty-nine acres of thermal park are in a lovely area lined with trees, lawns, and flowers.

If you want to combine the experience of natural spa treatments with a stay at a palace hotel, Schloss Feyregg, near Bad Hall, is the answer.

THE PAST 🐚 Located just one kilometer from the town of Bad Hall, Schloss Feyregg was once the summer residence of the abbots of the monastery of Stift Spital am Phyrn. The palace actually dates back to the

Middle Ages, but extensive renovations by the Baroque architect Johann Michael Prunner obliterated most traces of its origins.

THE PRESENT 🐚 This attractive Baroque palace provides privacy and quiet. Most of the furnishings are genuine antiques as old as the house itself. Vaulted ceilings suggest the building's early origins. Elegant and spacious guest rooms are done in either period or modern furnishings.

A-4540 Bad Hall, Oberösterreich. Tel: 011-43-7258-2591. Fax: None. **Rooms:** 11, including 5 singles and 6 doubles; all with bath. **Rates:** Expensive; doubles from AS1800; includes breakfast, service, and tax. **Dates closed:** Open all year. **Dining facilities:** None. **Children:** No discounts. **Facilities for disabled:** None. **On-site recreation:** None. **Nearby diversions:** Spa town of Bad Hall; swimming pool; golf; hiking; cycling. **Proprietor:** Ruth Maria Harmer. **Operated as a hotel since:** 1969. **U.S. representative:** Schlosshotels.

Directions: Bad Hall is about 30 kilometers south of Linz along route 122. It is connected by train to Linz and Salzburg.

Hotel Schloss Fuschl

A Fifteenth-Century Castle

Many of the lake resorts outside Salzburg are overrun by tourists during the summer and on weekends. But even though the lake of Fuschl lies closer to Salzburg than does the lake of Saint Wolfgang, it doesn't seem to attract as many people.

Lake Fuschl is surrounded by woodland, some sections of which are a protected nature reserve. Hotel Schloss Fuschl sits in a magnificent locale with a romantic and lovely view across the deep-blue water to forest-covered hillsides and snowcapped mountains.

THE PAST 🐏 The archbishops of Salzburg built this castle as a hunting lodge in 1450. For centuries aristocratic society came here for special hunting parties and festivals. During the secularization program of the Habsburgs, the estate was turned over to the government of Austria. Under

Franz Josef, society flocked to the nearby resort of Bad Ischl. In the nineteenth century Schloss Fuschl was auctioned, leased, and, for the first time, placed in private hands.

In 1938 Hitler came and set up headquarters at Salzburg's Klessheim Palace. The Nazis seized Schloss Fuschl, and von Ribbentrop took up residence there, hosting frequent visits from Mussolini. After the war ended, the Americans arrived. A rumor circulating at the time claimed that one hundred crates of gold were hidden in the lake. Though special instruments have combed the lake bottom, nothing has ever been found.

The castle went through several more owners, and in 1977 Dr. Max Grundig Stiftung purchased it, enlarging and modernizing the building for today's guests.

Schloss Fuschl has hosted such luminaries as Eleanor Roosevelt, Randolph Hearst, Jawaharlal Nehru, and Nikita Khrushchev.

THE PRESENT 🐚 The main section of the castle is a very simple square building without much fuss or decoration, but the interior is stunning, with vaulted ceilings, an enormous fireplace, fine tapestries, Oriental carpets, and antique furniture.

Guest rooms are individually decorated, and all have views of the lake. The antique-filled suites located in the castle are definitely worth the splurge.

A path leads down through the trees to the lakefront where you may swim and sun. Alternatively, a swimming pool dedicated to Diana, the mythical goddess of hunting, is found in the castle's cellar under an impressive plaster vaulted ceiling.

Because the cuisine of this hotel is famed throughout Austria, reservations for meals are always a must. The dining rooms are lovely, decorated with antiques and paintings and offering fine views of the lake.

A-5322 Hof bei Salzburg. Tel: 011-43-6229-22530. Fax: 011-43-6229-2253-531.   **Rooms:** 84, including 29 suites; located in the castle, in lakefront bungalows, and in a hunting lodge; all with bath. **Rates:** Very expensive; doubles from AS2600; includes breakfast, service, and tax. **Dates closed:** Open all year. **Dining facilities:** 3 restaurants (jacket and tie required for dinner); covered terrace; bar. **Children:** Age 9 and younger sharing with parents free, with breakfast surcharge of AS240; age 10 and older AS490, includes breakfast. The lakefront bungalows are popular with families. **Facilities for disabled:** None. **On-site recreation:** Indoor swimming pool; spa; tennis; sailing; fishing; 9-hole golf course. **Nearby diversions:** Alpine and cross-country skiing; horseback riding; 18-hole golf course; Salzburg; Berchtesgaden. **General Manager:** Stefan Lauda. **Operated as a hotel since:** 1948. **U.S. representative:** Leading Hotels of the World.

Directions: Fuschl is about 20 kilometers east of Salzburg on route 158. Transfer by hotel limousine is available. A public bus service runs between Fuschl and Salzburg.

Schloss Haunsperg

A Fourteenth-Century Castle

An alternative to staying in Salzburg is to lodge a short distance south of the city in the little village of Oberalm. The neighboring town of Hallein was once the prize of the archbishops and is now one of Salzburg's major tourist attractions. The Dürrnberg Salt Mines offer popular tours through the underground salt chambers and toboggan rides on logs downhill into the mines.

Oberalm is an especially good place to stay if you're traveling by car: The highway passes right by, and you're in a good location for excursions to Berchtesgaden and the mountains.

THE PAST Though it was built around 1320, historians disagree on Haunsperg's exact origins. One theory suggests that a watchtower existed on the site since Roman times, while another proposes the Romanesque style of the castle's chapel dates from the Middle Ages.

THE PRESENT 🌼 The outside building and towers are covered with gray and pink stucco with white trim and a gray roof. An ornate gilt Baroque chapel is attached to the castle; a plaster ceiling and wrought-iron gate separate the inner chapel and vestibule. Services are often held here.

The rooms and vaulted corridors of the delightful castle are treasure-troves of antiques and fine paintings. Fine carpets adorn the parquet and tile floors, and chandeliers hang from above.

A charming music room resembles a fine salon in a private home. Famous musicians such as Pierre Boulez and Bruno Walter have played its Bösendorfer grand piano. Carrying out the musical tradition at Haunsperg, the proprietor's great-grandfather wrote the words to the unofficial Austrian anthem—"The Blue Danube."

Fine paintings, carved antique armoires, and settees furnish the six spacious guest rooms.

Schloss Haunsperg has been in the von Gernerth family for more than a century. Mrs. Erika von Gernerth welcomes guests to her home with warmth and graciousness. If you need help in making dinner reservations or finding tickets to various events in Salzburg, she can help. Drinks and snacks are served on request, but the hotel has no restaurant.

A-5411 Oberalm bei Hallein. Tel: 011-43-6245-80-6-62. Fax: 011-43-6245-85-6-80. **Rooms:** 6; all with bath or shower. **Rates:** Expensive; doubles from AS1700; includes breakfast, service, and tax. **Dates closed:** Open all year. **Dining facilities**: None. **Children:** Age 11 and younger sharing with parents 20 percent discount; baby-sitting. **Facilities for disabled:** None. **On-site recreation:** Tennis. **Nearby diversions:** Swimming pool; fishing; horseback riding; Dürrnberg Salt Mines; Berchtesgaden. **Proprietors:** von Gernerth family. **Operated as a hotel since:** 1969. **U.S. representative:** Schlosshotels.

Directions: Oberalm is just south of Salzburg. From the E-14 autobahn, exit at Hallein.

Hotel Schloss Leonstain

A FIFTEENTH-CENTURY CASTLE

Among the popular summer resort destinations in Carinthia is the Wörthersee, a lake with temperatures reaching as high as eighty degrees in summer. Situated on a small peninsula, Pörtschach—with its long, flower-decorated promenade, hillside villas, and fine hotels—is one of the nicest of the delightful villages dotting the shoreline.

THE PAST 🥨 Pörtschach's Hotel Schloss Leonstain has stood on its present site only since the fifteenth century. When the secretary of the duke of Carinthia felt that he could no longer comfortably live in Leonstain Castle (its ruins can be seen nearby), he built a small château with an adjacent farmhouse. Ownership changed over the years, with the Jesuits taking possession in 1645. Emperor Joseph II later confiscated all Jesuit property, and in the nineteenth century the Crown passed Leonstain over to the Benedictines.

The most famous guest at the castle was Johannes Brahms, who was inspired to write the Symphony in D-flat, the Concerto for Violin, and the Sonata in G-flat during the summers of 1877 and 1878.

The family of the present owner, Aldo Neuscheller, purchased Leonstain around the beginning of the century and modernized it.

THE PRESENT 🐚 Although Leonstain is a modern hotel, many medieval touches remain, including vaulted or wood-beamed ceilings, stonework, and fireplaces. The restaurant has a fine reputation; you may dine either by candlelight in the dining room or outside in the courtyard. In the summer weekly chamber music concerts are held in the courtyard.

The exceptionally lovely grounds feature walkways surrounded by flower gardens, large trees, and lawns. The hotel sits across the street from the lake, and lounge chairs and boats are available at the hotel's private waterside park. Water sports, tennis, and health treatments are popular here.

A-9210 Pörtschach, Kärnten. Tel: 011-43-4272-28-16-0. Fax: 011-43-4372-28-23. **Rooms:** 33; all with bath. **Rates:** Expensive; doubles from AS1920; includes breakfast, service, and tax. **Dates closed:** October through April. **Dining facilities:** Restaurant; outside terrace; café; bar. **Children:** Discount offered for age 12 and younger sharing with parents; children's menu; playground; baby-sitting. **Facilities for disabled:** None. **On-site recreation:** Tennis; boating; swimming pool; sauna. **Nearby diversions:** Horseback riding; golf; hiking. **Proprietor:** Christoph Neuscheller. **Operated as a hotel since:** 1950. **U.S. representative:** Schlosshotels; Euro-Connection.

Directions: Pörtschach is on the north side of the Wörthersee along route 83. It has a train station. The hotel is on the main highway.

Schloss Matzen

A TWELFTH-CENTURY CASTLE

It's not every day an American inherits a real castle. But Christopher Kump and his wife Margaret Fox, owners of the well-known Cafe Beaujolais restaurant in Mendocino, California, did, and now find themselves commuting halfway around the world to extend their hospitality Austrian-style.

Situated high in the Austrian Alps in the picturesque northwestern province of Tyrol, their cozy castle bed and breakfast is surrounded by twenty-five hundred acres of parkland. It is just ten minutes from excellent skiing, a half-day from Vienna, and conveniently close to Italy, Switzerland, and Germany—making it a convenient stopover spot.

THE PAST 🏵 A Roman sentry first stood watch on this strategic site above the Inn river valley over two thousand years ago. Only a tower existed then. Using smoke signals to spread important news through the empire, from tower to tower, the site served as a vital communications link for the ancient world. The Romans named the site "Masciacum"; the name Schloss Matzen was taken from this word. It is one of the few castles in Austria that has always remained in private hands.

The present structure dates back to 1167 and the first family of record—the Freundsbergs. Over the years, they fortified the castle with a second tower and extensive walls.

During the fifteenth century the wealthy Turndl family bought the property and turned the castle into a stunning home. Parapets were transformed into cloistered arcades, and glass—an unheard of luxury—was set into the enlarged windows. Then a succession of families, most of whom were involved with the silver and copper mines in the valley, took over the castle.

Life was prosperous until the Napoleonic Wars, when the ancient Roman tower of Schloss Matzen supported field guns in defense of the town. A peasant army led by Andreas Hofer stood up to Napoleon's army. Though Napoleon won the battle and Hofer was killed, he was highly

regarded for leading the revolt. (A castle room is named in honor of Hofer.) The war devastated this area of the Tyrol, and with no money for upkeep, the last owners moved out of the castle and into the stables.

In 1873 Fanny Read Grohman, an Irishwoman, bought the property and restored it. Her son William Baillie-Grohman continued her work, wrote a number of books about the history of the valley, and once even hosted Theodore Roosevelt on a hunt. The family maintained the castle through two World Wars, returning to Britain when the fighting got too close.

The fourth generation of the family sold the castle in 1957 to the American architect Ernest Kump, who was of Austrian background. Kump carefully installed modern bathrooms, plumbing, and central heating while preserving the integrity of the castle's medieval architecture. In 1994 his son Peter, who founded the prestigious Peter Kump's New York Cooking School, planned to open the castle to guests but died the next year. Peter's son Christopher carried out his plans and introduced Schloss Matzen as Austria's newest castle hotel in 1996.

THE PRESENT You don't need to pack your tiara when visiting this informal country castle. Its interior reveals the medieval architectural charm of Gothic cloisters, carved marble doorways, high beamed ceilings, and intricately decorated wrought iron hinges and locks.

Most of the stately guest rooms in this sixty-eight-room, five-floor castle have high ceilings and thick stone walls and feature antique furniture found by the Kumps in the attic. Choose the extra-large Baillie-Grohman Room for its marble fireplace and three-sided view of the valley, or the Teddy Roosevelt Room—the highest room—for its views of the valley and Alps.

Sherry and snacks are offered in the late afternoon. A lavish buffet breakfast, which includes regional foods and delicious pastries from the town bakery, is usually served in an interior cloistered corridor overlooking the central castle courtyard and background mountains.

You can explore the premises on your own or take a guided tour. Highlights include a five-story Roman watchtower, a Baroque chapel, a knights' dining hall, and two dungeons. Very old manuscripts and rare books and maps in the library can be perused with assistance. Among the castle diversions are playing billiards on an antique pool table, playing table tennis in the vaulted gallery, and swimming in a rock-lined pool just outside the walls.

A-6230 Reith, Brixlegg, Tyrol. Tel: 011-43-5337-62-679. Fax: 011-43-5337-66-581.   **Rooms:** 11; all with bath. **Rates:** AS1700; includes breakfast; does not include 11 percent room tax; 2-night minimum stay. **Dates closed:** Dates change each year. **Dining facilities:** No restaurant. **Children:** No discounts. **Facilities for disabled:** None. **On-site recreation:** Billiards; swimming pool. **Nearby diversions:** Hiking; alpine and cross-country skiing; ice skating; fishing; river rafting; tennis; golf; rock climbing and mineral baths in Brixlegg; excursions to nearby Rattenberg—the oldest medieval village in Austria and famous for its glass and crystal—and to Alpbach, called the most beautiful village in the Alps; cogwheel train from nearby Jenbach to lake for ride on a lake steamer. **Proprietor:** Christopher Kump and Margaret Fox. **Operated as a hotel since:** 1996. **U.S. representative:** Christopher Kump (owner); Tel: 888-837-0618, Tel/Fax: 707-937-0618; E-mail: cafebeau@mcn.org; Website: www.cafebeaujolais.com.

Directions: Brixlegg is located about 30 minutes from Innsbruck. Take the autobahn toward Salzburg/Kufstein. Exit at Kramsach/Rattenberg/Brixlegg. Go to the left toward Rattenberg and Brixlegg. At the traffic circle, take the road to the right, which is the main road just outside Brixlegg. Drive straight for 1 kilometer. Continue through a small traffic circle found just after a VW car dealership, and continue about 2/10 of a kilometer to a blinking yellow traffic light. Turn left onto a narrow gravel lane that leads to the castle gates. Trains run from Innsbruck to Jenbach, and from Salzburg or Munich to Worgl; taxis make the 10-minute drive to the castle. A reasonably priced shuttle bus is available from the Munich airport to the castle.

Hotel Schloss Mönchstein

A Fourteenth-Century Castle

Nature did not let Salzburg down in matters of physical beauty. Admirers from all over the world regularly return to enjoy the magnificent setting of mountains and Alpine valleys. The picturesque old town—with its towers, church domes, palaces, medieval streets, arcaded courtyards, and tall narrow houses—lies between the river Salzach and Mönchsberg Hill. The manmade city and lovely physical setting harmonize perfectly. No less important is that this is the city of Mozart. Although he was unappreciated in his lifetime, Salzburgers honor him now with the Mozartium music academy and the famous Salzburg Festival held each year from the end of July through the end of August.

THE PAST 🌸 Known as the "German Rome," Salzburg was designated as an archbishopric in 798. For over one thousand years the prince archbishops ruled autocratically over the region, increasing their great personal wealth by control of the salt trade. If you were a peasant living back then, your life was a miserable one of hard physical labor. Merchants fared a little better, and talented artisans were greatly honored. Although the bishops were generally a selfish, arrogant lot, they did support the craftsmen who built the lovely city we are fortunate to enjoy today.

Originally built by the archbishops in 1358 as a guest house, Schloss Mönchstein became the estate of the Mülln monastery three hundred years later. Shortly after that, the University of Salzburg bought it for their professors' leisure-time enjoyment.

Baron Leitner, a famous Salzburg banker, acquired the property in the nineteenth century and built the first elevator coming up from the town below, as well as a road that winds up the mountain and many walking paths. Upon his death in 1918, the castle was sold again and renovated.

The present owners, the von Mierka family, took possession in 1956.

THE PRESENT 🌸 Rising above the center of Salzburg, the Mönchsberg is like a large city park of wooded paths, flowers, and chirping birds, with benches provided for contemplating the view. The hotel, located at the north end of the park, offers an idyllic atmosphere of privacy and tranquillity and is the perfect place to unwind after a day of sightseeing in Salzburg. The exclusive salons, gardens, and terraces offer splendid views of the city.

The unique exterior is a mixture of towers and step gables partially covered by clinging ivy. Brilliantly colored flowers accent the lawns. The elegant and refined interiors feature crystal chandeliers, leaded windows, Oriental carpets, and brocade upholstery. A small chapel dating from 1500 is popular for weddings. Guest rooms are elegantly decorated, reflecting the regal stature of Mönchstein's former guests: Czarina Katharina of Russia and Empress Elisabeth of Austria. The romantic tower room found in the former observatory is very special.

Offering a splendid view of Mirabell Castle below, the elegant Paris Lodron restaurant serves international cuisine in an intimate atmosphere. Twice a week a chamber music concert is performed either inside or on the outdoor terrace.

Mönchsberg Park 26, A-5020 Salzburg. Tel: 011-43-662-84-85-550. Fax: 011-43-662-84-85-59. Rooms: 17, including suites; all with bath. **Rates:** Very expensive; doubles from AS2400; includes service and tax. **Dates closed:** Open all year. **Dining facilities:** Restaurant. **Children:** Age 6 and younger sharing with parents free; playground nearby. **Facilities for disabled:** None. **On-site recreation:** Tennis. **Nearby diversions:** The old town of Salzburg: Hohensalzburg, St. Peter's Church, Archbishop's residence, Mozart's birthplace. **Proprietor:** von Mierka family. **Operated as a hotel since:** 1949. **U.S. representative:** Relais & Châteaux; Utell International; Euro-Connection.

Directions:: The hotel is situated on top of the Mönchsberg overlooking Salzburg. You can reach it by car through a maze of streets up the hillside; on foot, take the Mönchsberg lift from Anton Neymayr Platz. Signposts lead the way.

Hotel Schloss Moosburg

A Fifteenth-Century Castle

If you would like to be near the activities on the Wörthersee and at the same time stay in quieter surroundings, visit Moosburg. Located a few kilometers north of Pörtschach, this attractive little village sits snugly at the foot of the mountains and enjoys expansive unspoiled views.

THE PAST 🦪 Carolingian King Karlman built the first castle at Moosburg in 888. King Arnulf next governed the property. Formerly the duke of Carinthia, he deposed his uncle, the Holy Roman emperor Charles the Fat, and became king of Germany.

In 1500 Emperor Maximilian I inherited the extensive lands of the extinct counts of Görz—the previous owners. He sold this property to Knight Georg von Ernau, one of a long line of valiant warriors: Ulrich liberated the town of Friesach from Hungarian invaders; Leonhard and Jakob were killed during a Salzburg peasant revolt in 1525; and Christoph and Balthasar defended Vienna. The family also excelled in serving in the Carinthian parliament. The Ernau family met its doom during the Reformation of the early seventeenth century: They converted to Protestantism, emigrated to Germany, and died out within three generations.

The next owner of Moosburg Castle, Baron Georg Andreas von Kronegg, bought and sold the castle, then bought it again. He and his wife, Regina von Dietrichstein, built the Baroque altar in the chapel. In 1708 Count Peter Goëss acquired both Moosburg and the nearby Ratzengg Castle.

Today, the main castle we see dates from the fifteenth century. Another section, connected by a pretty archway, dates from the sixteenth century.

THE PRESENT 🦪 Dominating the little village of Moosburg, the castle is partly surrounded by forests and a small picturesque lake. The grounds are interesting to explore. If you look carefully above the iron gateway and along the iron railing on the main staircase, you can find the coats of arms of the various families who owned Moosburg. The area's sunny climate is perfect for swimming, tennis, fishing, boating, and walking, and the Wörthersee is only a few kilometers away.

Moosburg once offered self-catering apartments but is now a three-star hotel. No longer do you have to cook your own dinner. Instead, you can dine in an award-winning restaurant considered to be one of the best in Carinthia. And you can stay on the upper stories of the castle in guest rooms and suites decorated in either period or modern style.

Dating from 1650 and filled with stunning pieces of furniture and valuable carpets, the late-Gothic Baronial Hall hosts concerts and readings during Moosburg's annual "Summer of Culture" festival.

A-9062 Moosburg, Kärnten. Tel: 011-43-4272-832-06. **Fax:** 011-43-4272-832-06-23. **Rooms:** 17, including 2 suites; all with bath. **Rates:** Expensive; doubles from AS1700; includes breakfast, service, and tax. **Dates closed:** November through March. **Dining facilities:** Restaurant. **Children:** Age 3 and younger free; age 4 through 8 sharing with parents 40 percent discount; baby-sitting. **Facilities for disabled:** None. **On-site recreation:** Tennis; swimming pool. **Nearby diversions:** Lake Wörthersee; Pörtschach. **Proprietor:** Graf Leopold Goëss. **Operated as a hotel since:** 1994. **U.S. representative:** Schlosshotels.

Directions: Moosburg is north of Pörtschach. Signposts lead the way. The castle is visible at the entrance to the town.

Hotel Schloss Pichlarn

AN ELEVENTH-CENTURY CASTLE

When you get tired of sightseeing, consider settling into one of Austria's picturesque green valleys surrounded by mountains. The resort at Schloss Pichlarn is a fine place to relax and unwind. Every season here offers its diversions, whether swimming, riding, golf, tennis, downhill and cross-country skiing, hunting, fishing, or ice-skating. There's even someone to look after the kids. But this elegant hotel is run more like an elegant country club than a camp.

THE PAST 🌀 The castle originated more than nine hundred years ago to help protect the river Enns valley. In 1074 history first mentions the name Püchlern when priests from the village of Irdning laid the original foundation. (Two priests from Irdning went on to become popes.) Through the centuries, additions were made to the original structure, then torn down, and rebuilt again.

THE PRESENT 🌀 Today the old and new sections of the five-story castle blend harmoniously. The main entryway has an interesting arched door covered with chevron designs, while the interior features arched ceilings with hanging crystal chandeliers and floors covered with Oriental carpets.

Though antiques fill every room—including the spacious, pretty guest rooms—you won't find tapestries and suits of armor. A modern atmosphere prevails. Two attractive dining rooms feature a beautifully presented cuisine that changes with the season.

Throughout the year special tours of the Styria region of Austria and both music and cooking programs are scheduled.

Gatschen 28, A-8952 Irdning, Ennstal, Steiermark. Tel: 011-43-3682-228-41-0. Fax: 011-43-3682-228-41-6. **Rooms:** 117; all with bath. **Rates:** Very expensive; doubles from AS3000; includes breakfast, service, and tax. **Dates closed:** Open all year. **Dining facilities:** Restaurant. **Children:** Age 11 and younger sharing with parents free; age 12 through 17 in own room, 50 percent discount; baby-sitting. **Facilities for disabled:** Yes. **On-site recreation:** Tennis; 18-hole golf course; outdoor and indoor horseback riding; outdoor and indoor swimming pools; fitness center; hiking. **Nearby diversions:** Alpine and cross-country skiing. **General Manager:** Andreas Plischke-Delabro. **Operated as a hotel since:** 1969. **U.S. representative:** Schlosshotels; Euro-Connection.

Directions: Irdning is about 110 kilometers east of Salzburg. Trains and buses connect the area with Salzburg.

Romantik Hotel Post

A Sixteenth-Century Palace

Villach, located in Carinthia, is called the "Gateway of the South" since it lies just over the border from Slovenia and Italy. Though it's not exactly in the mainstream of Austria's sightseeing areas, should you find yourself here, the Romantik Hotel Post offers interesting and historic accommodations. Located in the heart of the old town, this city palace displays an impressive façade of carved stone, bay windows, and wrought iron.

The Past 🍥 The Hotel Post has hosted famous heads of state for centuries. One of the richest and most distinguished families of Carinthia, the counts of Khevenhueller, built the palace around 1500. They were also the owners of nearby Landskron and Hochosterwitz castles. During the sixteenth century they hosted Emperor Charles V, Archduke Charles II of Austria, King Henry III of France, and Archduchess Margarethe of Habsburg, when she was on her way to Spain to marry Philip III. In 1628 the Khevenhueller family, who were devout Protestants, were forced to sell their possessions and exiled.

Count Widman, a wealthy businessman who had made his fortune trading with Venice, bought the palace and reconstructed it after a great fire. When Empress Maria Theresa bought the estates of the bishops of Bamberg in 1759, she, too, lived at the palace, then known as the Gasthaus zur Post. A hundred years later, Crown Prince Rudolf, the son of the Emperor Franz Josef, resided here, and Jerome Bonaparte, nephew of Napoleon I, was once a guest.

During World War II part of the house was destroyed by bombing. Another part was later occupied by British officers. In 1952 the Post once again resumed its duties as a hotel.

The Present 🍥 The Post is still charming, and many of its elegant rooms remain fit for a royal visit. Vaulted ceilings, chandeliers, and antique prints create a special atmosphere. Guest rooms vary widely from elegant to simple.

A former coach room (or garage), a hunting room, and another room with a vaulted ceiling serve as restaurants. If you can't stay for the night, do plan to have a meal here. The hotel's restaurant ranks among the top two

hundred in Austria. Delicious schnitzels, pâtès, cheeses, soups, local game, and plenty of butter and cream on everything guarantee to destroy any diet you might think you're on.

Hauptplatz, 26 A-9500 Villach, Kärnten. Tel: 011-43-4242-26101-0. Fax: 011-43-4242-26101-420. **Rooms:** 52, including 3 suites; all with bath. **Rates:** Moderate; doubles from AS1070; includes breakfast, service, and tax. **Dates closed:** Open all year. **Dining facilities:** 3 restaurants. **Children:** Age 11 and younger sharing with parents free. **Facilities for disabled:** Yes. **On-site recreation:** Sauna; gym. **Nearby diversions:** Swimming pool; horseback riding; winter sports; golf. **Proprietors:** Kreibich family. **Operated as a hotel since:** 1748. **U.S. representative:** Euro-Connection.

Directions: Villach is in southern Austria near the Slovenian border. It has train service from major cities. The hotel is located in the center of town, with parking at the rear.

Hotel im Palais Schwarzenberg

AN EIGHTEENTH-CENTURY PALACE

In a city boasting a palace on every corner, the Schwarzenberg Palace might appear to be just another elegant and stately Viennese building. But on second glance, you see that this is a palace you can live in. No cordoned off musty rooms and faded glory here.

The Schwarzenberg is a *real* palace with a real prince. Prince Karl Johannes von Schwarzenberg stays here when he isn't tending his other castle and vineyards in Styria. And when you stay at his palace, you, too, can live like royalty and stroll in the prince's beautiful nineteen-acre private park and dine in the grand salon.

THE PAST 🦋 After the second Turkish siege of Vienna in 1683, reconstruction projects began all over the city. Duke Heinrich von Mansfeld-Fondi commissioned the famous Baroque architect Lucas von Hildebrandt to build a regal palace. Duke Adam Franz von Schwarzenberg, equerry-in-chief to the imperial court, bought the palace eighteen years later and

finished it with the help of another equally famous architect, Johann Bern-
hard Fischer von Erlach. The Schwarzenbergs have lived here during the
summers for more than three hundred and fifty years.

During World War II the palace was confiscated by the Gestapo as
punishment for the anti-Nazi stance taken by the Schwarzenberg family.
Priceless pieces of furniture were shipped to Bohemia, where they were
seized after the war by the Czechoslovakian state. At the end of the war,
when the southern railroad was bombed, two bombs fell on the palace and
twenty on the park; this damage has been repaired.

The family opened their palace to the public in 1962 as a bed and
breakfast, adding a full-service restaurant six years later.

THE PRESENT 🐏 The old section of the palace, with an elegant Baroque
central hall, is now used for private functions and special concerts. The interiors dazzle with gilt, chandeliers, mirrors, and priceless art objects, and
ceilings are painted with cavorting cherubs. The Baroque gallery, or Marble
Hall, is the only one in Vienna that still exists in its original form. It boasts a
fine series of paintings. Another hall exhibits two works by Rubens:
Ganymede and *Romulus and Remus*.

The wing of the palace where most of the guest rooms are located probably was once the servants' quarters. Now an antique collection, abundant fresh flowers, chandeliers, striated marble, and rich French fabrics create a charming, intimate atmosphere in each room. All guest rooms are furnished in period style. Some suites overlook the garden. Rooms 15 and 19, with their high ceilings and long windows, are exceptionally lovely; in the high season they are usually the first to be booked.

The restaurant is in a glass-enclosed area with views of the garden. Awarded a one-star rating from Michelin, it serves a light classical Viennese and international menu that changes daily. Temptations such as medallions of veal with crab, lamb with cinnamon, and pheasant with juniper and cabbage sometimes appear on the menu. The wine cellar holds nearly forty thousand bottles.

You can spend time outdoors on eighteen acres with rows of chestnut trees, manicured lawns, fountains, and ponds. A walk through the park takes you to the Belvedere Palace—a Baroque palace built by the architect Lukas von Hildebrandt as a summer residence for Eugene of Savoy. A ten-minute walk in the opposite direction delivers you to the heart of Vienna.

Schwarzenbergplatz 9, A-1030 Vienna. Tel: 011-43-1-798-45-15. **Fax:** 011-43-1-798-47-14. **E-mail:** schwazberg@nethotels.com.　**Rooms:** 38, including 4 suites; all with bath. **Rates:** Very expensive; doubles from AS3300; includes service and tax; Christmas, New Year's, and honeymoon packages. **Dates closed:** Open all year. **Dining facilities:** Restaurant (jacket and tie required for dinner); café; outdoor terrace. **Children:** Age 11 and younger sharing with parents free; baby-sitting. **Facilities for disabled:** Yes. **On-site recreation:** Tennis courts; 3 kilometers of jogging paths in hotel's private park; croquet. **Nearby diversions:** The palaces of Vienna: Schönbrunn, Hofburg, Belvedere; Fine Arts Museum and Historical Museum of Vienna; St. Stephen's Cathedral; homes of Haydn, Mozart, Beethoven, Freud; State Opera House; Spanish Riding School; coffeehouses. **Proprietor:** Prince Karl Johannes von Schwarzenberg. **General Manager:** Gerhard Schwendner. **Operated as a hotel since:** 1962. **U.S. representative:** Relais & Châteaux; Utell International; Preferred Hotels.

Directions: Schwarzenbergplatz is in the center of Vienna, just south of the Ringstrasse. Helicopter service directly to the hotel can be arranged.

More Hotels

Hotel Burg Bernstein

This thirteenth-century castle in southeast Austria has been owned by the same family for generations. A ghost is said to haunt one of the rooms.

A-7434 Bernstein, Burgenland. Tel: 011-43-3354-63-82. Fax: 011-43-3354-65-20.

Schloss Kapfenstein

Located in southeast Austria, this fortified castle is family-run and commands views of Slovenia and Hungary. Wines produced from the surrounding vineyards are served at dinner.

A-8353 Kapfenstein, Styria. Tel: 011-43-3157-22-02. Fax: 011-43-3157-22-024.

Jagdschloss Kühtai

This charming hunting palace dates back to the thirteenth century. Count Karl Stolberg-Stolberg—the great-grandson of Emperor Franz Joseph—presides and dines every night among his guests in the wood-paneled dining room.

A-6183 Kühtai, Tyrol. Tel: 011-43-5239-201. Fax: 011-43-5239-2814.

Burg Oberanna

The towers and walls of this family-run castle date back to the twelfth century. Interiors have been lovingly restored.

A-3622 Mühldorf, Lower Austria. Tel: 011-43-2713-82-21. Fax: 011-43-2713-83-66.

France

For hundreds of years the French monarchy moved at whim from château to château—hunting, attending tournaments, and dancing at lavish balls. They left a tradition of unsurpassed beauty and elegance. Of course, it is impossible to re-create their world for the modern traveler, but you can catch a glimpse of it by driving in your contemporary carriage, moving as the monarchy did through pastoral countryside from château to château. You'll be greeted with warmth and kindness and experience some of the world's finest cuisine and wine.

No visit to France is complete without exploring the magnificent châteaux of the Loire Valley, or picnicking on pâté and truffles in the Dordogne region, or gazing at the brilliant colors of Provence. Each region of France offers you something unique and special.

The country's castle and palace hotels reflect the same individuality. Their original purposes varied widely. Some were architectural expressions of the noble families who built them. Some were fortresses built in defense against the British, Saracens, or Germans. One was built to protect pilgrims, another was a honeymoon retreat, and another was a pleasure palace for a famous perfumer.

But one thing they all have in common is the gracious hospitality of their current owners, who give attention to every detail—decorating with exquisite furnishings, planting idyllic gardens, and serving food that satisfies even the most demanding gourmet. They genuinely care that every guest enjoys their stay and leaves impressed.

For a rare insight into country life in a French château, contact the Château Accueil, an association of private château owners who are often counts or marquises in whose family the estate has been handed down for centuries. These member châteaux are truly splendid. You'll be greeted by owners who make you feel like their personal guests. Only a limited number of guest rooms or apartments are available in each château, with dinner served by request. A detailed guide with photographs of each property costs buyers in non-European Community countries FF70 (includes postage and handling) and can be ordered with a credit card from: Pegasus, Mr. Gérard Potel, 47 rue de la Harpe, 27000 Evreux, France, Tel: 011-33-32-38-58-21, Fax: 011-33-32-39-76-82. Be sure to include your address, credit card number, expiration date, and signature.

Most of the French hotels listed here are located outside the cities. You'll need a car to reach them. Directions are given for each hotel, but since many are found near tiny villages, the appropriate Michelin road map can be indispensable in helping you find them.

For information to help you plan a vacation to any of the regions of France, write the French Government Tourist Office at: 444 Madison Avenue, New York, New York 10020-2452; or 676 North Michigan Avenue, Suite 3360, Chicago, Illinois 60611-2819; or 9454 Wilshire Boulevard, Suite 715, Beverly Hills, California 90212-2967. Tel: 900-990-0040 (calls cost 50 cents per minute). Website: http://www.fgtousa.org.

Chateau d'Artigny

Château d'Artigny

An Eighteenth-Century Palace

Some travelers find a special joy in staying in charming little inns, while others travel in the grand manner of visiting royalty. The Château d'Artigny suits this second group perfectly. It is reminiscent of Newport, Rhode Island during the twenties.

This château was the dream of the famous perfumer François Coty, who spent twenty years building his fantasy home.

THE PAST 🐚 From the eleventh century until 1769, a castle stood on this site. Then a new owner, the king's treasurer René Testard de Bournais, tore the castle down and built a new palace in its place. It was spared during the French Revolution, and a succession of aristocratic families owned it until Coty bought the estate in 1912. He pulled down the second structure and began his lifelong ambition of building an eighteenth-century-style cream-puff palace.

Famous guests include Haile Selassie, the emperor of Ethiopia, Henry Ford II, Richard Burton, and Elizabeth Taylor.

THE PRESENT 🐚 Coty spared little expense, as is evidenced in the massive polished limestone staircase, brass-inlaid marble floors, and grand ballroom. A cupola overhead with a trompe l'oeil fresco by C. Hoffbauer depicts a scene from the château's past in which Monsieur and Madame Coty enjoy a costume ball.

Part of the fun of staying here is exploring all the little reminders of past excess: the cold-meat storage area that was once the closet for Mme Coty's furs (she is said to have had two thousand wardrobe and linen closets); a room lined in pink marble that was once the pastry room; the kitchen—placed upstairs so ascending food smells would not "corrupt" sensitive noses used for sniffing perfumes.

The guest rooms furnished in period style are by far the most interesting. Some are small; others are spacious with high ceilings. Room 74 has ornate columns. Ask for room 36 and you can enjoy using Mme Coty's personal bathroom. Outside the château, an exact but unfinished replica of Louis XIV's chapel at Versailles is now the Pavillon d'Ariane, which also contains several apartments.

The restaurant menus feature seasonal choices such as lamb cutlets, pigeon with heather honey, and fresh fish with mussels and saffron. Two

sommeliers help you choose from a seventy-five-page wine list describing the fifty thousand bottles in the château's wine cellar.

As in the other hotels operated by René Traversac, life here is very formal and elegant. Candlelight concerts are held in the Regency ballroom.

Route de Monts, 37250 Montbazon (Indre-et-Loire). Tel: 011-33-2-47-26-24-24. Fax: 011-33-2-47-65-92-79. Rooms: 43, including 2 suites and 23 rooms in annex; all with bath. **Rates:** Moderate; doubles from FF650; includes service and tax. **Dates closed:** January 1 through 13, month of December. **Dining facilities:** 2 restaurants; bar. **Children:** Inquire about discounts when booking; children's menu. **Facilities for disabled:** None. **On-site recreation:** Tennis; swimming pool. **Nearby diversions:** Hunting; fishing; flying club; ballooning; horseback riding; Loire châteaux. **General Manager:** Patrice Puvilland. **Operated as a hotel since:** 1959. **U.S. representative:** Relais & Châteaux.

Directions: Montbazon is 12 kilometers south of Tours. The château is just west of Montbazon on D-17.

Domaine de Castel Novel

A Thirteenth-Century Castle

If you enjoy exploring abandoned châteaux or prehistoric caves, visiting antique shops, and driving on uncrowded roads through peaceful rolling hills, then head for the enchanting Dordogne region of France. You'll want to plan a riverbank picnic of fresh local pâté de foie gras and truffles, and to stay in one of the fine country castle hotels.

THE PAST This site has been occupied since ancient times. (Excavations on the grounds have turned up Roman coins and pottery.) The oldest section of the castle is the round tower, dating back to the Middle Ages, when it was used as a military fortification.

The earliest mention of it in any document is 1289, when the castle was associated with the family of Pida of Castel Novel. During the Hundred Years' War the English captured the castle, but they gave it back nine years

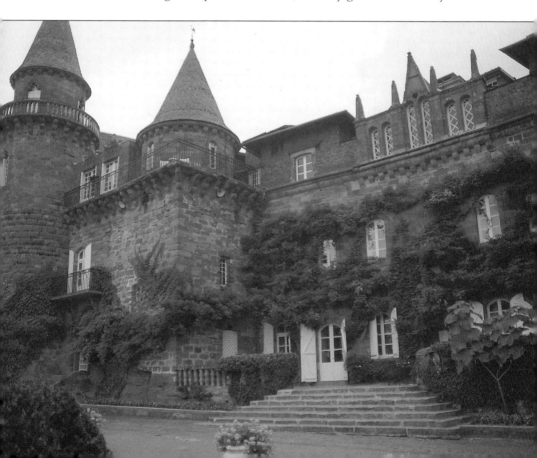

later. Castel Novel was once given away as a wedding gift and later sold for two thousand gold crowns. In 1500 Françoise de Beaupoil, the lady of the castle, married Gilles d'Aubusson, and the castle remained in this family for three hundred and fifty years.

One of the more recent owners of the castle was Henri de Jouvenal—journalist, orator, politician, and ambassador to Rome. His wife, the writer Colette, wrote several of her novels here, and her influence is still felt.

THE PRESENT 🐚 Castel Novel is an utterly charming and romantic hideaway. From the time you arrive and are greeted at your car door until you leave, you are treated with every kindness and courtesy. The proprietor, Albert Parveaux, is possibly one of the most charming men in France. He sincerely cares that his guests leave with a good impression of his hotel.

Each guest room is furnished with antiques and lovely fabrics. You'll find a superb pair of carved wooden canopy beds in one suite that also features a beamed ceiling. One tower room is done in very feminine pastel floral fabrics; another more masculine counterpart is mostly stone. Colette's room is now the Louis XVI suite.

Michelin has awarded a two-star rating to the hotel's cuisine. The menu features such temptations as duck foie gras prepared at the castle and marinated in Sauternes wine, salmon smoked at the castle, truffle omelets, duck breast roasted in wine and walnut sauce, and lobster. You can dine in either the Louis XIII room with its grand fireplace, or in a room with a charming painted ceiling, or outside on a French country-style terrace.

Monsieur Parveaux certainly enjoys the hotel business. When Castel Novel closes each October, he's off to the French Alps and his other hotel—the Pralong 2000—which opens for the season in December.

19240 Varetz (Carrèze). Tel: 011-33-5-55-85-00-01. Fax: 011-33-5-55-85-09-03. E-mail: dcn19@calvacom.fr. **Rooms:** 32, including 5 suites and 10 rooms in the Maitairie annex; all with bath. **Rates:** Moderate; doubles from FF595; includes service and tax. **Dates closed:** October 17 through May 4. **Dining facilities:** 3 restaurants. **Children:** 30 percent discount. **Facilities for disabled:** Yes. **On-site recreation:** Tennis; swimming pool; golf. **Nearby diversions:** Canoeing; fishing; mountain biking. **Proprietor:** Albert Parveaux. **Operated as a hotel since:** 1965. **U.S. representative:** Relais & Châteaux.

Directions: Varetz is a short distance northwest of Brive in the Dordogne region. Follow D-901, turn south on D-152, and follow the signposts to the château.

Château de la Caze

A Fifteenth-Century Castle

The Gorges du Tarn offer some of the most dramatic scenery in France. Sheer limestone cliffs tower straight up from the valley to heights of over fifteen hundred feet. Whether exploring the canyon by car or boat, you'll be awed and delighted by the constantly changing but always breathtaking vistas. In the middle of the most beautiful stretch, between the villages of Sainte-Enimie and Les Vignes, the Château de la Caze stands out as a romantic hideaway forgotten by the world.

THE PAST 🌀 This perfectly preserved little castle, built during the reign of Charles VIII, was not designed as a defensive fortification, nor has it ever been attacked.

Soubeyrane Alamand, niece of the prior of Sainte-Enimie, loved a section of land along the Tarn that belonged to her family. Engaged to the sire of Monclar, she had the castle built for them to honeymoon in. The two never had any children, and the property passed to the Mostuejouls family.

Bertrand de Mostuejouls was a renowned swordsman. Named Captain de la Caze, he made a career out of fighting the Huguenots. His daughter married M. de Malian, and their union produced eight girls. Reputed to be very beautiful, the daughters attracted every young man in the district to secret visits in the garden. Portraits of the young ladies are painted on the ceiling of the room in the south tower. (To preserve them, the tower and portraits are not open for general viewing but may be seen by request.)

THE PRESENT 🐚 One of the first castle hotels in France, the Château de la Caze opened its doors in the early 1900s. Through the centuries the château has retained its romantic atmosphere. You'll find it an ideal hideaway. Tall rocky bluffs and a tributary from the nearby river form its moat. Stone staircases and vaulted rooms have remained unchanged for centuries. Antiques fill the public rooms.

The beautifully decorated guest rooms inside the castle feature beamed ceilings and canopy beds. Each carries the name of a former inhabitant of the château, and all look out onto the river and canyon. The Ferme contains six suites in what was once the barn.

The excellent dining room has a one-star Michelin rating and offers items such as duckling and trout fresh from the river.

The château hosts summer music festivals, and each year the "*Sortilège des Nymphes*" and the "*Nocturnes de Soubeyrane*" take place in its chapel, followed by a special candlelight dinner. The Festival of the Gorges du Tarn Valley concert takes place in the park while guests dine under the stars.

Route des Gorges du Tarn, 48210 Sainte-Enimie (Lozère). Tel: 011-33-4-66-48-51-01. Fax: 011-33-4-66-48-55-75. **Rooms:** 19, including 6 suites in an annex; all with bath. **Rates:** Moderate; doubles from FF500; includes service and tax. **Dates closed:** End of November through March 31, and Wednesdays in low season. **Dining facilities:** Restaurant and outside terrace; restaurant open to non-guests except on Wednesdays. **Children:** Age 14 and younger sharing with parents free. **Facilities for disabled:** None. **On-site recreation:** Swimming pool. **Nearby diversions:** Fishing; canoeing; hiking; rock climbing. **General Managers:** Jean Paul and Sandrine Lecroq. **Operated as a hotel since:** 1970. **U.S. representative:** None.

Directions: The Tarn region of France is northwest of Montpellier. The château is 5 kilometers northeast of La Malène on D-907.

Château de la Chèvre d'Or

An Eleventh-Century Castle

For over a thousand years the little village and castle of Eze have stood watch over the Mediterranean. A distinct anachronism amid all the glitter and high life of the Côte d'Azur, Eze would win any vote for the most charming hideaway along the coast. You can cross its narrow twisting streets only by foot, moving through dark vaulted or arched passageways. Curved tiles and ancient ironwork decorate the tiny houses. Nothing seems to have changed here in centuries.

THE PAST A legend relates that the Saracens built Eze, but in fact it was originally a Ligurian (northwest Italian) settlement. For centuries Phoenicians, Romans, and Saracens took turns ruling the town. Though the inhabitants had to leave the security of the walls to find food and water, the castle offered protection from Germanic invasions and Muslim pirates. Gradually economic conditions made its protection unnecessary. Security in general improved, and so did communications and agriculture.

The name "Chèvre d'Or" comes from the twentieth-century discovery of the castle ruins. In 1924 an American violinist and his wife were hiking in the late afternoon and spotted a small goat in the distance. The rays of the sun had given it a golden glow. As they approached the goat, they found the ruins of the castle.

THE PRESENT At the same time Eze-Village was restored, this charming château built into the original fortifications was opened as a hotel. Featuring sweeping views of the Mediterranean twelve hundred feet below, it is beautiful and romantic throughout. Interiors feature fine stonework and beamed

ceilings and are furnished with French and Italian antiques. Outside walls covered with ivy and bougainvillea surround a terraced swimming pool, and a patio sheltered under graceful arched colonnades makes an idyllic spot to while away time.

Many of the cozy guest rooms open onto terraces. Each is furnished with antiques and has a private bath.

The very best part of staying at the Chèvre d'Or is dining on its sun-drenched terrace and enjoying the splendid view up and down the coast. Michelin gives the outstanding kitchen a high rating of four forks and one star. You can indulge yourself with fresh foie gras, oysters with champagne, loin of lamb, or a warm raspberry soufflé.

When you arrive in the village of Eze, you'll find a parking lot at the bottom of the hill. Though you must walk up to the hotel, passing through a narrow gate and tiny streets filled with art shops and boutiques, you needn't worry about your luggage—pack mules will carry it up.

Moyenne corniche, rue du Barri, 06360 Eze-Village (Alpes-Maritimes). Tel: 011-33-4-93-10-66-66. Fax: 011-33-4-93-41-06-72. **Rooms:** 29, including 8 suites; all with bath. **Rates:** Very expensive; doubles from FF1300; includes service and tax. **Dates closed:** November 30 through end of February. **Dining facilities:** Restaurant (closed Wednesdays during low season); terrace; bar. **Children:** Age 6 and younger sharing with parents free. **Facilities for disabled:** None. **On-site recreation:** Swimming pool. **Nearby diversions:** Tennis; golf; rock climbing. **General Manager:** Thierry Naidu. **Operated as a hotel since:** 1956. **U.S. representative:** Relais & Châteaux.

Directions: Eze is halfway between Nice and Monaco. On the autoroute from Nice, exit at La Turbie; coming from Italy, exit at Monaco.

Château de Chissay

A Fifteenth-Century Castle

Travelers come to the Loire to see the river and the magnificent, stately châteaux that lie along it. But another lure is the drive through lovely countryside full of woods and greenery, traveling from one old village to the next on lightly traveled roads. The Château de Chissay is the kind of place that suddenly appears on one of these drives and delightfully surprises you when you discover that it's actually a hotel.

The Past This Renaissance château had its beginnings in the thirteenth century and was finished three hundred years later. It belonged to the dukes of Choiseul and later to Pierre Bèrard, treasurer to Charles VII. The king came to stay here in 1452 and again in 1454. Ten years later King Louis XI paid several visits, and in 1940 General Charles de Gaulle stayed for a few days.

The Present The grounds of the castle are so peaceful and serene, you'll want to whisper so as not to break the silence. Most guest rooms have antiques, fireplaces, and views of the Loire Valley. A fine restaurant opens onto a terrace, and private dining salons in the Gothic-style cellars are also

available. The management prefers that guests stay for at least three days, on either a half-pension or full-pension plan.

Just eight kilometers away is one of the loveliest of all the Loire châteaux—Chenonceaux. This former home of the legendary Diane de Poitiers and Catherine de Medici is open for tours.

Chissay-en-Tourraine, F-41400 Montrichard (Val de Loire). Tel: 011-33-2-54-32-32-01. Fax: 011-33-2-54-32-43-80. Rooms: 31, including 25 doubles and 6 suites; all with bath. **Rates:** Expensive; doubles from FF750; includes breakfast, tax and service. **Dates closed:** November through March. **Dining facilities:** Restaurant and private salons. **Children:** Inquire about discounts when booking. **Facilities for disabled:** None. **On-site recreation:** Swimming pool; tennis. **Nearby diversions:** Chenonceaux. **Proprietor:** Patrice Longet. **Operated as a hotel since:** Not known. **U.S. representative:** Euro-Connection.

Directions: Chissay is east of Tours. From Montrichard, it is just a few kilometers west on D-176.

Hôtel de la Cité

AN ELEVENTH-CENTURY PALACE

The medieval city of Carcassonne conjures up romantic images of fair damsels, knights on horseback, and itinerant troubadours, but this magnificent fortress city also has a long and brutal history of warfare and continual sieges. With its double row of ramparts and narrow winding streets, this picturesque city is one of the great attractions of France.

Today only one thousand people live within the walls of the old city. One of the town's major sites—the eleventh- and twelfth-century Cathedral of Saint-Nazaire—contains some of the finest stained glass in southern France.

THE PAST 🌸 The city was first built during Gallo-Roman times. The Visigoths built the inner rampart, which later repelled a siege by Clovis in 506. The Moors captured the city in 728 and were driven out twenty-four years later by Pepin the Short, father of Charlemagne. During one five-year siege by Charlemagne, the populace was on the verge of starvation and surrender when a woman named Dame Carcas had the idea of feeding the last bits of grain to a pig and then tossing the pig over the wall. The idea was that when it burst the invaders would see the grain and think there was an unlimited food supply inside the walls. This ruse must have worked, since the enemy abruptly ended their siege and left. In 1355 Edward, the infamous Black Prince, burned down the city.

Through the centuries Carcassonne was continually being rebuilt—walls were fortified, additions made. By the middle of the seventeenth century, new methods of warfare meant the end of Carcassonne's strategic advantage. The city fell into such decay that in the nineteenth century builders of the new lower city removed sections of the ancient wall to use as construction material. When the French government realized that a treasure was slipping away, it commissioned Viollet-le-Duc, who had led the restoration of Notre Dame, to restore the walls.

Standing between the cathedral and the city walls, the Hôtel de la Cité was once the site of a bishop's

palace. A *Who's Who* of the Middle Ages and Renaissance lived or visited here: Pope Urban II (1096), Pope Clement V (1309), King François I (1553), Charles IX and Catherine de Medicis (1565), Henri IV (1565), and Louis XIII (1662). Since the building was opened as a hotel in 1909, hundreds of famous personalities have signed in—from the king and queen of Portugal and sultan of Morocco to Mary Astor, from Rudyard Kipling and J. Pierpont Morgan to Mary Pickford and Douglas Fairbanks.

THE PRESENT It's easy to see why they came. With thick stone walls and leaded Gothic windows, this charming inn has maintained both its medieval architecture and atmosphere. Ceiling-high fireplaces provide warmth in the public rooms (there is also central heating). The beautiful furnishings are either antiques or very good reproductions, and a cozy bar boasts superb carved wood panels.

The charming guest rooms feature views of the garden, ramparts, or rolling countryside through leaded windows covered with filmy white curtains or tapestry prints. One room also has a wooden bed with an outstanding medieval canopy; others have brass beds.

The dining room, which features arched leaded windows and a rich wood ceiling, is decorated with gold fleurs-de-lis against blue walls. A variety of excellent menus are offered, with *coquilles Saint Jacques au Champagne* and *cassoulet* among the mouthwatering temptations. Michelin has awarded two stars and Gault Millau three *toques* to the cuisine.

During the summer season you can watch drama festivals held in an open-air theater, or take a night tour (led in French) of the brilliantly floodlit old city.

Place de l'Eglise, 11000 Carcassonne. Tel: 011-33-4-68-25-03-34. **Fax:** 011-33-4-68-71-50-15. **Rooms:** 26; all with bath. **Rates:** Expensive; doubles from FF1050; includes tax and service. **Dates closed:** Open all year. **Dining facilities:** 2 restaurants; piano bar (open June through August). **Children:** No discounts. **Facilities for disabled:** None. **On-site recreation:** Swimming pool. **Nearby diversions:** The old city; golf; tennis; horseback riding. **General Manager:** Alexandre Pierre Faidherbe. **Operated as a hotel since:** 1906. **U.S. representative:** Small Luxury Hotels of the World.

Directions: Carcassonne is southeast of Toulouse in the south of France. It is connected by train to all major cities. The hotel is inside the city wall near the Cathedral of Saint-Nazaire.

Château de Codignat

A FIFTEENTH-CENTURY CASTLE

Stone turrets peering above the surrounding woods direct you to this medieval castle hidden deep in the heart of France. Its pastoral location and pleasant views contribute to its peaceful atmosphere. Finding yourself far from the tourist track, you can enjoy quiet excursions through the unspoiled Auvergne countryside.

THE PAST Local knights built this castle overlooking the little village of Bort-l'Etang (which means "edge of the pond") as a defensive structure against any enemies who might march down the valley to capture the nearby arkose quarry. (Arkose—a granite sandstone—was the preferred building material of the time for castles, cathedrals, and sarcophagi.) The original size of the castle was four times larger than what we see today. By the eighteenth century, it had been abandoned and sacked and its stones scavenged by builders of new homes. In the early part of the twentieth century, all that remained was the present building with a sunken roof.

After World War I, Prince Obolenski, a member of Russia's Romanov family, sought temporary refuge here. (The name Codignat is derived from

de Codonhac—one of the noble families who once lived here.) The present proprietors, Monique Barberan and her son Guy, discovered the property covered over in ivy and bushes in 1971 and proceeded to turn it into a stunning hotel.

THE PRESENT Monique Barberan has done an outstanding job maintaining a medieval atmosphere in her castle: Renaissance tapestries hang on rough-hewn stone walls, heraldic arms emblazon open fireplaces, and fine antique furniture fills the public lounges. Individually decorated guest rooms feature wooden canopy beds and Louis XIII furniture. The spacious bathroom in the mauve and burgundy Queen Victoria suite—located in one of the stone towers—has a Jacuzzi and a trompe l'oeil wall painting. The Jacques Coeur room, embellished in shades of gold, has a wood-beamed ceiling.

Another of the towers holds the dining room, where meals, using fresh produce from the château's own gardens, are served by candlelight. Occasionally barbecues are held outside by the pool.

Lezoux, 63190 Bort-l'Étang (Puy-de-Dôme). Tel: 011-33-73-68-43-03. Fax: 011-33-73-68-93-54. **Rooms:** 19, including 4 suites; all with bath. **Rates:** Moderate; doubles from FF650; includes service and tax. **Dates closed:** November 3 through March 20. **Dining facilities:** Restaurant. **Children:** Age 12 and younger sharing with parents free; playground; baby-sitting. **Facilities for disabled:** Yes. **On-site recreation:** Tennis; swimming pool; fitness room. **Nearby diversions:** Hunting; fishing; horseback riding; helicopter excursions over Auvergne volcanos and Puy mountains. **Proprietors:** Monique Barberan and Guy Vidal. **Operated as a hotel since:** 1975. **U.S. representative:** Relais & Châteaux.

Directions: From Clermont-Ferrand, drive east towards Thiers on N-89. When you reach Lezoux, continue on D-223 towards Courpière. Turn again on D-309 and follow the signpost to Bort l'Étang. If you go into the village of Bort l'Étang, you've gone too far.

Château de Coudrée

A Twelfth-Century Castle

This elegant castle, splendidly situated on the banks of lovely Lake Geneva, is near the French Alps and the spa town of Evian (the popular bottled water comes from here). While offering all the facilities of a modern hotel, Château de Coudrée retains the charm of its ancient origins.

THE PAST ❀ The first fortress, which was nothing more than a wooden tower, was built on this site in the sixth century. Moats, palisades, and earth embankments helped protect this tower and other structures to the side, which were probably used for storage. Because of the lack of elevation, builders had to rely on water to provide defense—the lake on the north side of the property and a moat on the other three sides.

The property first belonged to the Abbey of Saint Maurice d'Agaune, and one of its priors made his home here. No one knows the exact origin of the name "Coudrée," but it is derived from either the shape of the gulf or from an old French word mean-ing "drained land." By the time the property changed owners in 1245 from the priory to Beatrix de Grey-zier, widow of Henri d'Allinges, the tower had become a massive stone fortress.

Through the centuries Bernese, Savoyard, and Genevese soldiers laid siege to the castle, inflicting varying amounts of damage. After each siege the castle was rebuilt and its defenses adjusted to account for new styles of warfare: a better drawbridge, staircases to replace clumsy ladders, and a new style of window. These improvements were in place for only a few years when a fire nearly razed the castle to the ground in 1590.

Two hundred years later, a relative of the Allinges family, Count Vittorio Alfieri, the famous Italian tragic poet, came to live at Coudrée with the Countess of Albany, widow of the Stuart pretender to the English throne. When the last Marquis of Allinges died in 1840 without a direct heir, the estate passed to Cesare Alfieri di Sostegno, a cousin of the poet. His heir was the Italian statesman, Cavour, but there is no evidence he ever visited Coudrée. Neglected, the castle became little more than a farm, with the workers living in the east wing and the animals and supplies in the west wing.

The Bartholoni family took possession in the nineteenth century. Prince Louis Bonaparte conferred the position of deputy for the Haute-Savoie on Anatole Bartholoni. His nephew married Louise Grimaldi, a relative of the reigning family of Monaco. He undertook the complete restoration of the castle, rebuilding the walls, gateways, portcullises, and arrow-slit windows. The moats were re-excavated and the interiors decorated in the style of the Italian Renaissance.

THE PRESENT ❧ Coudrée appears as an ivy-clad mansion surrounded by a park and flanked by two towers. But when you pass through the entryway, you'll feel like you're entering a small museum. The castle features Italian painted, coffered, and paneled ceilings. A painting above the fireplace in the François I drawing room is part of a Florentine fresco, while the sixteenth-century paneling of the hotel bar is of Spanish origin. Another public room features a grand fireplace rescued from a French manor house whose owners, friends of King Henri IV, felt their home was too modest to receive the king and so ordered renovations. The Flemish tapestries in this room were gifts from Louis XIV to Colbert, though it is not known how they arrived here.

Guest rooms and suites are furnished with antiques that include carved canopy beds, Oriental carpets, and roll-top desks. A wood-beamed ceiling and stone walls provide a medieval ambiance to the dining room, where you can enjoy such specialties as fricassee of pigeon and scalloped duck liver with sweet curry.

Domaine de Coudrée-Bonnatrait, 74140 Sciez-sur-Léman (Haute-Savoie). Tel: 011-33-4-50-72-62-33. Fax: 011-33-4-50-72-57-28. Rooms: 19, including 5 suites; all with bath. **Rates:** Moderate; doubles from FF580; includes service and tax. **Dates closed:** End of October through April. **Dining facilities:** Restaurant. **Children:** Age 12 and younger sharing with parents free; gameroom; nearby playground; baby-sitting. **Facilities for disabled:** None. **On-site recreation:** Tennis; swimming pool; lakeside beach. **Nearby diversions:** Golf; water sports; medieval village of Yvoire. **Proprietor:** Laden family. **Operated as a hotel since:** 1962. **U.S. representative:** Relais & Châteaux.

Directions: Sciez-sur-Léman is on the south bank of Lake Geneva, northeast of the city of Geneva.

Château d'Esclimont

A Sixteenth-Century Castle

As graceful as the swans populating its lake, the Château d'Esclimont provides an elegant retreat into a noble past. This lovely towered and moated château stands in one hundred and fifty acres of forest, lakes, rivers, and gardens. If your image of the ideal fairy-tale castle includes an exquisite setting, priceless antiques, handcrafted crystal chandeliers, marble fireplaces, and elaborate ceiling frescoes, you'll be pleased to find it all here.

THE PAST ✿ Originally built in 1543 by Etienne de Poncher, archbishop of Tours, this château has passed through the hands of many noble families. Philippe Hurault, count of Cheverny and chancellor of France under King Henri III, was one owner. Another owner, Claude de Bullion, was a favorite of Richelieu, who sat as an advisor at the side of Marie de Medicis and Cardinal de la Rochefoucauld. Louis XIII named de Bullion as first president of Parlement in 1634.

The château was acquired through marriage by the Rochefoucauld family, one of the most prestigious in France. L. F. Sosthène de la Rochefoucauld was the director of the Beaux Arts who named the composer Rossini as director of the Paris Opera. His descendants continued living at

the château until its sale in 1981. His granddaughter, Laure de Mailly-Nesle, still lives in a smaller house on the grounds.

THE PRESENT 🌸 René Traversac, who is also responsible for such elegant hotels as the Château d'Artigny, Le Prieuré, Domaine de Beauvois, and the Château d'Isenbourg, spent more than twenty million francs remodeling Esclimont, and it shows. Of all Monsieur Traversac's hotels, this one is the ultimate in luxury and style. This lovely country house presents a Renaissance façade as you approach. Towers, dormer windows, turrets, and a moat complete the fanciful scene.

Over the doorway the inscription of François de la Rochefoucauld— "C'est mon plaisir" ("This is my pleasure")—invites you to begin a divine experience. Accommodations are in four sections, and no two guest rooms are alike. Many look out over the lake and are furnished with exquisite antiques, chandeliers, and Persian carpets. One apartment has its own tower with a painted ceiling fresco of clouds and birds. Room 14 holds a stunning Louis XVI bed.

Four restaurants, designed in a Louis XIII and Louis XV style, overlook the park. The traditional, classical cuisine includes such temptations as filet of sole with a dark lobster sauce and a light champagne cream sauce. From November to April, Parisian musicians come to perform classical music soirees.

The primary reason you come to the Château d'Esclimont, though, is to enjoy a romantic interlude. The atmosphere is so idyllic here, you might never want to leave.

28700 St-Symphorien-le-Château (Eure-et-Loir). Tel: 011-33-2-37-31-15-15. Fax: 011-33-2-37-31-57-91. Rooms: 53, including 5 suites, in four sections: Château, Donjon, Pavillon de Chasse, or Les Trophées; all with bath. **Rates:** Moderate, doubles from FF650; includes tax and service. **Dates closed:** Open all year. **Dining facilities:** 4 restaurants (jacket and tie required for dinner). **Children:** Age 12 and younger sharing with parents free; baby-sitting. **Facilities for disabled:** Yes. **On-site recreation:** Tennis; swimming pool; bicycles; fitness trail. **Nearby diversions:** Golf; excursions to Versailles, Rambouillet, and Chartres; wildlife park. **General Managers:** Raymond and Nicole Spitz. **Operated as a hotel since:** 1981. **U.S. representative:** Relais & Châteaux.

Directions: The château is 50 kilometers southwest of Paris near Chartres. From Paris, take autoroute A-10 to A-11 west to Pont de Saint Cloud; exit at Ablis, and continue west on N-10 for 5 kilometers; turn right in Essars for Saint-Symphorien Le-Château. Or take the train from Gare Montparnasse in Paris to Rambouillet; from there, take a taxi to the château.

Château d'Igé

A Thirteenth-Century Castle

Apart from its reputation for fine wines, the Burgundy region is known for its Romanesque architecture and traditional French cooking. You'll find *boeuf bourgignon, coq au vin,* Dijon mustard, and *escargot* on every menu. Once cultivated by the monastic orders for their religious services, the vineyards of Burgundy now produce millions of bottles of commercial wine every year.

THE PAST 🦋 This ancient, turreted castle began life as a feudal lord's manor for the counts of Mâcon, the region's largest landowners in the thirteenth century. Under Saint Louis, the property was taken over by the Crown and later by the Abbey of Cluny. Eventually the counts of Morangiers took possession, but abandoned it after they were bankrupted by the French Revolution. The castle sat in ruin until this century, when it found new life as a beautifully restored castle hotel.

THE PRESENT 🦋 Set amid several acres of gardens and surrounded by woods, meadows, and vineyards, Château d'Igé couldn't be lovelier or more romantic. Inside the ivy-covered stone walls and towers, stone-flagged floors contribute to a medieval atmosphere, while outside ducks glide picturesquely to the edge of a stream seeking offerings of food.

Worn stone stairs lead to spacious, comfortable guest rooms in the turret. They are furnished with antiques, and many have views of the garden and village.

An enormous open hearth, a massive beamed ceiling, and stone walls in the dining room reflect the castle's ancient origins. Since the castle is in the heart of Burgundy, you can be assured of a long wine list featuring Burgundy wines to complement the regional cuisine.

 71960 Igé (Saône-et-Loire). Tel: 011-33-4-85-33-33-99. Fax: 011-33-4-85-33-41-41. Rooms: 13, including 6 suites; all with bath. **Rates:** Moderate; doubles from FF480; includes service and tax. **Dates closed:** December 1 through February 28. **Dining facilities:** Restaurant. **Children:** Age 12 and younger sharing with parents free; playground; baby-sitting. **Facilities for disabled:** None. **On-site recreation:** None. **Nearby diversions:** Swimming pool; tennis; golf. **Proprietor:** Henri Jadot. **Operated as a hotel since:** 1973. **U.S. representative:** Relais & Châteaux.

Directions: From Lyon, drive north on A-6 and exit at Mâcon Sud. Continue north on N-6 a short way, then bear west on N-79 towards Montceau, la Roche Vineuse, Verzé, and Igé.

Château de Marçay

A Twelfth-Century Castle

After a long day spent exploring the magnificent châteaux of the Loire Valley, you might decide that the best castle of all is the one you are temporarily calling home. There's nothing quite like walking outside the front door after a fine dinner and watching the moon illuminate the white stone walls of "your" castle, or noticing the lamp glowing from the window in "your" turret room. On quiet nights you might even forget what century you're in.

THE PAST 🌀 Proudly standing in a large open field surrounded by vineyards, the Château de Marçay has witnessed over eight hundred years of French history. Built in 1150 by the Knights Templar, it was soon expanded as a fortress to protect the royal castle at nearby Chinon. In 1152 Henry II of England, count of Anjou and Plantagenet through his marriage to Eleanor of Aquitaine, reigned over a tremendous empire rivaling that of the French Capet kings. Henry built the greater part of Chinon Castle and used Marçay as a royal hunting lodge. After Henry's death the fortress of Marçay soon fell into the hands of the French Philippe Auguste.

It's hard to imagine this lovely, quiet, and dignified white castle as a symbol of bloody warfare, but even the Loire Valley was the scene of invasions and battles. During the Wars of Religion Marçay sustained some damage and was diminished in size.

Abandoned for nearly one hundred and fifty years, it remained the property of the clergy of Poitou. Eventually the castle was restored in a Renaissance style, with archery slits in the four great towers converted to windows. During the French Revolution, the fleurs-de-lis that used to be displayed on the towers were scratched off as "ornaments of feudalism."

THE PRESENT 🌸 A medieval atmosphere still exists in this castle. It features timbered ceilings, secret passageways, delightful tower rooms, and period furniture (some pieces date back to the twelfth century). Be sure to ask for one of the fifteen guest rooms inside the castle. They are gorgeously decorated with fine fabrics and feature exposed wood beams, stone walls, leaded windows, paneling, and fireplaces. Room 25 has a fabulous turret bathroom with an open-beamed ceiling and blue-and-white tiled walls and bathtub.

Dining at Marçay is first-rate. Michelin gives a one-star rating to the cuisine and Gault Millau two red *toques*. Specialties such as oysters and duck with currants are served in a dining room converted from the ancient kitchen; it retains the original ovens, a chimney, and beams for hanging game. If the weather is pleasant, you can dine on an outside terrace.

On occasion, the château hosts musical soirées.

37500 Marçay-Chinon (Indre-et-Loire). Tel: 011-33-2-47-93-03-47. **Fax:** 011-33-2-47-93-45-33. **Rooms:** 38, including 4 suites; some rooms in annex; all with bath. **Rates:** Moderate; doubles from FF495; includes service and tax. **Dates closed:** End of January through mid-March. **Dining facilities:** Restaurant closed Sunday evenings and Mondays from November through end of April, except holidays; bar. **Children:** Inquire about discounts when booking; playground. **Facilities for disabled:** None. **On-site recreation:** Swimming pool; tennis. **Nearby diversions:** Fishing; ballooning; canoeing; horseback riding; wine tasting; Loire châteaux. **Proprietor:** Philippe Mollard. **Operated as a hotel since:** 1971. **U.S. representative:** Relais & Châteaux; Marketing Ahead.

Directions: From Tours, take D-751 southwest to Chinon. Continue south on D-116. The château is signposted.

Château de Mercuès

A Thirteenth-Century Castle

Just south of the Dordogne region is Quercy, an area with a unique historical and cultural identity. The region has much to offer. Cahors, the capital, was once one of the greatest university towns and economic centers in France.

You can't miss the castle. As it has since ancient times, it sits high above the valley and Cahors.

THE PAST 🌀 The name "Mercuès" comes from the Roman god Mercury. A fortified temple dedicated to this god once stood on the site. Eventually the bishops of Cahors took possession, retaining it for nearly twelve hundred years. During the Albigensian Crusade in the thirteenth century, the castle was enlarged by the bishop to protect Cahors from the heretics.

During the Hundred Years' War the Château de Mercuès bounced back and forth between the French and English armies like a Ping-Pong ball. For years both the English and French laid siege to Mercuès, capturing and pillaging it until the two sides finally reached a stalemate, with the French buying the castle back for the sum of sixteen hundred sheep and a

piece of damask cloth. That's not much for a castle, you might think, but the English were quite eager to leave since the French were clearly gaining the advantage.

No sooner had the English gone home than the Wars of Religion broke out and the Huguenots arrived. At one point a captain of the castle turned traitor and set Mercuès on fire. The bishop, nearly asphyxiated, jumped out of a window to save himself and landed in the arms of the Huguenots. He was made to watch Mercuès torn apart and looted. When this ordeal was over, the Huguenots dressed him in his Episcopal robes, turned inside out, and sent him off on an ass. Mercuès was recaptured, but the castle remained in sorry condition for some time.

Restored in the seventeenth century, it was again looted during the Peasant Revolt. Fortunately, starting with Monseigneur Alain de Solminihac, several bishops did a considerable amount of work rebuilding the castle, having new rocks and dirt brought up from the valley below.

Luckily the French Revolution had little effect on Mercuès. In 1904, when France enacted a law separating church and state, the bishops had to put the castle up for sale.

THE PRESENT 🐚 Even the bishops didn't live in accommodations as deluxe as today's regally furnished guest rooms featuring fine antiques and carpets. If your budget permits, book a room inside the château. Less expensive rooms are in the Allée des Cédres Pavillon.

The elegant restaurant has a one-star Michelin rating. You'll find local specialties such as cold foie gras, artichoke hearts, and Cahors' fine, deeply colored red wine.

46090 Mercuès (Lot). Tel: 011-33-5-65-20-00-01. Fax: 011-33-5-65-20-05-72. **Rooms:** 30, including 6 suites; some rooms in the Allée des Cèdres Pavillon annex; all with bath. **Rates:** Expensive; doubles from FF700; includes service and tax. **Dates closed:** November 1 to Easter. **Dining facilities:** 2 restaurants; 1 restaurant closed on Wednesdays except in July and August; bar. **Children:** Age 10 and younger sharing with parents free; playground; game room; baby-sitting. **Facilities for disabled:** Yes. **On-site recreation:** Swimming pool; tennis. **Nearby diversions:** Fishing; horseback riding; mountain biking. **Proprietor:** George Vigouroux. **Operated as a hotel since:** 1944. **U.S. representative:** Relais & Châteaux.

Directions: Cahors is just south of the Dordogne region. The château is 8 kilometers west of Cahors on D-911. The nearest train station is in Cahors.

Château de Meyrargues

A Seventeenth-Century Castle

The clear blue skies and varied landscape of Provence inspired the masters of modern art. Van Gogh, Cezanne, Gauguin, Renoir, and Matisse all lived and found inspiration in this lovely region. Towns filled with Roman ruins and fountains, and idyllic hills covered with vineyards, lavender, and mimosa make Provence a spectacular area to drive through.

The imposing Château de Meyrargues is situated on a hilltop in the heart of Provence on one of France's most ancient fortified sites.

THE PAST A Celtic settlement existed here as far back as 600 B.C. For over nine hundred years, a long line of noble families has lived at Meyrargues. (The castle's name "Meyrargues" is thought to come from "Meyran"—a common family name in Provence.)

In 1024 a bull (a papal document) of Pope Benedict VIII first mentions Hugues, lord of Les Baux and Meyrargues, but the estate itself was then under the political control of the archbishop of Aix. In 1291 the Hugues family sold the château to the count of Provence, and from then on it changed hands often among various counts and viscounts.

During the Wars of Religion, the castle was pillaged and wrecked by royalist troops. After the Treaty of Vervins, which ended the war, the castle's owner, Louis d'Alagonia, was suspected of a plot against Henri IV and decapitated. In 1720 a plague decimated half the population of the village, and barely a hundred years ago a businessman from Aix used the castle as a warehouse for almonds.

Through the centuries Meyrargues survived every assault on its dignity and now sparkles as a lovely castle hotel.

THE PRESENT 🏵 To enter the castle, you must climb a balustraded flight of stairs between impressive twin stone towers where medieval knights once rode. After passing through an ancient door, you can view a marble blazon bearing a coat of arms from one of the castle's former lords. The antique-filled public lounge contains rich wood accents and a large stone fireplace, and fresh flowers abound.

Each guest room is named after a famous personage or style of French history. Rosettes, garlands, and paintings of chivalrous scenes embellish the Marie-Antoinette Suite, which also has a modern whirlpool tub. Painted furniture, porcelain lamps, and a canopy bed hung with taffeta furnish the Pompadour Room, while a more austere decor is found in the Mazarin Room.

An outside terrace with a sweeping view overlooking the town and the valley of Durance makes a pleasant spot to eat breakfast or relax in the afternoon. You can explore the grounds in search of the remains of an ancient Roman aqueduct.

The stone-vaulted gourmet dining room has a three-fork Michelin rating for atmosphere. Local Provençal dishes such as foie gras, *coquilles Saint Jacques,* and Grand Marnier soufflé are offered.

Route de Château, 13650 Meyrargues (Bouches-du-Rhône). Tel: 011-33-4-42-63-49-90. Fax: 011-33-4-42-63-49-92.   **Rooms:** 11, including 2 suites; all with bath. **Rates:** Expensive; doubles from FF700; includes service and tax. **Dates closed:** Open all year. **Dining facilities:** 2 restaurants; bar; medieval banquets. **Children:** Age 11 and younger sharing with parents free; cribs available; children's menu. **Facilities for disabled:** None. **On-site recreation:** Swimming pool; jogging path through forest. **Nearby diversions:** Hiking; tennis; horseback riding; golf; wine tasting. **Proprietor:** Maurice Binet. **Operated as a hotel since:** 1952. **U.S. representative:** None.

Directions: Meyrargues is about 15 kilometers northeast of Aix-en-Provence on N-96.

Château de Nieuil

A Sixteenth-Century Castle

This lovely white château is everything you could ask for in comfort and elegance. The setting is close to fairy-tale perfect. Symmetrical towers, a moat, formal gardens, and surrounding woods paint a storybook picture of handsome princes, fair damsels, and romantic interludes. This gracious château provides excellent accommodations in a central location for exploring the nearby Cognac region and the famous porcelain town of Limoges.

THE PAST King François I built Nieuil as a hunting castle. This sixteenth-century monarch embodied the romantic ideal of the medieval knight-king steeped in cultivated humanism and the art of the Renaissance. The château later became the property of various titled families. In 1937 the Fougerat family, who have lived in the Charente region since the fourteenth century, opened it as one of the first castle hotels in France.

THE PRESENT Jean-Michel Bodinaud, a grandson of the Fougerat family, and his wife, Luce, now manage the hotel. A very kind and gracious man, he takes an interest in his guests and welcomes them to his hotel with warm hospitality. He once taught art and now enjoys giving tours of an

outbuilding that holds an art gallery with fine paintings and Aubusson tapestries in one room, and an outstanding collection of turn-of-the-century posters (which are for sale) in another. The hundred acres of grounds are a delight to stroll through, and paths lead down to the château's own lake.

An imposing marble staircase leads to the beautiful guest rooms furnished with antiques. The immense rooms are decorated with chandeliers, tapestries, mirrors, and paintings. All overlook the gardens. One outstanding suite encompasses three floors of an ancient tower. A very unusual table in the reception area is crosscut from one tree that had nearly a five-foot diameter.

The lovely paneled dining room displays many valuable silver pieces. Luce Bodinaud oversees the kitchen, which has been awarded a Michelin star for cuisine. Regional specialties made with fresh produce are featured. Should you leave on an excursion for the day, the staff will pack you a lunch.

 16270 Nieuil (Charente). Tel: 011-33-5-45-71-36-38. Fax: 011-33-5-45-71-46-45. **Rooms:** 14, including 3 suites; all with bath. **Rates:** Moderate; doubles from FF700; includes service and tax. **Dates closed:** November 4 through April 27. **Dining facilities:** Restaurant; bar. **Children:** Age 12 and younger sharing with parents free; baby-sitting. **Facilities for disabled:** Yes. **On-site recreation:** Tennis; outdoor swimming pool. **Nearby diversions:** Fishing; mountain biking; town of Limoges (famous for porcelain). **Proprietors:** Luce and Jean-Michel Bodinaud. **Operated as a hotel since:** 1937. **U.S. representative:** Relais & Châteaux; Marketing Ahead.

Directions: Nieuil is 63 kilometers west of Limoges and 42 kilometers northeast of Angoulème. Coming from Angoulème on N-141, watch for signposts at Fontafie or Suaux. The château is on D-739 between the villages of Fontafie and Nieuil. Public transportation is not practical in the area.

Château de Pray

A Thirteenth-Century Castle

The Château de Pray was one of the first Loire castles to open as a hotel over forty years ago. Located near the magnificent Château d'Amboise in the Loire Valley, it permits you to sample fine living at moderate prices. The proprietors have created the atmosphere of a French country manor house.

THE PAST Since the Loire is easy to cross at this point, the site has always been strategically important. A fortress has existed here since the sixth century. Named after Geoffroy de Pray, the Château de Pray has been home to a long line of families closely connected with the French royal court who resided at the Château d'Amboise.

This circa 1244 Renaissance house was built around the same time as the Château d'Amboise. Perhaps because of its small size, the Château de Pray always had an owner to protect it from the ravages of time—Elizabeth I's commissioner of artillery in 1631, a councilor to the kings of Spain and France in the eighteenth century, and, later, one of Lafayette's officers (whose portrait now hangs above the fireplace).

THE PRESENT 🦋 After a day of sightseeing, you can relax in the château's cozy lounge among a nineteenth-century tiled fireplace, rich dark-wood paneling, antiques, and leaded-glass windows, or sit in the garden with its lovely views of the Loire. An attractive staircase leads to the charming guest rooms, decorated with period furniture. The delightful Sorbiers room holds a four-poster bed with turned-wood columns.

The highly regarded dining room features such seasonal specialties as Loire salmon, lamb, and roast guinea hen, and the wine list offers a fine selection of Loire wines.

37400 Amboise (Indre-et-Loire). Tel: 011-33-2-47-57-23-67. Fax: 011-33-2-47-57-32-50. Rooms: 19; all with bath. **Rates:** Moderate; doubles from FF470; includes service and tax. **Dates closed:** January. **Dining facilities:** Restaurant. **Children:** Age 4 and younger sharing with parents free; children's menu. **Facilities for disabled:** None. **On-site recreation:** None. **Nearby diversions:** Golf; horseback riding; tennis; cycling; Loire châteaux; wine tasting. **Proprietor:** M. and Mme Cariou. **Operated as a hotel since:** 1955. **U.S. representative:** None.

Directions: The hotel is located 2 kilometers east of Amboise on D-751.

Château de Rochegude

A Twelfth-Century Castle

Both wine connoisseurs and history lovers will find the beautiful Rhône Valley appealing. Driving through miles of vineyards that produce the popular Châteauneuf du Pape wine takes you to such towns as Orange, with one of the best-preserved Roman theaters in the world, and Avignon, with its immense palace inhabited in the fourteenth-century by French popes.

Rochegude, which is just a few miles down an ancient Roman road from Orange, offers excellent accommodations in an extensive château set on thirty-seven acres of parkland. Peace and tranquillity reign here, and you'll also find plenty of authentic medieval atmosphere.

THE PAST 🐚 The château originally belonged to the Marquis de Rochegude, who used it as his summer residence. The surrounding region sat astride the frontier of France and the papacy from 1274 to 1797. The village and château were governed by two sovereigns and two priors—one representing the French king, the other the pope. This arrangement worked well until the Huguenots entered the area in the sixteenth century. Baron des Adrets, a Huguenot captain, attacked the fortified castle and did some

damage, but he was driven back. The château was eventually restored, and some new terraces were added in the eighteenth and nineteenth centuries.

THE PRESENT 🍂 The bare stonework of this medieval castle's exterior belies the ornate style inside. The guest rooms are individually decorated with antique period furnishings and feature four-poster beds, tapestries, crystal, mirrors, and plenty of gilt. Each room is done in the style of a different period.

The lounge, with its huge carved baronial fireplace, makes a cozy spot to read. The medieval armory is now a flower-filled dining room opening onto a cobblestone courtyard. Michelin has awarded one star and Gault-Millau two *toques* to the cuisine, which includes dishes such as sea bass flavored with basil, tournedos with truffles, and stuffed quail. Barbecues are held outdoors by the pool on sunny days. And, of course, the Rhône Valley provides a fine selection of wines.

Vaulted stone corridors, an ancient dungeon, and huge underground cellars that have been excavated only recently invite exploration.

26790 Rochegude (Drôme). Tel: 011-33-4-75-04-81-88. Fax: 011-33-4-75-04-89-87. Rooms: 29, including 4 suites; all with bath. **Rates:** Moderate; doubles from FF650; includes service and tax. **Dates closed:** End of January to beginning of March; Mondays during low season. **Dining facilities:** Restaurant; bar. **Children:** Age 12 and younger sharing with parents free; playground. **Facilities for disabled:** None. **On-site recreation:** Swimming pool; tennis; walking paths; horseback riding; wine seminars. **Nearby diversions:** Golf; fishing; Grigan castle. **General Manager:** André Chabert. **Operated as a hotel since:** 1975. **U.S. representative:** Relais & Châteaux.

Directions: Rochegude is a short distance east of the Rhone River and 12 kilometers north of Orange. The château is at the junction of D-117 and D-8.

Château de Roumégouse

A Tenth-Century Castle

At first glance, this château looks too cute to be a real castle, but it has stood here for nine hundred years protecting pilgrims on their way to nearby Rocamadour. Now the Château de Roumégouse opens its doors to visitors exploring the fascinating Dordogne region of France.

Rocamadour is a tiny town of ancient houses, towers, and oratories perched precariously on cliffs sixteen hundred feet above a gorge. It is an incredible sight and the biggest attraction of the Dordogne.

THE PAST In 1166 a townsman desired to be buried under the town's Chapel of the Virgin. Workmen digging his grave found the body of another man and placed it near the altar. Soon after miracles mysteriously started taking place. Theories abounded about whose body had been found, the most prevalent being that it was that of Zaccheus, husband of Saint Veronica and a disciple of Jesus. The miracles soon brought people on pilgrimage from all over Christendom. Kings and saints—Henry II of England, Philip IV and Philip VI of Spain, Louis XI of France, Saint Bernard, Saint Dominic—all came to kneel and pay homage. Sinners, with chains around their arms and

necks, were required to come here, climb the two hundred and sixteen steps of the Great Stairway, and pray for forgiveness.

Money came and greed followed. The town was sacked by the English, who helped themselves to treasure during the Hundred Years' War, and by the Huguenots during the Wars of Religion, when the body of Saint Amadour was thrown into the flames (when it would not burn, the Protestant captain took an ax to it).

Although the centuries left Rocamadour less renowned than it once had been, pilgrims still come here.

THE PRESENT 🐚 Just four kilometers east of Rocamadour is the Château de Roumégouse. The gracious hosts take pride in ensuring their guests' comfort, and you'll feel as if you're in a large country home rather than a hotel. A nature preserve surrounds the castle, so peace and quiet are assured. A library and music room are available for your use, and the public rooms are full of antiques and tapestries that are for sale.

Guest rooms are decorated in the style of Louis XIV, Louis XV, Louis-Philippe, and Napoleon III. The best room is the Roumégouse room, which features an antique carved bed.

The castle's single tower houses a bar, and the breakfast room is accented with heart-shaped chairs. In the Louis XIII dining room, the house specialties, which include cold and warm foie gras, are served upon pewter tableware.

Route de Rocamadour, Rignac, 46500 Gramat (Lot). Tel: 011-33-5-65-33-63-81. Fax: 011-33-5-65-33-71-18. E-mail: smth10@calvacom.fr. **Rooms:** 15, including 2 suites; all with bath. **Rates:** Moderate; doubles from FF600; includes service and tax. **Dates closed:** October 30 through April 4. **Dining facilities:** Restaurant closed on Mondays except in July and August. **Children:** Age 12 and younger sharing with parents free; family plan available; baby-sitting. **Facilities for disabled:** Yes. **On-site recreation:** Swimming pool. **Nearby diversions:** Tennis; fishing; hunting; biking; ballooning. **Proprietor:** Luce and Jean-Louis Lainé. **Operated as a hotel since:** 1966. **U.S. representative:** Relais & Châteaux.

Directions: Located in the heart of the Dordogne region, Roumégouse is 4 kilometers east of Rocamadour on N-140. The hotel is signposted.

Château de la Treyne

A Fourteenth-Century Castle

After spending five minutes exploring the grounds of this enchanting white stone château, you'll feel as if you've been dropped into the middle of a fairy tale. Situated on a low cliff above the Dordogne River and surrounded by woods, the castle's spectacular setting has hardly changed in hundreds of years.

THE PAST The Dordogne flows so peacefully by this idyllic spot, it's hard to imagine why the local lords needed to build a fortress. In 1342 the Vicomte de Turenne gave his permission for a defensive keep at a place called La Treyne. After various owners, the de la Ramière family took over the property in 1553. During the Wars of Religion the castle was burned; it was rebuilt later during the reign of Louis XIII. In 1711 Marie de la Ramière married her cousin, Jean de Cardaillac-Vegennes, and the castle remained in the Cardaillac family until 1910.

THE PRESENT The elegant proprietress, Michèle Gombert-Devals, welcomes her guests with flair and genuine warmth, giving her castle the atmosphere of a private home. The lovely salon features a large fireplace and

a handsome wood-paneled bar, plus antiques and comfortable sofas that entice you to linger.

Individually decorated guest rooms feature period furnishings and pretty tile bathrooms. One room has a fur bedspread, and another is graced by a wood-beamed ceiling, antique furnishings (including a carved four-poster bed), and Oriental carpets on its polished wood floor.

Eating is very important at la Treyne. Candlelight dinners are served in either the elegant Louis XIII salon or on an outside terrace overlooking the river. One of the most romantic dining spots in all of France is at the edge of this terrace—where a small tower holds just one table. Since you're in the heart of the Dordogne region, foie gras and truffles feature prominently on a menu that has been awarded two red Gault Millau *toques*. Naturally, the wine is superb. In the morning, tables are set up under the trees in the garden for breakfast.

This castle is surrounded by three hundred acres of parkland that include graceful formal gardens bordered by several massive ancient trees—among them two cedars of Lebanon. Concerts and exhibitions are often held in the Romanesque chapel, which is topped by two capitals from Segovia, Spain.

64200 Lacave (Lot). **Tel:** 011-33-5-65-27-60-60. **Fax:** 011-33-5-65-27-60-70. **E-mail:** treyne@ calvacom.fr. **Rooms:** 14, including 2 suites; all with bath. **Rates:** Expensive; doubles from FF700; includes service and tax. **Dates closed:** November 15 through March 31. **Dining facilities:** Restaurant for hotel guests only; closed for lunch on Tuesdays and Wednesdays except during July and August. **Children:** Age 10 and younger sharing with parents free; playground; game room; baby-sitting. **Facilities for disabled:** None. **On-site recreation:** Swimming pool; tennis. **Nearby diversions:** Horseback riding; hunting; fishing; golf; excursions to Rocamadour. **Proprietor:** Mme Michèle Gombert-Devals. **Operated as a hotel since:** 1982. **U.S. representative:** Relais & Châteaux.

Directions: La Treyne is situated along the Dordogne River off D-43, 10 kilometers northwest of Rocamadour. The nearest train station is in Souillac.

Château de Trigance

An Eleventh-Century Castle

The Gorges of Verdon is often referred to as the Grand Canyon of France. Thanks to the Verdon River, which cuts its way through canyons ranging from two hundred and fifty to seven hundred meters in height, this isolated area has a rugged beauty unparalleled in Europe.

You'll need a car to best appreciate the spectacular views, scenic meadows, and eye-catching wildflowers. Traffic is light, so you can drive at a leisurely pace.

You can enjoy this region even more with the Château de Trigance as a base for your excursions. Perched high on a hill, with spectacular views of the valley below and mountains in the distance, you'll feel like an eagle in its aerie. Since the château is definitely not on the beaten tourist route, it takes some effort to get here, but you'll be rewarded by a fine hotel in an out-of-the-way place.

THE PAST 🌸 The earliest trace of habitation at Trigance dates back to the ninth century, when monks from the monastery of Saint Victor of Marseilles found it the ideal spot for meditation. The counts of Provence took possession next. The most famous count, Raimond de Provence "Le Gros," was from an eminent family of Italian origin. As knight of the Order of Malta, he came to France at the head of a military troop serving Queen Jeanne, who gave him title to the lands.

The château was destroyed during the French Revolution. Most of the records were burned, and the castle itself met the sad fate of being used as a rock quarry for the village below. In 1961 M. and Mme Hartmann fell in love with the site and the ruins and spent ten years gradually bringing the castle back to life. The Jean-Claude Thomases carry on their work with great success. If you stay at the castle, be sure to ask to see the scrapbook of the before-and-after-restoration photos. It's a fascinating documentation of the tremendous amount of work that goes into castle restoration.

THE PRESENT 🌸 The approach to the castle up a long winding road is an exciting one. After you reach the parking lot, you'll have at least eighty steps to climb to reach the castle. Don't worry about your luggage—the staff will bring it up for you. But all the effort is well worth the trouble, as the views from the top are exhilarating and the acoustics are so good that you can actually hear conversations from the village below.

The medieval stone-vaulted guest rooms come equipped with comforts such as modern bathrooms, canopy beds, and carpets on the tile floors. Each has an outside entrance. Winding stone stairways and small terraces lead to the warm, cozy lounge, where you are greeted by the gracious and friendly staff. This is the perfect place to talk to other guests or read a good book, perhaps while sipping an apéritif.

From the lounge, stone steps lead to candlelight dining under a vaulted stone ceiling. The menu emphasizes regional cooking that is well prepared and elegantly served. At your request the staff will bring breakfast to your room in the morning.

83840 Trigance (Var). Tel: 011-33-4-94-76-91-18. **Fax:** 011-33-4-94-85-68-99.   **Rooms:** 10, including 2 suites; all with bath. **Rates:** Moderate; doubles from FF550; includes service and tax. **Dates closed:** November 2 through March 23. **Dining facilities:** Restaurant closed for lunch on Wednesdays during low season. **Children:** Age 12 and younger sharing with parents free. **Facilities for disabled:** None. **On-site recreation:** None. **Nearby diversions:** Tennis; fishing; rock climbing; mountain biking; summer theater; Baroque music festival. **Proprietor:** Jean-Claude Thomas. **Operated as a hotel since:** 1966. **U.S. representative:** Relais & Châteaux.

Directions: Château de Trigance is near the Gorges du Verdon in southeast France, about 44 kilometers northwest of the city of Grasse. It is located on D-955 and is signposted.

MORE HOTELS

Château de Gilly

Located deep in the heart of Burgundy, this Cistercian
abbatial palace has origins in the sixth century. The property
is surrounded by vineyards and a water-filled moat.

Gilly-lès-Cîteaux, 21640 Vougeot (Côte d'Or). Tel: 011-33-4-80-62-89-98. Fax: 011-33-4-80-62-82-34.

Château de Madières

Perched above the Vis river gorge in the south of France,
this fourteenth-century fortress is built into the town's ancient
walls and arches. Part of the castle is still a ruin.

34190 Madières, Gard. Tel: 011-33-4-67-73-84-03. Fax: 011-33-4-67-73-55-71.

Hôtel du Vieux Château

One lord of this castle was an officer to William the Conqueror
in the eleventh century. The hotel is located in the oldest part
of the structure, and the fourteenth-century tower dungeon
now houses a museum.

4 cours du Château, 50260 Bricquebec, Normandy. Tel: 011-33-2-52-24-49.

Germany

By the close of the fourteenth century, more than five thousand castles dominated Germany's countryside. Before unification every prince, king, and robber knight ruled over a little mini-kingdom behind the towering walls of his own protective castle. Dozens of these castles now provide the traveler with some of Germany's most interesting accommodations. There is a castle hotel here to suit every budget, taste, and fantasy.

Most of the German castles were built by serfs who spent their days breaking rocks and building the massive walls and towers for their feudal overlords. The castles not only provided protection for their inhabitants, but increased the wealth and power of their owners. On one stretch of the Rhine River over thirty tollgates were imposed to tax all commerce. As a result kings, adventurers, and profiteers came to take advantage of the economic opportunity, and the castles soon became battlegrounds and changed owners regularly.

The Rhine between Koblenz and Bingen (a sixty-kilometer stretch), where castles dot the landscape for as far as the eye can see, is the source of legends. Exciting stories of robber knights, the Nibelung treasure, and the Lorelei originated here. The area has gained even more romance for us through the inspiration of Wagner and his *Ring* operas and the poetry of Goethe, Hugo, and Longfellow.

Over the centuries, the German castles met their downfall for a variety of reasons. On the Rhine, the robber knights had become so powerful that in 1254 twenty-six Rhenish towns, resenting the disruption of river traffic, formed the Rhenish League association to stop the brigandage. It took twenty years and the help of King Rudolf of Habsburg to effectively destroy the fortresses of the robber knights.

Then the Thirty Years' War brought soldiers from Sweden, France, and Spain who plundered, occupied, and destroyed castles all over Germany. In 1688 and 1689 the soldiers of the French king Louis XIV destroyed over a dozen castles in their effort to gain German territory. The final blow came from the French Revolution, when the advance of revolutionary troops forced the German army to withdraw behind the Rhine. Unable to withstand attack from modern weaponry and explosives, the castles were damaged one by one and then eventually fell into decay.

Not until the nineteenth century did restoration attempts begin to preserve the heritage of the German castle—and to provide summer homes for the nobility. Today many of these castles are open to the public as either museums or castle hotels.

You might wonder about the difference between a "burg" and a "schloss." A burg is a fortified defensive structure, and a schloss is a softer version, more like a palace. However, the two terms are used interchangeably today.

Many of the castles in this section belong to the Gast im Schloss association, which represents many of Germany's finest castle hotels. All are noted for their beautiful locations away from big cities. A number of special programs are offered, including individual tours of the Grimm Brothers' fairy-tale castles and of the water-moated castles of northern Germany. The "Wandern—Gast im Schloss" is organized so that you can walk from castle to castle along quiet forest paths without your luggage (it is transported for you). A Castle Gift Voucher good for any of the association's hotels is also available. For more information, contact Gast im Schloss Hotels & Restaurants at: D4, 9-10, P.O. Box 120620, D-68057 Mannheim, Germany, Tel: 011-49-621-12662-0, Fax: 011-49-621-12662-12.

For general information on Germany, contact the German National Tourist Office at: 122 East 42nd Street, New York, New York 10168-0072, Tel: 212-661-7200, Fax: 212-661-7174; or 11766 Wilshire Boulevard, Suite 750, Los Angeles, California 90025, Tel: 310-575-9799, Fax: 310-575-1565.

Parkhotel Wasserburg Anholt

A TWELFTH-CENTURY CASTLE

Rising majestically from the flat countryside of Westphalia next to the Dutch border, the Parkhotel Wasserburg (which means "water castle") Anholt, presided over by the Prince zu Salm-Salm, is encircled by a wide moat and lake. The only approach to the castle is through a large park and over a narrow stone causeway and drawbridge.

THE PAST 🌀 This impressive building began as a "thick tower," which was said to be the only safe place in the marshes in which people could take

refuge back in Roman times. Further construction around the tower and lower wall date from the twelfth century. Other additions date from the thirteenth and fourteenth centuries. The castle is still in remarkable condition, considering that it has been in the path of every marching and conquering army imaginable.

After the Thirty Years' War proved the inadequacy of most castles' defensive structures, Anholt was transformed into a residence. But not until relatively recently did it suffer its greatest damage: During World War II two air raids destroyed part of the structure. After the war, Prince zu Salm-Salm meticulously restored the castle using ancient tiles and bricks.

THE PRESENT 🐚 The modern interiors of the hotel section, done in shades of cream and beige, are lovely. Guest rooms are also contemporary in style, although the two in the tower have four-poster beds.

Two restaurants and a bar serve well-prepared meals, and, when weather permits, an outside terrace just off the moat is also available for dining.

The quiet and peaceful setting at Anholt invites you to take long walks through the gardens and park. You'll find many fascinating places to explore. The park and a museum with a collection of Dutch portraits, Flemish tapestries, and Japanese and Chinese porcelains are open to non-guests.

Kleverstrasse, D-46419 Isselburg. Tel: 011-49-2874-4590. Fax: 011-49-2874-4035. Rooms: 28, including 6 singles and 22 doubles; all with bath, some with showers. **Rates:** Expensive; doubles from DM220; includes breakfast, service, and tax. **Dates closed:** January, and December 24 and 25. **Dining facilities:** Restaurant, closed Monday and Sunday evenings; café-restaurant Treppchen; outdoor terrace; bar. **Children:** Age 11 and younger sharing with parents 15 percent discount; crib DM20. **Facilities for disabled:** None. **On-site recreation:** 18-hole golf course; cycling; hotel museum; animal park. **Nearby diversions:** Excursions to Holland. **Proprietor:** Fürst zu Salm-Salm. **Operated as a hotel since:** 1970. **U.S. representative:** Euro-Connection.

Directions: From the A-3 autobahn, exit just before Dutch border at Bocholt-Rees, Isselburg. Follow signposts.

Hotel Schloss Auel

AN EIGHTEENTH-CENTURY CASTLE

Fortified castles died out by the time of the Baroque era, and Schloss Auel, a fortified baronial mansion, was one of the first residences to usher in the new era. Originally moated, it was converted in the seventeenth century into a U-shaped structure around a large courtyard.

THE PAST 🌸 The family of the Marquis Philippe de la Valette St. George acquired this property through marriage. The most famous member of this family was the admiral and grandmaster of the Knights of St. John, who defended Maltese independence and stopped the expansion of the Ottoman empire under Suleiman II. (Valletta, the capital of Malta, was named after him.) All the manuscripts and memorabilia pertaining to the family are preserved at Schloss Auel.

En route to inspect his Rhine army, Napoleon Bonaparte stayed at Schloss Auel in 1811.(Today you can lie in the very same four-poster bed in which Napoleon slept.) A few years later, Tsar Alexander I was a guest here before completion of the Holy Alliance. At the turn of the century, Kaiser Wilhelm II often visited.

THE PRESENT  The la Valette family still lives here, bringing their guests centuries of tradition and hospitality. Baron de la Valette's passion today is aviation, and he is as eager to talk about flying as about the long history of his family and home.

Recently the hotel underwent a complete refurbishment. In keeping with the castle's historical atmosphere, lovely antiques fill the rooms. An oak stairway in the entry hall leading to the guest rooms is especially grand. Falling asleep under the namesake portraits in Napoleon's or Kaiser Wilhelm's room will remind you that history took place right here.

The restaurant features trout, venison, and wild fowl specialties.

Wedding ceremonies are conducted in an intimate chapel with a rococo altarpiece and paintings from the sixteenth and seventeenth centuries.

D-53797 Lohmar-Wahlscheid. **Tel:** 011-49-2206-60030. **Fax:** 011-49-2206-6003-222. **Rooms:** 20; all with bath. **Rates:** Expensive; doubles from DM250; includes breakfast, service, and tax. **Dates closed:** Open all year. **Dining facilities:** Restaurant. **Children:** Age 5 and younger sharing with parents free; playground. **Facilities for disabled:** None. **On-site recreation:** Tennis; horseback riding; swimming. **Nearby diversions:** Fishing; golf. **Proprietor:** Von la Valette St. George family. **Operated as a hotel since:** 1951. **U.S. representative:** None.

Directions: Lohmar is southeast of Cologne on route 484. The schloss is north of Lohmar.

Dornröschenschloss Sababurg

A FOURTEENTH-CENTURY CASTLE

If sleeping in a real fairy-tale castle spurs your imagination, you have something in common with the Grimm Brothers, who were once guests at Sababurg and modeled the castle in "Sleeping Beauty" after it. (But this is not the Sleeping Beauty castle of Disneyland. The Disney castle was styled after King Ludwig's Neuschwanstein in Bavaria.)

Sababurg has a unique character. Rising out of the woods, the castle appears empty. But upon closer inspection, you'll find the hotel operating in one of the two massive towers and in a newer connected annex.

THE PAST Sababurg was in existence long before the Grimm Brothers' visit. The castle was originally built in 1334 for the protection of pilgrims en route to Gottsbüren, a nearby village that found fame for a short time when what was thought to be the body of Christ was miraculously discovered there in 1330.

Soon the castle could not protect anybody and became an object of territorial contention between Mainz, Paderborn, Braunschweig, and Hessen. When the area no longer held any political or military value, the castle declined in status.

For the next four hundred years of its life, the castle was frequently damaged and rebuilt. For a while the grounds were used for keeping wild horses; later, Philip I used the castle as a hunting lodge.

THE PRESENT 🌀 Today no one seems to pay much attention to the castle's true origins. The fairy-tale theme dominates the interiors, with spinning wheels and antiques furnishing the public rooms. A small gift shop sells souvenir pottery pieces with fairy-tale scenes painted on them.

Guest rooms are warm, cozy, and decorated in period style. The seven rooms in the tower are the most expensive but also have the most charm. However, the rooms in the attached annex are attractive and comfortable and have fabulous views of the quiet countryside and adjacent animal park. Rooms aren't numbered but instead bear animal names dating back to the sixteenth century—*In der wilden Sau* (In the Wild Sow) and *Das Einhold* (The Unicorn).

The restaurant also has a stunning view of the surrounding woodlands and features a menu of wild game and fish. In summer, café meals are served on an outside terrace.

The portion of the castle that is in ruins is open to the public for exploration. In summer, the ruins provide the setting for performances of the Grimm Brothers' fairy tales as well as for concerts and exhibitions. Inside, the castle vaults now serve as a private theater.

The surrounding woods and magnificent oak forests makes for idyllic hiking. It's also possible to walk to nearby Trendelburg Castle to spend a night and have your luggage taken over to meet you. The five hundred and thirty-acre Tierpark Sababurg located just below the castle is a low-key hiking zoo with a children's petting area, a playground, and a hunting museum. Europe's oldest animal park, it is populated with European bison, wild horses and ponies, and reindeer with lineages dating to pre-historic times.

D-34369 Hofgeismar (Sababurg). Tel: 011-49-5671-808-0. Fax: 011-49-5671-808-200. **Rooms:** 17; all with bath. **Rates:** Expensive; doubles from DM265; includes breakfast, service, and tax. **Dates closed:** Mid-January through mid-February. **Dining facilities:** Restaurant; outside terrace café. **Children:** Cribs free; age 5 and younger extra bed charge DM15; age 6 through 12 extra bed charge DM30. **Facilities for disabled:** None. **On-site recreation:** Fitness room; sauna; hiking; theater performances. **Nearby diversions:** Animal park; cycling; steamer trips on the Weser River; tennis; pilgrimage church at Gottsbüren. **Proprietor:** Koseck family. **Operated as a hotel since:** 1960. **U.S. representative:** Euro-Connection.

Directions: Sababurg is about 30 kilometers north of Kassel. Take the Hannover-Frankfurt autobahn (E-4) and exit at H. Münden/Werratal; continue northwest on route 80. The hotel is signposted.

Wald & Schlosshotel Friedrichsruhe

AN EIGHTEENTH-CENTURY CASTLE

In your rush to get to the Romantic Road, don't overlook some of the quieter, less-touristy areas located between the Swabian Forest and the Tauber Valley, where tradition still reigns in tiny rural towns. Castles with typical German Renaissance features, such as round carved gables, abound throughout the Hohenlohe Plain.

THE PAST 🐚 The Hohenlohes have dominated this region of Germany for centuries. Up the road from Friedrichsruhe in the town of Neuenstein, one of the Hohenlohes' beautiful sixteenth-century Renaissance castles is now a museum showing what daily life was like in a small German court. In the village of Öhringen, a cemetery at a late-Gothic church holds several members of the family. The nearby village of Waldenburg was once a moated fortified town from where the Hohenlohes commanded the region.

Prince Johann Friedrich zu Hohenlohe-Öhringen built Friedrichsruhe as a summer residence and hunting castle in 1712. (In fact, "Friedrichsruhe" means "Friedrich's refuge.") The family lived here off and on until the Wald (which means "forest or woods") and Schlosshotel

opened. Today Prince Kraft zu Hohenlohe-Öhringen presides over his ancestor's elegant and luxurious eighteenth-century hunting castle, which is now both a wildlife preserve and resort.

THE PRESENT ᠁ In an atmosphere of traditional refinement, the Schlosshotel Friedrichsruhe gives you a peek at the old style of German country life. The hotel is divided between the original residence and a new section housing the reception area, restaurant, and indoor pool. The grounds are lovely at any time of year, and the surrounding woods and parkland make for pleasant walking excursions.

Furnishings are a combination of modern and antique. Fine art pieces and tapestries from the family's collection are displayed in some public rooms. Special antique pieces furnish many of the guest rooms, the best of which are in the castle.

Gourmet cuisine rated two stars by Michelin is served in the castle's elegant restaurant. Specialties include lobster with fried leeks, tender venison, breast of dove, and marzipan ice cream. The Jägerstube—an informal yet atmospheric restaurant decorated with mounted antlers, an antique porcelain stove, and carved chairs—offers simpler fare.

D-74639 Friedrichsruhe-Zwieflingen. Tel: 011-49-7941-60870. **Fax:** 011-49-7941-61468. **Rooms:** 49, including 14 suites; all with bath; guest rooms are in the castle, tower house, and garden house. **Rates:** Expensive; doubles from DM295; includes breakfast, service, and tax. **Dates closed:** Open all year. **Dining facilities:** Main restaurant closed on Mondays for everybody, also on Tuesdays for non-guests; informal restaurant; outdoor terrace. **Children:** Crib DM25; extra bed DM50. **Facilities for disabled:** Yes. **On-site recreation:** Indoor and outdoor swimming pools; sauna; tennis; 18-hole golf course. **Nearby diversions:** Hiking; hunting; fishing; horseback riding. **Proprietor:** Fürst Kraft zu Hohenlohe-Öhringen. **Operated as a hotel since:** 1969. **U.S. representative:** Relais & Châteaux.

Directions: Friedrichsruhe is east of Heidelberg. From the E-12 autobahn, exit at Öhringen and go north.

Burghotel Götzenburg

A Fifteenth-Century Castle

On the Romantic Road, halfway between the medieval town of Rothenburg and the university town of Heidelberg, lies the Hohenlohe Plain—an area of picturesque sleepy villages and German Renaissance castles. For a glimpse at a more traditional side of Germany, take a one-day detour to explore this untouristed region.

THE PAST ✺ Götzenburg Castle at Jagsthausen was the birthplace of the famous German knight Götz von Berlichingen (1480-1562). Also known as Götz of the Iron Hand, he was an imperial knight romanticized as a German Robin Hood. (His "iron hand" was a replacement for one shot off during the siege of Landshut.) He fought in campaigns against the Turks in Hungary and with Charles V against the French. In between wars he kidnapped nobles and ransacked commercial convoys. Twice banished from the empire, he came back to lead a faction in the Peasants' War. Despite having led such an active and dangerous life, he lived to be eighty-two years old, wrote his memoirs, and died a peaceful death at nearby Hornberg Castle. Goethe dramatized his story, which is still reenacted every summer in the courtyard of Burghotel Götzenburg using authentic period armor from the castle's own collection.

THE PRESENT ✺ This unusual three-story Renaissance building, with steep gabled roofs and spires crowning its turrets, retains a medieval atmosphere. You can see the famous iron hand of Götz in a little museum on the grounds.

The spacious and warm public rooms are furnished with antiques, and many guest rooms, named after various German actors, contain massive, carved four-poster beds.

Generous helpings of traditional cuisine, including venison, are served in the wood-beamed dining room.

D-74249 Jagsthausen. Tel: 011-49-7943-22-22. Fax: 011-49-7943-82-00. **Rooms:** 15; most with bath or shower. **Rates:** Moderate; doubles from DM170; includes breakfast, service, and tax. **Dates closed:** November through February. **Dining facilities:** Restaurant; outside terrace. **Children:** Inquire about discounts when booking. **Facilities for disabled:** None. **On-site recreation:** Bowling alley; performances in courtyard. **Nearby diversions:** Tennis; fishing. **Proprietor:** Jürgen Bircks. **Operated as a hotel since:** Not known. **U.S. representative:** None.

Directions: From the E-12 autobahn, exit at Öhringen and go north.

Burg Hornberg

AN ELEVENTH-CENTURY CASTLE

The Neckar River flows past Heidelberg and is linked to the great Rhine. Several castles along the river overlook a lovely valley of woods, orchards, and vineyards. After a day of exploration, you can relax and enjoy watching all the activity on the river from the terrace of your very own castle.

THE PAST The famous German knight, Götz von Berlichingen, bought Hornberg castle in 1517 from the bishop of Speyer and lived here for forty-five years between campaigns and exile. During his times at home he dictated his autobiography to a priest. When he died, his grandson sold the castle to Freiherren von Gemmingen, in whose family the property remains. A museum in the castle exhibits Götz's armor.

THE PRESENT Burg Hornberg stands as a venerable landmark along the vine-covered hillsides of the Neckar. The main part of the castle lies mainly in ruins, but the surrounding buildings remain intact and now house the hotel.

Throughout the public rooms you'll find open-beamed ceilings, fireplaces, copper etchings, murals with medieval themes, blacksmiths' works, and pewter collections.

Guest room names include the Gunpowder Chamber, Arms Chamber, and Eagles Nest, and they are decorated in either modern or period style. Many have fireplaces, verandas, and river views through arrow-slit windows. Three rooms are in the turret.

The restaurant Im Alten Marstall operates in the former horse stable and has enjoyed a fine reputation since 1953. Charcoal-grilled meats are the specialty, and the wine comes from the castle's own vineyards.

D-74865 Neckarzimmern. Tel: 011-49-6261-924-60. Fax: 011-49-6261-924-644. **Rooms:** 24, including 3 singles and 21 doubles; all with bath. **Rates:** Moderate; doubles from DM195; includes breakfast, service, and tax. **Dates closed:** Mid-December through February. **Dining facilities:** Restaurant with English à la carte menu. **Children:** Inquire about discounts when booking. **Facilities for disabled:** None. **On-site recreation:** Tours through castle ruins. **Nearby diversions:** Tennis; horseback riding; fishing; swimming; excursions on the Neckar River. **Proprietor:** Freiherr B. von Gemmingen. **Operated as a hotel since:** 1972. **U.S. representative:** Euro-Connection.

Directions: Burg Hornberg is on the east bank of the Neckar River on route 37. It is about 50 kilometers east of Heidelberg, and 25 kilometers north of Heilbronn. The nearest train station is about 1 kilometer away.

Hotel Schloss Hugenpoet

A Seventeenth-Century Castle

An outstanding example of a moated German water castle, Schloss Hugenpoet offers its guests an elegant atmosphere, idyllic surroundings, and fine food. Though most visitors to Essen are businessmen and industrialists, this castle hotel is well worth seeking out for its own sake. It is inviting at any time of year: Its massive old fireplaces will warm you in winter, and the surrounding woods and gardens are delightful in summer.

THE PAST The area of Hugenpoet was first a manorial domain of Charlemagne in 778. A marshland probably existed here in ancient times, as the name Hugenpoet means "pool of toads."

As was typical of nobles of the time, the Barons von Nesselrode built Hugenpoet Castle in 1308 as a base from which to rob the passing commerce. The castle was besieged and burned one hundred and fifty years later, with only a few sections remaining unscathed. A new castle was built close by the old one, but it was ravaged by Swedish, French, Spanish, Hessian, and royal troops during the Thirty Years' War. The foundation of today's castle was laid in 1650.

At the beginning of the nineteenth century, Baroness Auguste von Nesselrode-Hugenpoet brought the property as a dowry to her husband, Baron von Maercken zu Geerath. When he couldn't afford the upkeep, he sold the disintegrating castle to Baron Friedrich Leopold von Fürstenberg, in whose family it remained until recently.

The Fürstenbergs made it their home and enlarged it by adding another story. During the last few years of World War II, the castle served as a military branch office, and after the war Essen leased the property to house the contents of the destroyed Folkwang Museum. The cost of repairing and maintaining the castle was fast becoming a liability to the Fürstenberg family. To help offset the huge expenses, they leased the property to Dusseldorf hotelier Kurt Neumann in 1954. Over a million deutsche marks later, the castle opened its doors to its first guests.

Jürgen and Edda Neumann took over the management ten years later, and under a new contract with the Fürstenbergs it has become a first-class establishment of international reputation.

THE PRESENT 🦁 A striking black marble stairway greets you in the entry hall, and a splendid collection of antiques and fine art adorns the public rooms. The fireplaces, carved of Bamberg sandstone, are fine examples of the sixteenth-century Dutch art of the area (as influenced by the late Renaissance).

Many of the cozy guest rooms are furnished with their original sixteenth-century furniture, including elaborately carved four-poster beds.

Three elegant dining rooms present German and French cuisine that has been awarded one star by Michelin.

August Thyssen Strasse 51, D-45219 Essen (E-Kettwig). Tel: 011-49-2054-120-40. Fax: 011-49-2054-120-450. **Rooms:** 19, including 1 suite; all with bath. **Rates:** Expensive; doubles from DM265; includes breakfast, service, and tax. **Dates closed:** First week in January. **Dining facilities:** 3 restaurants. **Children:** Age 12 and younger sharing with parents free. **Facilities for disabled:** None. **On-site recreation:** Tennis. **Nearby diversions:** Swimming; golf. **Proprietors:** Jürgen Neumann and Michael M. Lübbert. **Operated as a hotel since:** 1954. **U.S. representative:** Relais & Châteaux; Euro-Connection.

Directions: Kettwig is 15 kilometers south of Essen. From the autobahn, exit at Kreuz:Breitscheid. You might need to stop and ask directions.

Schlosshotel Kronberg

A Nineteenth-Century Palace

Not all royal residences in Germany are massive, defensive structures that have been bombarded through the centuries. One of the most stunning hotels in Germany is a former palace secluded in fifty-six acres of woods, meadows, and gardens. The lounges, hallways, and rooms at Kronberg feel more like a museum than a hotel, except that every detail has been carefully thought out to provide you comfort.

THE PAST 🌰 Built in the early 1890s, Kronberg was the final home of the Empress Victoria—widow of the German emperor Frederick III, eldest daughter of Queen Victoria of England, and mother of Kaiser Wilhelm II. An intelligent, active woman, she did much to influence her husband with her progressive views.

Although her marriage was successful, and she did her best to serve her new country, the German ruling class never liked having an English empress in their midst. Chancellor Otto von Bismarck once remarked, "If the Princess can leave the Englishwoman at home and become a Prussian, then

she may be a blessing to her country." Even sadder for her was that her son, who took the throne after his father had reigned for only ninety-nine days, was bitterly opposed to the ideals and beliefs of his parents and openly displayed his dislike for his mother.

When her husband died, the question arose as to where the dowager empress should live. Fortunately, a property became available near the Taunus Mountains. The house standing there was razed and work began on Friedrichshof—today's Schlosshotel Kronberg. The architect, Ernst Eberhard von Ihne, was under orders to design a house according to the principle "nothing to attract attention, but everything to hold attention." He went to England to study country-house architecture and returned to build a sixteenth-century German Renaissance palace with English country manor and Gothic elements. Local stone was used for the outside and quartzite for the façades. Other areas were built with basalt and sandstone. No shortcuts in workmanship were allowed—fittings for electricity were handmade; floors, paneling, and glasswork were all expertly laid.

The gardens were designed in the English style. When visiting royal relatives came, each planted a tree. At one time plaques marked each planting, but unfortunately these have disappeared with souvenir hunters.

Victoria moved into the palace in 1894 and died here in 1901. Many of her relatives came to visit—her mother, Queen Victoria; her brother, Edward VII; the last tsar of Russia, Nicholas II. Others visitors include the kings of Italy and Denmark.

Shortly after her brother took the British throne, he heard that she was seriously ill. He came to Friedrichshof with his private secretary, Sir Frederick Ponsonby, and his own personal physician to check out the rumors. Victoria, bedridden and obviously dying, called for Ponsonby to ask him a great favor. She had a large collection of personal letters she wanted smuggled out of Germany and away from the clutches of her son, the kaiser. At one o'clock in the morning, two huge boxes covered with black oilcloth and marked "China—with care" and "Books—with care" were taken out with Ponsonby's personal luggage. In 1928 the letters were published, although Kaiser Wilhelm I, then a refugee in Holland, had tried furiously to prevent it.

Victoria's will specified that the house and belongings were to remain intact and left the responsibility to her youngest daughter, Princess Margaret, who was married to Prince Frederick Charles of Hesse, a member of an anti-Prussian family. They made it their home until circumstances forced them to move out into the cottage. Further tragedies struck the family during World War II, and when the Americans entered Germany, the schloss was requisitioned for use as a club for the American Army. Margaret was forbidden to set foot on the property and various collections were damaged. Later King George VI of England demanded that a collection of bound letters from Queen Victoria to her daughter be brought back from Kronberg to England for safekeeping; Queen Elizabeth eventually returned them to Margaret.

In 1953 Friedrichshof was returned to the family. Thanks to the efforts of the Empress Victoria's grandsons, the palace was preserved as a hotel under management of the nonprofit foundation Kurhessische Hausstiftung.

THE PRESENT 🌼 Once Empress Victoria invited an Englishwoman to stay at her palace. When dressing for dinner, the woman was startled when Victoria herself walked in unannounced and said, "I just wanted to make sure that you have everything you want." Today the service is almost as personal. Victoria would have been proud: Schlosshotel Kronberg is a fine tribute to her.

The palace remains a meeting place for international visitors. The British royal family has come here for eighty years. Recent guests have included German chancellor Helmut Schmidt, Henry Kissinger, and Paul Volcker—former chairman of the Federal Reserve.

Each public room retains the atmosphere of its early days. The inside of the schloss is a showcase for the empress's extensive collections of paintings, *objets d'art,* and books. Several salons can be rented. The Blue Salon, highlighted by an exquisite crystal chandelier, is perfect for intimate occasions, while the Red Salon is large enough to hold a banquet.

Guest rooms are decorated with antique furniture, paintings, and Oriental carpets. Some have fireplaces. A splurge on the Royal Suite buys you a night in the room where the Empress Victoria slept.

A small, octagonal dining room is decorated with antique ceramics and glass; the larger dining room has walls bearing brass sconces and paintings by Titian and Holbein. (Paintings by Turner and Reynolds grace the walls of the hotel bar.) The extensive menu offers such delicacies as cream of smoked trout soup, quail stuffed with mushrooms, and tandoori lamb, and on occasion violins serenade diners from the balcony.

Hainstrasse 25, D-61476 Kronberg. Tel: 011-49-6173-70101. Fax: 011-49-6173-701267. **Rooms:** 58, including 24 singles, 27 doubles, and 7 suites; all with bath. **Rates:** Very expensive; doubles from DM480; includes service and tax. **Dates closed:** Open all year. **Dining facilities:** Restaurant; outdoor terrace; bar. **Children:** Crib DM30; age 12 and younger sharing with parents, extra bed charge of DM80; baby-sitting. **Facilities for disabled:** Yes. **On-site recreation:** 18-hole golf course available if you belong to an international golf club and have a handicap. **Nearby diversions:** Swimming; tennis; spa town of Bad Homburg. **General Manager:** Hartmut Althoff. **Operated as a hotel since:** 1954. **U.S. representative:** Relais & Châteaux; Utell International.

Directions: Kronberg is a short distance northwest of Frankfurt. It is the final stop on one of Frankfurt's metro lines. From the station, the hotel is about a 15-minute walk through the park. By car, turn off the B455 at Kronberg. With advance notice, a hotel car can pick you up at the Frankfurt airport.

Burghotel Lauenstein

A Tenth-Century Castle

Lauenstein is northwest of Bayreuth, right on the border of former East Germany. Its remoteness from the usual tourist centers is one of its attractions. Here you can see a Germany untouched by the developments of the last fifty years. At nearly two thousand feet elevation, the landscape of mountains and wooded valleys is beautiful and a promising sportsman's paradise.

THE PAST King Konrad I built this fortress in 915. He belonged to the powerful Franconian dynasty—the Conradines, who spent their reign upholding Carolingian kingship against the up-and-coming Saxon, Swabian, and Bavarian nobility. The Hohenzollern family later acquired the property and held it for centuries.

THE PRESENT The approach to the castle is up a winding narrow road—one knights rode up on horseback during the Middle Ages. Once here, you'll have a fascinating experience exploring the thousand-year-old castle's battlements, moat, and vaulted halls.

The hotel actually operates in a manor home. Hand-decorated furniture from the region fills the pleasant guest rooms. Those that do not have

private bathrooms share a tower facility outfitted with oversize bathtubs.

The restaurant, decorated in rustic style, serves game and fish dishes.

D-96337 Lauenstein-Ludwigsstadt. Tel: 011-49-9263-4930. Fax: 011-49-9263-7167. Rooms: 21, including 9 singles and 12 doubles; most with bath. **Rates:** Inexpensive; doubles from DM68; includes breakfast, service, and tax. **Dates closed:** Open all year. **Dining facilities:** Dining room; enclosed veranda. **Children:** Age 4 and younger sharing with parents free. **Facilities for disabled:** None. **On-site recreation:** None. **Nearby diversions:** Tennis; swimming; forest walks; skiing; tobogganing. **General Manager:** Helmut Wagner. **Operated as a hotel since:** 1897. **U.S. representative:** None.

Directions: Lauenstein is northwest of Bayreuth off route 85. If traveling by car, beware of police radar traps. Lauenstein can also be reached by train.

Schlosshotel Lembeck

A Twelfth-Century Castle

To reach this moated water castle, which is more museum than hotel, you must cross through a large park, over two moats, through a wall and gateway, and then continue down a long drive with a series of Baroque doorways and roofs. The layout of the castle is very unusual: As you enter, the main body is the axis, with the towers jutting out into the water.

The Past 🐾 In 1017 Emperor Heinrich II gave the land to the bishops of Paderborn, who later built a defensive castle on the site. In the seventeenth century the castle passed into the hands of the lords of Westerholt, who transformed it into a residence. Much of the castle's decor dates from this time.

THE PRESENT 🦚 Guest rooms are located in the rear wing and are stylishly furnished with many antiques. The bridal suite has a four-poster bed, Oriental carpets, chairs covered in tapestry fabric, and windows looking out over the grounds. Two rooms are in a turret.

A narrow stairway leads down to a small restaurant with a brick vaulted ceiling and medieval atmosphere. Michelin has awarded two forks to the gourmet cuisine.

The castle's grounds are lovely, with peacocks strutting through the gardens and water lilies blooming in the moat. On weekends many sightseers come to visit the castle and grounds and to tour the museum displaying items of everyday use from the Middle Ages—furniture, fine china and porcelain, handwoven tapestries, and fine carvings. Weddings are held in a chapel adjacent to the hotel.

Schloss 1, D-46286 Dorsten-Lembeck. **Tel:** 011-49-2369-7213. **Fax:** 011-49-2369-77370. **Rooms:** 10; all with baths. **Rates:** Moderate; doubles from DM118; includes breakfast, service, and tax. **Dates closed:** Open all year. **Dining facilities:** Restaurant; in summer snacks are served outside on the lawn. **Children:** Additional bed DM48; children's play area. **Facilities for disabled:** None. **On-site recreation:** Museum tours. **Nearby diversions:** Swimming; horseback riding. **Proprietor:** Josef Selting. **Operated as a hotel since:** 1968. **U.S. representative:** None.

Directions: Lembeck is just north of Essen. The easiest way to find it is to take autobahn A-3 toward Arnheim and exit at Wesel-Schermbeck. Drive east on B-58. Shortly before the town of Wulfen, a signpost points north to Lembeck and Reken.

Hotel Restaurant Burg Reichenstein

A Thirteenth-Century Castle

Castles on the Rhine bring to the contemporary mind romantic images of brave knights atop their fine steeds rescuing beautiful maidens held captive in locked towers by evil brutes. Surely the Rhine robber barons, who had their feudal serfs build these castles, were devoid of these romantic notions. Battering-rams, catapults, and mangonels ruled the day, and if these didn't do the job, quicklime, burning oil poured from towers, and flaming arrows did. Who would have thought that hundreds of years later people from all over the world would come to gaze at these castles for romantic inspiration?

THE PAST Trechtingshausen was first inhabited in the eighth century, when construction began on defensive fortresses along the river. Historical documentation of the castle dates back only to 1213, when the abbey of Kornelimünster-Aachen was named as owner. Later it fell into the hands of robber knights, and then to the Bolanden family. In 1253 the League of Rhenish Cities destroyed it. After its reconstruction, the archbishop of

Mainz took possession, but the castellans rebelled and King Rudolf of Habsburg destroyed it again in 1282.

A Rhine legend tells a story about the fall of the Bolanden family. The condemned knight of Reichenstein had begged the king to spare Philip, the youngest of his nine sons. King Rudolf agreed on the condition that the father show his repentance by cutting off his own head and walking toward his son. Well, the knight's head rolled, and the body got up, staggered to his son, and fell. King Rudolf was so impressed that he spared not only Philip but all the sons. History records that eight of the sons went into the service of the Habsburgs but that Philip stayed on at Reichenstein to rebuild the castle, although it never again was as powerful.

For some years ownership of the castle was a matter of dispute in a power struggle between the electorates of Mainz and the Palatinate. After the French destroyed Reichenstein in 1689, the castle remained a ruin until the end of the nineteenth century, when new owners began restoration work.

THE PRESENT 🍂 Today's castle is in excellent condition. Part of it houses the hotel while another section is a museum that displays a full-size functioning drawbridge. The library and music room hold a small art collection and some antiques, and the knight's hall retains a medieval ambiance complete with standing suits of armor. The restaurant, which occupies the former stable, specializes in steaks.

D-55413 Trechtingshausen. Tel: 011-49-6721-6101. Fax: 011-49-6721-6198. Website: http://www.caltim.com/reichenstein/ (though not an official web address, this is an excellent site). Rooms: 10, including 2 singles and 8 doubles; 5 with showers. Rates: Moderate; doubles from DM140; includes breakfast, service, and tax. Dates closed: November 15 through February 28. Dining facilities: Restaurant. Children: No discounts. Facilities for disabled: None. On-site recreation: Castle museum. Nearby diversions: Rhine cruises; red deer wildlife park; St. Clements chapel. Proprietor: Egon Schmitz. Operated as a hotel since: Not known. U.S. representative: None.

Directions: From the autobahn, exit at Stromberg and head east toward Bingerbrück. Trechtingshausen is just north. The Koblenz-Bingen Line train stops at the town station.

Schloss Hotel auf Burg Rheinfels

A THIRTEENTH-CENTURY CASTLE

Situated above the town of St. Goar on the west bank of the Rhine, Rheinfels commands an extraordinary view of the valley and of the famed "Cat and Mouse" castles on the opposite bank. The hotel is in a newer building tastefully incorporated into the extensive ruins of the original castle.

THE PAST 🐚 Count Diether von Katzenelnbogen, a friend of Emperor Frederick II, built Rheinfels castle around 1245 for the purpose of imposing tolls on Rhine traffic. (His family also owned Burg Katz across the river, thereby completely dominating this section of the river.) For ten years Rheinfels stood as one of the most powerful fortresses on the Rhine. The Rhenish League besieged the castle in vain for over a year with eight thousand foot soldiers, one thousand horsemen, and fifty armed boats. The family remained at Rheinfels for generations, until one of the later descendants was burned at the stake in Cologne in 1472 for "attempting to destroy the countess by infusing poison into her sacramental wine." The family soon

died out, and the castle passed into the hands of the Landgraviate of Hesse, who converted it into a magnificent Renaissance-style castle with gables and half-timbering.

In 1692 Rheinfels withstood a siege by a French army of twenty-eight thousand whose commander had promised Louis XIV the castle as a New Year's gift. The French finally did take it one hundred years later when its defenders surrendered without a fight after a man who said he was a French deserter sneaked into the castle and claimed it was to be stormed in the morning. Within four hours every man in the castle had fled in terror. A butcher in St. Goar tried to stop the fleeing general with an ax, crying, "You coward! I would brain you!" Within three years Rheinfels was destroyed by the French.

In 1812 the ruins were sold at an auction for one hundred pounds to a local townsman who proceeded to ship pieces of it downriver for the reconstruction of Ehrenbreitstein Castle near Koblenz. In 1843 Prince William, who later became emperor of Germany, bought the castle to prevent further destruction. Restoration was begun in 1925.

THE PRESENT 🐚 You can view models and plans of the castle's former glory in a museum located in the former chapel. A maze of walled passages, towers, and gates in the ruins take about an hour to explore.

Guest rooms are modern and elegant, and many have romantic views of the Rhine.

From the outside terrace and dining room, you can enjoy splendid views of the Rhine. For large groups, the hotel can arrange a medieval feast with venison as the entrée.

Schlossberg 47, D-56329 Saint Goar am Rhein. Tel: 011-49-6741-8020. Fax: 011-49-6741-7652. **Rooms:** 57, including 3 singles, 50 doubles, and 2 suites; all with bath. **Rates:** Expensive; doubles from DM210; includes buffet breakfast, service, and tax. **Dates closed:** Open all year. **Dining facilities:** Restaurant; outside terrace. **Children:** Age 7 and younger sharing with parents free. **Facilities for disabled:** None. **On-site recreation:** Indoor pool; sauna. **Nearby diversions:** Rhine cruises. **General Manager:** Gerd Ripp. **Operated as a hotel since:** 1973. **U.S. representative:** Euro-Connection.

Directions: From the Koblenz-Mainz autobahn, exit at Pfalzfeld to St. Goar. Follow the signposts up the hill. The castle is visible on the north side of town. St. Goar is a train stop on the line between Koblenz and Bingen.

Burg Hotel-Restaurant auf Schönburg

A TENTH-CENTURY CASTLE

North of Reichenstein Castle the Rhine narrows and twists so that especially trained pilots are required to guide commercial barges. At the point where the river narrows to one-quarter its normal width, a slate rock rises four hundred and seventy feet above the water. This rock is the famous Lorelei, named after the beautiful siren who was said to comb her golden hair and sing to the fishermen, luring them to crash their boats onto the rocks below. (Overcome by love herself, she also plunged into the river to her death.)

Just past the Lorelei on the west side of the river is the village of Oberwesel and its castle hotel, Schönburg. Oberwesel, with its eighteen watchtowers and Gothic church, has been called "the most beautiful refuge on the Rhine of the Romantic period." You'll enjoy visiting the charming antique shops, craft shops, bakeries, and German country restaurants.

THE PAST 🐏 Schönburg Castle dates back to 966. One thousand years later, it remains one of the better preserved Rhine castles. In 1116 Barbarossa of the Holy Roman empire presented the castle to one of his men. At one time it housed many families, each getting a share of the profits from the river tolls and the surrounding vineyards.

The most renowned member of the Schönburg family was Frederick, general in the army of the English William III. The English made him a duke and peer of England and grandee of Portugal, while the French made him a marshal to reward his service to the French army of Louis XIV. He was killed by a shot in the neck at the Battle of the Boyne while exposing French Papist traitors in the ranks of King James.

The French eventually burned Schönburg in 1689, and within thirty years the Schönburg family died out.

Note: This castle is depicted on the front cover; the terrace restaurant is depicted on back cover.

In the 1880s the castle was acquired by an American whose ancestors had lived across the Rhine. The family restored it over the years and, after World War II, they modernized the front part facing the river and sold the castle to the town of Oberwesel.

THE PRESENT 🐚 Schönburg Castle is now three interconnected fortresses surrounded by a wall. The massive stone towers, stairways, and narrow halls with secret chambers looking out over the Rhine are yours to explore. The modernized part of the structure is well hidden and does not detract from the medieval atmosphere. In fact, the exterior walls are painted red in deference to the medieval custom of indicating wealth with brightly painted walls.

Guest rooms are delightfully furnished. The most romantic rooms are inside the turrets and have four-poster canopy beds and antiques. Some have views through lead-paned windows of the Rhine or vineyards.

You can sit and relax in front of an open fire in the lounge, which also contains a small library. Or you can dine on whiskey steaks, lamb, and duck specialties in the highly rated candlelit restaurant located in the knight's hall. (An outdoor terrace has a spectacular view of the Rhine.) And, should you want to be married here, the castle chapel can provide the services.

D-55430 Oberwesel. Tel: 011-49-6744-93930. Fax: 011-49-6744-1613.   **Rooms:** 21, including 3 singles, 17 doubles, and 2 suites; all with bath. **Rates:** Expensive; doubles from DM230; includes breakfast, service, and tax. **Dates closed:** January 1 through March 20. **Dining facilities:** Restaurant; outdoor terrace; closed on Mondays and December 23 and 24. **Children:** Cribs free; children's menu; baby-listening. **Facilities for disabled:** None. **On-site recreation:** None. **Nearby diversions:** Rhine cruises; charming antique and craft shops in Oberwesel. **Proprietors:** Hüttl family. **Operated as a hotel since:** 1957. **U.S. representative:** Euro-Connection.

Directions: From the autobahn, take the Laudert exit and follow the signs to Oberwesel. Oberwesel is also a train stop on the Koblenz-Bingen line. A footpath leads from the town directly to the castle.

Burghotel Schwalenberg

A THIRTEENTH-CENTURY CASTLE

The quaint village of Schwalenberg has changed little over the centuries. Streets are still lined with half-timbered houses bedecked with flower boxes in their windows, and the town's castle still boasts a splendid view of the Lippe countryside and its dense forest known as the Teutoburger Wald.

THE PAST 🐚 Through the centuries this castle has been repeatedly destroyed and reconstructed. Built in 1231 by the counts of Schwalenberg, it was located strategically on the important Flanders-to-Saxony commercial

highway. Descended from an ancient family that held important positions under Karl the Great, the counts became "robber-knights" in the Middle Ages, involving themselves in conspiracies and murder. To atone for their criminal lives, they built a number of monasteries in Germany. A hundred years later, the castle became the property of the powerful Lippe princes and the See of Paderborn.

THE PRESENT 🐚 Items through-out the public rooms remind you of the castle's turbulent past: suits of armor, a cannon, assorted weapons. Ancient rifles decorate the Knights Room bar.

Guest rooms are furnished in a contemporary style accented with an occasional antique piece. The Wedding-Room features a carved mahogany four-poster bed and Oriental carpet. Views are of the valley, park, or inner courtyard.

The main attraction here is the restaurant, where you can enjoy the view below while dining. It is a particularly good choice for lunch.

The surrounding woods have fine walking trails through a wildlife area. During the holidays the hotel schedules special Christmas programs.

D-32816 Schieder-Schwalenberg. **Tel:** 011-49-5284-5167. **Fax:** 011-49-5284-5567. **Rooms:** 15; all with bath. **Rates:** Moderate; doubles from DM170; includes breakfast, service, and tax. **Dates closed:** January and February. **Dining facilities:** Restaurant and café. **Children:** Cribs available; children free if sharing parents' bed; children's menu. **Facilities for disabled:** None. **On-site recreation:** None. **Nearby diversions:** Horseback riding; golf; tennis; covered wagon tours through the forest; animal park. **Proprietor:** Saul-Feuchter family. **Operated as a hotel since:** 1971. **U.S. representative:** Euro-Connection.

Directions: Schwalenberg is about 70 kilometers southwest of Hannover. From Detmold on route 1, Schwalenberg is about 11 kilometers east on route 239.

Hotel Schloss Spangenberg

A Sixteenth-Century Castle

A short drive from the Grimm Brothers' home of Kassel takes you to Schloss Spangenberg—a massive stone castle overlooking the red tile roofs and half-timbered houses of the picturesque town of the same name. When you enter the castle through its outer walls, you cross over a drawbridge above a dry moat and pass into a cobblestone courtyard—entering a world of well-preserved history.

THE PAST The knights of Treffurt started building Spangenberg between 1214 and 1238. Additions were made in 1350 by the counts of Hesse, one of Germany's most powerful families. Three hundred years later,

Count Wilhelm IV fortified it into one of the most powerful of Hessian castles. Count Wilhelm, also known as "The Wise," was an accomplished economist and astronomer and spent much of his rule trying to reconcile the Calvinists and Lutherans.

Despite the walls, the moat, and the towers, the French seized the castle in 1758 during the Seven Years' War. The castle was damaged by bombing in World War II but is now restored to a fine condition.

THE PRESENT Today you can walk completely around the castle on the walls beside the moat. You can also visit a small museum devoted to hunting that gives insight into traditional German country life.

Guest rooms are individually furnished in a contemporary style. The Princes Room has an ornate rococo bed, and room 16 has a charming alcove with a small table and chair. Ideally suited to families, the gatekeeper's house has a small living room, bedroom, sleeping loft, and two bathrooms. Many of the rooms have views of the valley and town below.

Wild game dishes are popular in the restaurant. When the weather is sunny, you may eat lunch on an outdoor terrace. The hotel sometimes caters banquets in the great knights' hall.

 D-34286 Spangenberg. Tel: 011-49-5663-866. Fax: 011-49-5663-7567.   Rooms: 23, including 1 suite; all with bath. **Rates:** Moderate; doubles from DM180; includes breakfast, service, and tax. **Dates closed:** December 22 through December 25. **Dining facilities:** Restaurant (closed on Thursdays January 1 through March 15); outside terrace; medieval banquets. **Children:** Age 3 and younger free; age 4 through 10, DM45 for an extra bed for the first night only. **Facilities for disabled:** None. **On-site recreation:** Hunting museum. **Nearby diversions:** Hiking. **General Managers:** Wilfried and Angela Wichmann. **Operated as a hotel since:** 1985. **U.S. representative:** Euro-Connection.

Directions: Spangenberg is about 40 kilometers southeast of Kassel. From the Hannover-Frankfurt autobahn (E-4), exit southeast on B-83, pass through Melsungen, and go east on B-487.

Burghotel Trendelburg

A THIRTEENTH-CENTURY CASTLE

The Weser valley is rich with pretty villages filled with half-timbered Renaissance houses. Of special note is Bodenwerder—the town of eccentric Baron Münchhausen—and Hamelin—home of the Pied Piper.

Burghotel Trendelburg, a romantic medieval castle offering both comfort and atmosphere, sets the stage for excursions into the region. Along with nearby Sababurg Castle, it provided inspiration for many of the Grimm Brothers' fairy tales. Today its charming rooms, lovely views overlooking the valley and Reinhard Forest, and attentive staff provide an experience you'll long remember.

THE PAST 🌀 Burg Trendelburg was destroyed and rebuilt four times during its long history. In fact, it's surprising anything is left for us to see today. No one knows how long the castle existed before 1300, when the first records were kept.

Burggrave Hans von Stoghusen (the landgrave of Hessia) and the bishop of Paderborn each owned half the castle. They continued this arrangement for four generations until the castle was destroyed by fire. In the late fifteenth century the landgrave of Hessia and the bishop of Paderborn began to have such violent quarrels that the region was soon devastated and

the peasants had to seek refuge behind the town walls. During the Thirty Years' War soldiers captured both the town and castle, later destroying them. In the eighteenth century the Seven Years' War brought further hard times. For four hours the castle sustained a cannonade of eight hundred shots that damaged the southeast tower. French troops, and later English troops, captured the castle.

Not until 1900 did the von Stockhausen family regain possession of their ancestral home. By then it was almost uninhabitable, but they restored it according to some historical drawings. After World War II American troops stayed here. Then war refugees adopted the castle. The von Stockhausens opened the doors of their castle home as a hotel in 1949.

THE PRESENT 🐚 When you arrive at the castle, park your car by the great tower, cross over the deep, dry moat on the drawbridge, and enter the grounds through a tiny doorway into the courtyard. The rooms inside are warm and friendly—from the entry hall with its grand staircase and dark wooden walls, to the library and fireplace room where the legendary Baron von Stockhausen once told stories from the castle's past.

Guest rooms are furnished in period style, and many have fine views. Located across from the main building, the honeymoon tower holds several guest rooms and is a special treat. Rooms here have open-beamed ceilings and lacy curtains, and a spinning wheel hangs above the doorway to some.

A former chapel, with a vaulted ceiling and carved wooden sidings, now serves as a dining room. The menu features a selection of well-prepared meat and fish dishes.

Another chapel is available for weddings.

Steinweg 1, D-34388 Trendelburg. Tel: 011-49-5675-9090. Fax: 011-49-5675-9362. **Rooms:** 22, including 4 singles and 18 doubles; all with bath. **Rates:** Moderate; doubles from DM190; includes breakfast, service, and tax. **Dates closed:** Open all year. **Dining facilities:** Restaurant; outside terrace. **Children:** Cribs available; extra bed DM35. **Facilities for disabled:** None. **On-site recreation:** None. **Nearby diversions:** Horseback riding; tennis; swimming; fishing. **Proprietor:** Mrs. H. Lohbeck. **Operated as a hotel since:** 1949. **U.S. representative:** None.

Directions: Trendelburg is about 35 kilometers north of Kassel on route 83.

Hotel Schloss Waldeck

A TWELFTH-CENTURY CASTLE

The Waldeck is one of the most popular tourist regions of central Germany. The deep forests, Eder River, Edersee (a lake), and Bad Wildungen spa attract people from all parts of Germany. And situated high above the Edersee, the exceptionally well-preserved massive stone fortress of Waldeck offers a view into the area's medieval past.

THE PAST From 1120 this castle was the home of the counts of Waldeck. Over the centuries additions were built. Sections were damaged during a siege in the Seven Years' War. At one point it served as a prison, and it was completely abandoned in the seventeenth century. By 1906 the entire castle was restored, and a small section was opened as a hotel.

THE PRESENT Driving up the steep road leading to the castle, you will enjoy spectacular views of the Edersee. Most of the castle is now preserved as a museum. Two galleries display objects from the Waldeck counts, and

for a small fee you can visit the Sorceress's Tower with its dungeons and prison cells.

A rough-hewn spiral stairway leads up to many of the guest rooms, which are furnished in contemporary style. A recently added wing also holds guest rooms. Although there is no difference in decor between rooms in the castle and the annex, it is more desirable to stay in the castle. Many rooms have views of the Edersee.

One large dining room has beamed ceilings and wood paneling, while another more intimate candlelit dining room, Alte Turmuhr, features rugged stonework and vaulted ceilings. Specialties include local game and fish from the Edersee. On occasion, the hotel offers medieval banquets using old, traditional recipes.

During holidays and weekends when the weather is pleasant, the castle attracts many visitors and tour groups. But most come only for lunch, leaving the castle a more peaceful place in the evening.

The hotel management offers many unusual activities: nightly torchlight castle tours of the thirteenth-century kitchen, vaults, dungeons, and former jail; walks and carriage rides through the woods with a picnic waiting at the end; fireworks set off from the terrace of the Clock Tower. Wedding packages are available complete with printed invitations, flowers, photographer, carriages, minstrels, fireworks, torchlight procession, and costumes for a courtly ceremony.

D-34513 Waldeck. Tel: 011-49-5623-589-0. Fax: 011-49-5623-539-289. **Rooms:** 41, including 2 singles, 35 doubles, and 4 suites; all with bath; some guest rooms are in a new wing. **Rates:** Expensive; doubles from DM270; includes breakfast, service, and tax. **Dates closed:** Open all year. **Dining facilities:** 3 restaurants; medieval banquets. **Children:** Discounts upon request. **Facilities for disabled:** None. **On-site recreation:** Swimming pool; sauna; solarium; museum; castle tours. **Nearby diversions:** Water sports; horseback riding; tennis; golf; aviation school. **Proprietor:** Karl F. Isenberg. **Operated as a hotel since:** 1905. **U.S. representative:** Euro-Connection.

Directions: Waldeck is about 35 kilometers southwest of Kassel. Take route 251, then turn south on route 485. A train station is just 2 kilometers away.

MORE HOTELS

Schloss Fürsteneck

Located in the hills of Bavaria near the Czech Republic and
Austrian borders, this castle's tower dates back to the twelfth century.
Short on frills but long on charm, the castle is a treasure found
for the budget-minded traveler.

D-94142 Fürsteneck. Tel: 011-49-8505-1473.

Burghotel Schnellenberg

This impressive thirteenth-century castle lies deep in the
woods east of Düsseldorf. Guest rooms in the oldest part are reached
by winding stairs in the turret. A small museum displays medieval
weapons and suits of armor.

D-5952 Attendorm am Biggesee. Tel: 011-49-2722-6940. Fax: 011-49-2722-694169.

Schloss Sommersdorf

Turrets, bridges, and a moat provide lots of atmosphere at this
small castle. Operated as an intimate bed and breakfast inn,
the castle is located on the famous Romantic Road.

D-91595 Sommersdorf. Tel: 011-49-981-647. Fax: 011-49-981-9707950.

Schloss Weitenburg

Located south of Stuttgart on a hilltop overlooking the Neckar
River, this castle dates back to 1062. The von Rassler family has lived
here since 1720. The present baron maintains a medieval ambiance
with displays of antiques, massive wood furnishings,
ancestral portraits, and hunting trophies.

D-72181 Weitenburg. Tel: 011-49-7457-9330. Fax: 011-49-7457-933100.

Great Britain

When we think about English castles, King Arthur and the Knights of the Round Table are usually the first images that come to mind. The great castles of such romantic legends still proudly dominate much of the English countryside, giving us a glimpse of a fascinating era of British history. Most are open for exploration, although surprisingly few have been converted into castle hotels.

Before the Norman Conquest only a few castles had been built in England and Wales, all of them of the wooden motte and bailey variety. When the Normans invaded, they continued this type of construction, often erecting a "castle" in eight days.

Not until the reign of Henry II did stone castles begin to proliferate. When the Crusaders returned from the Holy Land, they brought back new and more sophisticated designs, such as the concentric style of castle, and castle-building reached its peak.

But by the time of the War of the Roses (1455–1485) castles no longer had any useful function and most began to fall into disrepair. When Henry VII came to the throne in 1485, he banned all private armies and forbade the wearing of heraldic family livery. Gunpowder became a government monopoly and was impossible to obtain without a license. The defensive function of the English castle ended once and for all, although castles continued to be important in Scotland for a while longer.

Just as important to British history are the great and stately Elizabethan, Jacobean, and Victorian manor homes that took the place of the traditional castle. Many of these manor homes include a number of castle-like features and are sometimes incorrectly referred to as castles.

Visitors to the great historic castles and manor homes number around thirty million each year. This vast support has kept many of these monumental houses, with their rich treasures, safe from the wrecking ball.

But the expense of maintaining these estates privately is astronomical, second only to the insatiable state tax known as the "death duty." When the head of a family dies, heirs have very few options left to preserve their property without an enormous sum of ready cash. To alleviate this financial burden, a popular option for the family is to open the house to tourists. An example is the famous Woburn House, which was opened to the public when the heir of the Duke of Bedford was faced with $7.5 million in estate duties. But this isn't as easy as it might sound; the property must be very special to keep the tourists coming. Other options include auctioning pieces of the artistic treasures to buy time, or selling the entire estate outright, or opening it as a hotel. Because of this last option, historic hotels exist today in nearly every area of Great Britain.

The National Trust preserves many historic properties but is entirely reliant on donors, members, and the general public for its existence. It can only accept an estate that comes with a substantial endowment to cover its own upkeep. A section of one of their properties—the magnificent Cliveden—is now open for overnight guests. The Landmark Trust, another organization that is dependent on donors and members for its existence, offers self-catering accommodations in unique historic buildings.

For further information on Great Britain, contact the British Tourist Authority at: 551 Fifth Avenue, Suite 202, New York, New York 10176-0799, Tel: 800-462-2748, 212-986-2200; or 625 North Michigan Avenue, Suite 1510, Chicago, Illinois 60611.

England & Wales

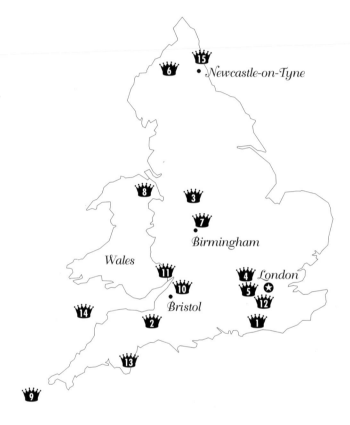

15 • Newcastle-on-Tyne

6

8

3

7

• Birmingham

Wales

11

10

14

• Bristol

4 London

5 ★

12

2

1

13

9

Amberley Castle

A Fourteenth-Century Castle

West Sussex offers some of the most picture-perfect countryside in England. Meadows, hop fields, and forests nestle in rolling hills where the only movement comes from grazing sheep and roaming deer. Charming thatched-roof cottages and country pubs seem untouched by modern civilization.

Between the South Downs and the expanse of the Amberley Wildbrooks—a preserved wetland and nature reserve—the massive fortified castle of Amberley welcomes you to a genuine castle experience.

THE PAST 🌸 Obviously, security was once an important consideration here. Marauding brigands and assaulting armies never had a chance when confronted by the castle's massive, sixty-foot-high stone walls, soaring battlements, iron portcullis, and moat.

In 672 the Saxon king Caedwalla gave the lands where the castle now sits to Saint Wilfred, first bishop of Selsey. Eventually the property passed to the bishop of Chichester.

Around 1100 Bishop Ralph Luffa of Chichester embarked on an ambitious building program in Sussex. (The first cathedral of Chichester and parts of the East Wing and Small Hall at Amberley still exist.) Not much is known of the period until 1377, when King Richard II granted a license to crenellate to Bishop William Rede. The bishop then built the castle's tremendous curtain wall.

Bishops lived quite a luxurious lifestyle back then, and their persons and possessions were coveted by peasants and French pirates who came up the Arun River from the coast. These men of the cloth required serious protection. Amberley's bishops could swiftly mete out justice to any local agitators and made use of the castle's oubliette. (Only one other still exists in such good condition in England.)

Not until the Civil War did Amberley suffer the ravages of battle. When the Royalist, John Goring, who lived in the castle in 1643, declared that he wasn't going to pay any more taxes to those "odious" Roundheads, Cromwell's soldiers laid the castle's Great Hall to waste. Several years later King Charles II visited the loyal Mr. Goring at the castle. A second royal visit from this king inspired the mural in the Queen's Room, which is now the dining room.

The fifteenth duke of Norfolk bought the property in 1893 and began the long restoration work that is being continued by the present owners.

THE PRESENT 🌸 The only threatening presence here nowadays comes from the peacocks who stand sentry duty on the walls and grass-covered moat, which now serves as a croquet lawn. Through the portcullis, you enter a large courtyard where a stone walkway leads to the hotel.

Guest accommodations have come a long way from the dank oubliettes. Each uniquely decorated room bears a medieval ambiance and is named for a Sussex castle. Proprietress Joy Cummings has furnished each with antiques, brass or four-poster beds, and fabrics in lovely shades of turquoise and terra-cotta or lilac and pale green. The Herstmonceux and Pevensey rooms each have a secret doorway leading to the battlements, and the Arundel and Amberley rooms have gas fireplaces and stunning windows set in stone recesses. The Chichester Room, decorated in shades of deep red and blue, not only has a fireplace and beamed ceiling, but a six-foot-long four-poster bed and an enormous bathroom with an outstanding view from its oversize whirlpool bath.

In the barrel-vaulted Queen's Room Restaurant, you can feast on classic French and traditional English cuisine served on Wedgwood china and Dartington crystal. Lancet windows provide views of the graceful English countryside.

Amberley, Nr. Arundel, West Sussex BN18 9ND. Tel: 011-44-1798-831-992. Fax: 011-44-1798-831-998. **Rooms:** 15; all with bath. **Rates:** Very expensive; doubles from £130; includes breakfast and tax. **Dates closed:** Open all year. **Dining facilities:** Restaurant. **Children:** No discounts. **Facilities for disabled:** None. **On-site recreation:** Archery; shooting; falconry; croquet; horseback riding. **Nearby diversions:** Golf; ballooning; Arundel Castle; Glyndebourne; Chichester Cathedral; Petworth House; Goodwood House. **Proprietors:** Joy and Martin Cummings. **Operated as a hotel since:** 1989. **U.S. representative:** Josephine Barr; Small Luxury Hotels of the World; Euro-Connection.

Directions: From London, take A24 south. Turn west on A283 to Storrington. In Storrington, continue southwest on B2139. The castle is on the right and is marked by a very small signpost. Try to arrive during daylight.

The Castle at Taunton

AN ELEVENTH-CENTURY CASTLE

The West Country boasts some of the most beautiful and historic country-side in England. Here quaint villages are sometimes announced by the tall spires of their parish churches sighted in the distance, and at other times by an overshadowing medieval Norman castle. This is the domain of the legend of King Arthur and Queen Guinevere, and of Lorna Doone's Exmoor—the beautiful wooded and heather-covered park where red deer and wild ponies run free.

THE PAST 🐚 Taunton Castle, which houses the hotel in one wing, is the site of England's earliest fortress. It dates back to two hundred years before any written historical records.

In 710 the King of Wessex—conqueror, lawgiver, and church reformer—built a wooden castle here. A record of it exists in the *Anglo-Saxon Chronicles,* the earliest history written in any modern language. Twelve years later, the castle burned down and was rebuilt. Queen Frithogytha of the West Saxons granted the property to the bishops of Winchester. (High on the wall of the hotel you can still see the painted arms of the See of Winchester, commemorating the episcopal ownership.) King Alfred is said to have stayed here at this time. In 1001 the Danes burned down the castle and town. By the time of the Norman Conquest, in 1066, another castle had taken its place.

At the end of the fifteenth century, Perkin Warbeck pretended that he was Richard, duke of York (the youngest of the child princes murdered in the Tower of London). With the support of the duke of Burgundy and the kings of Germany, Scotland, and France, Warbeck attempted to invade England and failed. He tried a second time and failed again. During one of his invasions, he succeeded in capturing Taunton Castle and proclaimed himself King Richard IV. Henry VII brought his army to Taunton and captured Warbeck, who later met his fate at the Tower of London.

Almost two hundred years later, in 1685, the duke of Monmouth, an illegitimate son of Charles II, came to Taunton and proclaimed himself king. He was defeated at the nearby Battle of Sedgemoor, and he and his men were executed in the streets of Taunton by the infamous and bloodthirsty Judge Jeffrey.

The castle was eventually dismantled, and almost three hundred years ago part of it was turned into a hotel. Since then, many royal personalities have enjoyed Taunton's hospitality. The hotel has hosted Queen Victoria, King Edward VII, King Edward VIII, a former queen of Portugal, the Queen Mother, and Princess Margaret. Other guests have included the duke of Wellington, Coleridge, and Disraeli.

THE PRESENT 🦋 The current proprietor, Christopher Chapman, has created a romantic English country hotel. He has carried out a family tradition started by his grandfather, who managed the London Savoy during the Edwardian era. Surely the former inhabitants never lived in such comfort.

In springtime, the beautiful lavender wisteria covering the hotel's entire façade belies the castle's turbulent history. The interior retains a medieval air.

The Bow Suite, named for its position just above the castle bow, contains a master bedroom, two bathrooms, and a sitting room with a fireplace. Other guest rooms have floral fabrics or mahogany and walnut accents, and many feature four-poster canopy beds and antique furnishings. Thoughtful touches such as small bouquets of flowers and miniature bottles of sherry are found in each room.

The restaurant dining room—with its high ceilings, chandeliers, tall windows draped with velvet curtains, and tables covered with white cloths—boasts a one-star rating from both Egon Ronay and Michelin. The menu changes with the seasons, but venison, tender lamb with wild mushrooms, and veal in a leek cream sauce are usually available. The wine cellar list offers three hundred choices, with some vintages dating back to 1924.

Castle Green, Taunton, Somerset, TA1 1NF. Tel: 011-44-1823-272-671. Fax: 011-44-1823-336-066. E-mail: reception@the-castle-hotel.com. Website: http://www.the-castle-hotel.com. **Rooms:** 36, including 12 singles, 8 twins, 11 doubles, and 5 suites; all with bath. **Rates:** Expensive. doubles from £120; includes breakfast, service, and tax. **Dates closed:** Open all year. **Dining facilities:** Restaurant. **Children:** Extra bed £18; baby-listening. **Facilities for disabled:** Yes. **On-site recreation:** None. **Nearby diversions:** County Museum; excursions to Exmoor National Park, Wells Cathedral, and Glasonbury Abbey—the legendary burial site of Arthur and Guinevere. **Proprietor:** Christopher Chapman. **Operated as a hotel since:** 1600s. **U.S. representative:** Josephine Barr.

Directions: Taunton is easily reached by the M-5 motorway; take Exit 25. The castle is located in the center of town. Taunton is linked by train to London's Paddington Station.

Caverswall Castle

A THIRTEENTH-CENTURY CASTLE

Hidden behind two ancient churches in the tiny village of Caverswall, this informal bed-and-breakfast castle is a delightful discovery. If you are fond of English ceramics, you'll have the opportunity here to visit countless big name factory outlets—Wedgewood, Royal Doulton, Spode, Port Meirion— and reap some heady savings.

THE PAST 🐚 The history of Caverswall Castle begins in the days of the Anglo-Saxons. When Ernulf de Hesding, a Saxon landholder, fled his timber and earthenwork home during the Norman invasion, the Caverswall family laid claim to the property. Two hundred years later, in 1270, Sir William de Caverswall built a medieval stone fortress. A stone Norman tower, dungeon, and outer walls are all that remain. (William Caverswall's grave can be viewed in the adjacent church cemetery.)

By the end of the fourteenth century, the direct line of Caverswalls died out, and the castle passed through the hands of various families who allowed the property to deteriorate. In the beginning of the seventeenth century, George Craddock built a grand Jacobean mansion next to the original tower. Each successive owner has left their signature on the property: Sir Percival Radcliffe drained the moat and planted the splendid gardens, and the Wedgwood family beautified the library's ceiling.

THE PRESENT 🐚 After driving over the dry moat and through the rustic gatehouse, you might be greeted here by enthusiastic dogs bounding to your car, followed by the cheerful proprietress welcoming you at the heavy mansion door. Inside, splendid carved oak woodwork and tile fireplaces grace many of the public rooms, and rich, dark wood paneling is seen throughout. A magnificent Victorian sideboard topped with a pewter collection is just one of the many exceptional antique furnishings, and a billiard room holds a Victorian snooker table that guests are welcome to try out.

The three guest rooms are all very special. The Bishop's Room— where visiting clergy once stayed—is dominated by an elaborately carved four-poster bed and has a private sauna. The King's Room bears an oversize bathroom and a regal carved four-poster canopy bed that is larger than king-size, while the Pink Room is lined with the oldest wood paneling in the house. Completely modern, yet cozy, self-catering apartments are fashioned into two of the four turrets in the wall outside the main house.

In season, you can swim in a glass-enclosed pool or fish in a picturesque lake situated just outside the castle wall.

Caverswall, Staffordshire ST11 9EA. Tel: 011-44-1782-393-239. Fax: 011-44-1782-394-590. Rooms: 5, including 2 self-catering apartments in detached turrets; all with bath. **Rates:** Inexpensive to moderate; doubles from L70; includes full English breakfast. **Dates closed:** Rooms closed November 2 through March 31; turrets open all year. **Dining facilities:** None. **Children:** No discounts. **Facilities for disabled:** None. **On-site recreation:** Seasonal swimming pool; seasonal trout fishing. **Nearby diversions:** Hiking and mountain biking in the Peak District; golfing; bargain porcelain factory shops and Wedgewood Centre in Stafford; Alton Towers. **Proprietor:** Michael and Yvonne Sargent. **Operated as a hotel since:** 1994. **U.S. representative:** None.

Directions: The village of Caverswall is located just off A520 running from Stone to Leek, or A50 from Uttoxeter to Stoke-on-Trent; the castle is signposted. London is approximately 2 1/2 hours south by car, and 2 hours by train from Stoke-on-Trent.

Cliveden

A Seventeenth-Century Palace

The ultimate in pure indulgence, Cliveden provides glorious surroundings, sumptuous rooms, and brilliantly prepared cuisine. It leaves you feeling like you've walked into the middle of a *Masterpiece Theater* series. And it's little wonder, since this grand estate is the only hotel in England that belongs to the National Trust.

THE PAST 🦪 Cliveden's reputation as a pleasure palace began in 1666 when the nefarious second duke of Buckingham built a hunting lodge along the banks of the River Thames. This once-trusted minister to King Charles II needed a love nest where he could carry on an affair with his mistress, the countess of Shrewsbury. This liaison led the duke and the countess's husband to engage in one of Britain's most famous duels. It is said that the countess held the reins of Buckingham's horse while he gave the fatal blow to her husband. The king eventually dismissed Buckingham, and he died leaving debts.

The estate passed into the hands of the earl of Orkney in 1696. His improvements shaped the palace and grounds we see today. Like everyone who has owned Cliveden, he loved to entertain. King George I, Queen Caroline, and Frederick, Prince of Wales were among his guests. Frederick and his wife, Princess Augusta, made Cliveden their home from 1737 to 1751. He preferred to live away from his father, King George II, whom he intensely disliked. During his residence in 1740, the composer, Thomas Arne, debuted "Rule, Britannia" at Cliveden.

The estate passed to the duke of Sutherland in the nineteenth century. He was responsible for the present house, which replaced the old palace destroyed by fire. The architect, Charles Barry, also designed the Houses of Parliament. By 1850 gala parties were back in full swing. Prime Minister Gladstone and Queen Victoria were frequent visitors. Years after the duke and duchess of Westminster honeymooned at Cliveden, they bought the property. The duke added a water tower, dovecote, and stable block.

However, it is the Astor family with whom we associate Cliveden. The American-born William Waldorf Astor bought the property in 1893 and added the exquisite pieces of art found throughout the house and gardens. He gave Cliveden as a wedding present to his son, Waldorf, and his new bride, Nancy. Lady Astor spared nothing to provide the most lavish

house parties in England. Edward, Prince of Wales, T. E. Lawrence, Rudyard Kipling, Henry James, Sarah Bernhardt, and Winston Churchill stayed here regularly. In 1919 Nancy Astor became the first woman elected to Parliament.

THE PRESENT 🦋 As you drive through the three hundred and seventy-five acres of peaceful grounds, you find worldly cares slipping away. No one rushes here. No one speaks in a loud voice. Life is civilized, sedate, and elegant. Yet there is nothing intimidating about all this grandeur, and the staff couldn't be more gracious or warm.

You can explore to your heart's content through the splendid gardens and parklands, including those areas operated by the National Trust. You can even take a guided walk using recorded tapes by Robert Hardy. When you tire of nature's beauty, step inside the grand palace itself and wander through endless public rooms with exquisite molded ceilings and fine paintings. Don't miss the fantastic Orkney tapestries, which are elegantly displayed next to carved wooden columns flanked by medieval suits of armor—all beneath a wood-coffered ceiling.

Named after Cliveden's former illustrious residents, most suites have sitting rooms, dressing rooms, and fireplaces. CD players permit the addition of atmospheric classical music. Books line the entrance hall to the Inchiquin Suite, with its lovely paintings and four-poster bed. The romantic

Lady Astor's suite features the original Elizabethan mantelpiece over the fireplace, a private sitting area and terrace, and sweeping views. Four staff members attend to each guest room, packing and unpacking suitcases and drawing baths.

After seeing the calorie-filled temptations presented throughout the day, you'll be thankful for the hotel's sports activities and spa. Breakfast begins with smoked salmon, kippers, croissants, brioches, and French toast. At lunch, you can arrange for a specially packed Edwardian picnic hamper to take along on an excursion, and high tea brings on sandwiches, scones, and eclairs. Cliveden's restaurants are considered among the finest in England. Six large windows overlook the gardens from The Terrace dining room. The more intimate Waldo's features gourmet cuisine that has won every conceivable award from Michelin, Egon Ronay, and the Automobile Association.

For the ultimate indulgence, two boats are available to cruise the Thames. An electric canoe commissioned by Lady Astor in 1920 can take you to a romantic spot on the riverbank for a picnic or afternoon tea. On summer evenings a 1911 launch, the *Suzy Ann,* goes out for a pre-dinner champagne cruise. The *Suzy Ann* also makes day excursions during the Henley Royal Regatta in July.

Taplow, Berkshire SL6 0JF. Tel: 011-44-1628-668-561. Fax: 011-44-1628-661-837.   Rooms: 21 doubles, including 6 in the garden wing, 9 on main floor, and 10 suites; all with bath. **Rates:** Very expensive; doubles from £210; tax not included. **Dates closed:** Open all year. **Dining facilities:** 2 restaurants; Waldo's is closed for lunch and on Sunday and Monday evenings. 3 private dining rooms. **Children:** Inquire about discounts when booking; playroom; baby-sitting; children's videos and menus. **Facilities for disabled:** Yes. **On-site recreation:** Indoor and outdoor pools; tennis; fitness center; sauna; squash; jogging routes; horseback riding. **Nearby diversions:** Boating; 2 golf courses; Windsor Castle. **General Manager:** Stuart Johnson. **Operated as a hotel since:** 1986. **U.S. representative:** Relais & Châteaux; Leading Hotels of the World; Grand Heritage Hotels International.

Directions: Taplow is 10 miles northwest of Windsor. From the M4 take Exit 7 at Slough West. Continue west on A4 towards Maidenhead, and then north on B476 towards Burnham. Trains depart for Taplow from London's Paddington Station.

Great Fosters

A SIXTEENTH-CENTURY ELIZABETHAN MANOR

It is hard to think of anything more romantic than visiting London while staying in a sixteenth-century Elizabethan country estate that once served as a royal hunting lodge. More than a hotel, Great Fosters is classified as a Grade I Historic Monument and is a splendid alternative to the costly London hotels.

THE PAST This enormous Tudor brickwork mansion was built around 1550 on a site that dates back another thousand years to the Anglo-Saxons. You can still see sections of the original moat. The manor was the property of the Chertsey Priory until the dissolution of the monasteries, when it probably joined in tenancy with the Crown.

Windsor Forest, the royal hunting grounds of the Tudors and Stuarts, reached all the way to Great Fosters. Hunting lodges were situated throughout the forest for the use of royalty, and records indicate that Great Fosters was one of their favorites. The regular tenants who occupied the property were probably courtiers.

King James I gave the estate over to his favorite judge, Dodderidge, better known as the "Sleeping Judge" because he always listened to his cases

with his eyes shut. The house passed eventually to a Sir Robert Foster, in whose family it remained until the nineteenth century, when it was bought by the husband of Queen Alexandra's lady-in-waiting, Baroness Halkett. Later owners included the earl of Dudley and the Honorable Gerald Montague.

THE PRESENT 🦀 Today, much of the historic atmosphere is maintained. As you enter the main doorway, look up to see the arms and initials of Queen Elizabeth I, dated 1598. The inner door has a wicket through which only one person at a time can enter. Stepping into the front hall, which features seventeenth-century pilastered paneling, takes you straight into another era. To one side, a Jacobean carved wooden chimney piece dates from 1620 (log fires blaze here during the winter months). You can gaze out to the formal gardens through a large mullioned window.

Off the front hall, the Anne Boleyn sitting room is adorned with a beautiful 1602 plaster ceiling displaying the emblems of the queen. These badges depict a falcon with a royal scepter in its claw, the lion passant, and the fleur-de-lis. By all means visit the Tithe Barn. An outstanding timbered hall even older than the house, it is now used for private parties, banquets, dances, and receptions. (A tithe barn traditionally stored the produce collected from the parish as a tax to support the church.)

Guest rooms are decorated in character with the house. Several very special ones are lavishly furnished with antiques and tapestries. The Tapestry Suite features a fine chimney and a stone mantelpiece carved with the story of Adam and Eve (*without* navels). Flemish tapestries cover its walls, which are crowned by an ornate plaster ceiling. In the Nursery Suite the remains of a secret staircase can be seen through a trapdoor in a cupboard. A story relates that Charlie Chaplin made use of it to watch his children at night. The Panel II and Queen Anne suites contain four-poster beds and both walnut doors and window boards made from an ancient tree that once stood in front of the house. And the Italian Suite has ornate quattrocento doors, gilt furniture, and walls covered in damask.

A small dining room decorated in the style of the French king François I presents English and continental entrées.

Stroude Road, Egham, Surrey TW20 9UR. Tel: 011-44-1784-433-822. Fax: 011-44-1784-472-455. **Rooms:** 43, including 11 period rooms and 20 in a separate conference center; all with bath. **Rates:** Expensive; doubles from £98.50; includes breakfast and tax; Christmas programs available. **Dates closed:** Open all year. **Dining facilities:** Restaurant. **Children:** No discounts. **Facilities for disabled:** None. **On-site recreation:** Seasonal outdoor swimming pool; tennis. **Nearby diversions:** Golf; horseback riding; boating; polo; Runnymede; Windsor; Hampton Court Palace. **General Manager:** J. E. Baumann. **Operated as a hotel since:** 1931. **U.S. representative:** None.

Directions: Egham is 7 miles southwest of Heathrow Airport outside of London. By train, it takes 35 minutes from Waterloo Station. In Egham, signposts lead to the hotel.

Langley Castle

A FOURTEENTH-CENTURY CASTLE

Too often people consider northeast England a burdensome distance on a map—an obstacle to drive through hurriedly on the way to Scotland. However, for those who adopt a slower pace, Northumberland promises to reveal romance and history at every turn.

The castle purist will appreciate that Langley is England's only remaining medieval fortified castle hotel.

THE PAST ✸ To keep check on the Scots who constantly attacked south of the border, defensive castles were erected across northern England. In 1415 a survey listed one hundred and thirteen castles in Northumberland alone.

After the Battle of Crecy during the Hundred Years' War, victorious English soldiers brought home from France new-found riches and military experience. Sir Thomas de Lucy, one of the heroes of Crecy, returned to Northumberland to rebuild his castle that was destroyed by a Scots army led by David Bruce. (In 1346 an English army commanded in part by de Lucy defeated Bruce at the Battle of Nevilles Cross.) Langley Castle took nearly twenty years to build, and de Lucy died soon after its completion. His daughter, married to the earl of Northumberland, Henry Percy, took possession of the estate. Percy conspired in a failed plot to overthrow the English King Henry IV and fled to Scotland. Langley Castle suffered the consequences of Percy's misjudged acts: King Henry IV's army on its advance north burned the castle.

By the seventeenth century, the Catholic earls of Derwentwater gained the property, although they never lived there. The third earl, James, and his brother, Charles, participated in the 1715 Jacobite Rebellion against the Protestant King George I. The brothers were summarily arrested and executed in the Tower of London.

The Crown took over the estate until 1882, when a local historian, Cadwallader Bates, bought the castle with the intention of restoring its former glory and making it a home for himself. Incorporating the remaining walls and towers, he built a new roof, stairway, and entry as well as battlements and floors. Nothing was added to detract from the original "fortress house in the great days of Crecy." After his death in 1902, his wife Josephine continued the restoration, adding a rooftop chapel consecrated in 1914 in memorial to her husband. She is buried next to him on the castle grounds.

Prior to its life as a hotel, the castle served as a military barracks during World War II, then as a school for girls, and then as a banqueting house.

THE PRESENT 🌸 Langley is built in a popular fourteenth-century style, featuring a grand oblong hall with seven-foot-thick walls. Four turrets at each corner contain the main rooms. An added fifth tower that once served a defensive purpose now holds the main entrance, stairway, and guardrooms. You can explore fully the quiet castle and its surrounding ten acres of peaceful woodlands.

A brochure available at reception points out the castle's more unusual features. The southwest tower holds the finest remaining examples of fourteenth-century garderobes in Europe. (A ditch running along the side of the castle had a stream redirected into it to wash away what was discharged from these three-story toilets. Fortunately for guests today, the plumbing at Langley has joined the twentieth century.)

Each of the "feature" guest rooms beautifully integrates with its unique architecture. The Josephine Room has a large alcove set in the wall where you may have breakfast and gaze at the view, while the Cadwallader Room features a stone archway over the bathroom sink and one wall of solid stonework. Each room features wall sconces, rich fabrics, and a different style of canopy bed. In a new annex across from the main castle, Castle

View rooms—so named because they have views *of* the castle, not *from* the castle—are furnished comfortably in keeping with the theme of the castle.

You can relax in front of an open fireplace in the impressive second-floor stone-walled drawing room (once the castle's main hall), perhaps with a pre-dinner drink from the adjoining oak-paneled bar. Featuring open beams, tapestries, and another fireplace, the Josephine Restaurant offers a traditional menu of seafood, pheasant and duck, beef, and seasonal fresh vegetables.

Occasionally on Saturday nights the castle hosts a "Ghostly Night Experience." After a champagne reception, a local theater group performs a mystery story. Between dinner courses, participants roam up and down the stone staircases by candlelight looking for clues. After the winner receives a suitable prize, music and dancing ensue.

Langley on Tyne, Hexham, Northumberland NE47 5LU. Tel: 011-44-1434-688-888. Fax: 011-44-1434-684-019. Website: http:/dialspace.dial.pipex.com/town/parade/ow51/. E-mail: langleycastle@dial.pipex.com. Rooms: 16, including 5 feature rooms in the main castle, 3 standard rooms, and 8 Castle View rooms in an annex across from the castle; all with bath. **Rates:** Expensive; doubles from £85; includes breakfast and tax; special mid-week and weekend rates. **Dates closed:** Open all year. **Dining facilities:** Restaurant; vegetarian menus upon request. **Children:** Children £15; cribs free; children's menu. **Facilities for disabled:** None. **On-site recreation:** None. **Nearby diversions:** Excursions to Hadrian's Wall, Roman Army Museum, Northumberland National Park, and historic market town of Hexham. **Proprietor:** Dr. Stuart Madnick. **Operated as a hotel since:** 1985. **U.S. representative:** None.

Directions: Langley is off A69—the main highway between Newcastle-upon-Tyne and Carlisle. Just west of Hexham, turn south on A686. The castle is signposted.

New Hall

A Twelfth-Century Moated Manor House

For eight hundred years Birmingham was little more than a poor backwater town with few inhabitants. The onset of the Industrial Revolution in the eighteenth century changed the face of the city forever. Situated in the Midlands, with ready supplies of coal and iron, hundred of factories popped up overnight. Cadbury chocolates, Dunlop tires, and Austin Rover cars all started here. With over one million inhabitants, Birmingham is Britain's second largest city. Not an obvious tourist destination, visitors pour into the city nonetheless for business, exhibitions, and sporting events.

Surprisingly, you don't have to travel far here to find green spaces, woodlands, and lakes. Only seven miles northeast of the city is one of Britain's highest rated hotels: New Hall—the oldest inhabited moated manor house in England.

THE PAST The land around New Hall and Sutton Coldfield (originally spelled "Sutone Colfield") first appears in history in 1071. Edwin, earl of Mercia and grandson of Lady Godiva, was one of the first property owners. After the Norman Conquest, Edwin was executed by William the Conqueror and his property confiscated. Fifty-five years later the land passed to

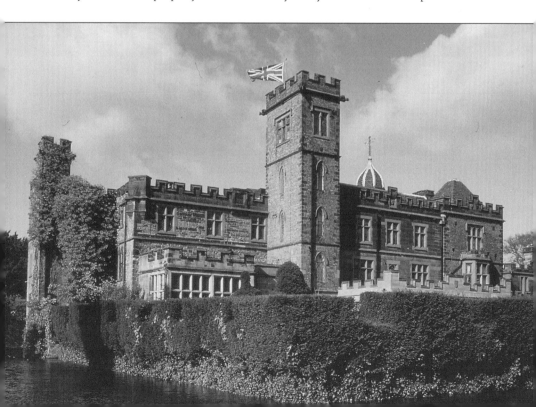

Roger de Newburgh, earl of Warwick, in whose family it remained for over two hundred years.

Defense was an important consideration in such turbulent times. A local style of castle construction utilized the abundant streams and springs to form a natural moat. In 1200 de Newburgh found the ideal spot on the land to build his grand stone house—where seven springs fed into a moat. This original structure forms part of the west range and south wing of today's manor.

For the next three hundred years, the property, which had now acquired the name of New Hall, passed to various knights and merchants.

In 1525 an impending visit by King Henry VIII instigated some renovations. A new wing was built of red sandstone, the Great Chamber enlarged, and gables and windows added. During his visit, King Henry nearly met with disaster while hunting when a wild boar charged him. Legend relates that an unseen marksman shot an arrow through the boar's heart at the last second, saving the king. The archer proved to be a young and beautiful markswoman whose family had been dispossessed of their property. The king not only restored the property but presented her with a Tudor Rose, now the emblem of Sutton Coldfield.

By the nineteenth century, the manor had survived both new additions and scandals. Illegitimacy, eccentrics, alchemy, and death by fire all played a part in its history. One of its ghost legends tells of a bodiless head seen at dusk drifting down Wylde Green Road across from New Hall.

During the twentieth century the estate sold to a succession of businessmen who preserved the integrity of the building while introducing modernized central heating and wiring. Thistle Hotels bought New Hall in 1985 and upgraded the property for its new life as a hotel.

THE PRESENT 🦋 Twenty-six acres of gardens are yours to roam through here, taking care, naturally, to step around the lily-filled moat. The terraced walkways date from the sixteenth or seventeenth centuries. Bird lovers particularly enjoy finding the rookery in the woods.

Floral bedspreads and drapes, four-poster beds, and over-stuffed armchairs give guest rooms the feeling of a country house, but views of the moat through latticed windows remind you of New Hall's true origins. Each room is named for a species of lily, many varieties of which thrive on the grounds from spring to fall.

The dining room features masonry dating back to 1250, and the tables are often decorated with lilies grown on the grounds. The traditional English cuisine has received a number of awards, including three rosettes

from the Automobile Association and an overall Blue Ribbon Award from the Royal Automobile Club.

Walmley Road, Royal Sutton Coldfield, Nr. Birmingham B76 1QX. Tel: 011-44-121-378-2442. Fax: 011-44-121-378-4637. **Rooms:** 62, including 12 luxury suites in the old part of the house, and 50 in a wing overlooking the courtyard; all with bath. **Rates:** Expensive; doubles from £135; includes tax. **Dates closed:** Open all year. **Dining facilities:** 3 restaurants. **Children:** No children younger than 8; no discounts. **Facilities for disabled:** None. **On-site recreation:** 9-hole golf course; putting green; tennis; croquet. **Nearby diversions:** Belfry golf course (home of the Ryder Cup); horseback riding; Warwick Castle; Stratford-upon-Avon; Cotswolds; pottery factories and outlet stores. **General Managers:** Ian and Caroline Parks. **Operated as a hotel since:** 1988. **U.S. representative:** Small Luxury Hotels of the World; Utell International.

Directions: Sutton Coldfield is 7 miles northeast of Birmingham near the M6 and M42. From the M42, get off at Exit 9 and go west on A4097. Continue through the round-abouts and turn north on Walmley Road. The gate for New Hall is on the left.

Ruthin Castle

A Thirteenth-Century Castle

A visit to northern Wales should include a day in beautiful Snowdonia National Park. Mountains, lakes, glacial valleys, and waterfalls provide some of the most superb landscape in Britain, and magnificent medieval castles dominate the countryside.

THE PAST 🌸 Llywelyn, a prince of northern Wales, was the only Welsh ruler officially recognized by the English as the Prince of Wales. For years he struggled to drive the English out of Welsh territory. When Edward I inherited the crown of England in 1274, Llywelyn refused to attend his coronation or to pay either homage or the annual tribute. Greatly offended by such bad manners, King Edward ordered his troops to invade Wales and seize most of Llywelyn's land. Edward built a series of castles as part of his plan to conquer and annex Wales, and in 1277 work was begun on Ruthin Castle. Ironically, Llywelyn's brother and rival, Dafydd, was first granted title to the castle, but within a few years Llywelyn had been slain and Dafydd executed. Edward reclaimed the castle and granted it to Reginald de Grey, baron of Wilton, in whose family it remained until 1508.

With seven one-hundred-foot-high round towers and eight-foot-thick walls that withstood uprisings, revolts, and the War of the Roses, the castle was quite impressive. In 1400 Welsh rebels kidnapped one of the de Greys. After paying an enormous ransom, the family never recovered financially and sold Ruthin Castle to the Tudors.

At one time one of Henry VIII's illegitimate sons, Henry Fitzroy, owned the castle. In 1646 Cromwell ordered that all fortresses in northern Wales be destroyed, and Ruthin was the first to go. With supplies brought in through an underground passage, the defenders held on for eleven weeks. The garrison surrendered only when they learned the walls had been mined with gunpowder. The castle was nearly destroyed. A free quarry was set up, and stones and timber were carted off.

In 1632 Sir Thomas Myddleton bought the property but later abandoned it. Not until the nineteenth century did a descendant, Maria Myddleton West, take an interest in her inheritance. She had the castle rebuilt, incorporating parts of the old structure with a new castellated building. The next few generations added more. Edward, Prince of Wales (later Edward VII), frequently visited the castle.

THE PRESENT 🐚 The interior features paneled rooms, wood floors, and gold-and-pink molded ceilings. Although not luxurious, the decor is tasteful, and an open fire warms guests in the Cornwallis Room.

Guest rooms are both large and small and are furnished in both traditional (one has a four-poster bed) and contemporary style. Each has a view of either the gardens or the ancient battlements.

Medieval banquets consisting of a four-course meal with wine, costumes, serving wenches, and entertainment are held most evenings in the banquet hall.

When strolling among peacocks on the castle's thirty acres of parkland, it's hard to believe that Ruthin has such a bloody history. But the dungeons, drowning pool, and whipping pit in the ancient ruins are silent reminders.

Corwen Road, Ruthin, LL15 2NU North Wales. Tel: 011-44-1824-702-664. **Fax:** 011-44-1824-705-978. **Website:** http://www.hotel-wales.co.uk/ruthin/ruthincastle/.   **Rooms:** 60; all with bath. **Rates:** Expensive; doubles from £88; includes breakfast and tax. **Dates closed:** Open all year. **Dining facilities:** Restaurant; medieval banquets (reservations required). **Children:** Age 15 and younger sharing with parents 50 percent discount. **Facilities for disabled:** None. **On-site recreation:** None. **Nearby diversions:** Mountain walks; trout and salmon fishing; pony trekking; tennis; golf. **General Manager:** K. Clayton. **Operated as a hotel since:** 1963. **U.S. representative:** Best Western.

Directions: Ruthin is in northern Wales, about 25 miles west of Chester on A494.

Star Castle

A SIXTEENTH-CENTURY CASTLE

Protruding several miles off the Cornish coast, the Scilly Isles have been known by mariners since ancient times. Even the Greeks and Romans spoke of the Scillys in their myths, and Celtic legend proclaims they were inhabited by holy men. Burial mounds and artifacts have established that man first came to these islands four thousand years ago. Warmed by the Gulf Stream, semi-tropical vegetation thrives here in a climate that seldom sees a winter frost, and geraniums grow seven feet tall.

THE PAST 🐚 The strategic location of the Scillys has determined much of their history. Star Castle was built in 1593 during the reign of Queen Elizabeth I as a needed defense against Spanish attacks after the defeat of their armada.

In 1643 the Prince of Wales (the future King Charles II) took shelter here when he was being hunted by Cromwell and his parliamentary army. The famous Royalist privateer, Sir John Grenville, later made the castle his headquarters until it was overtaken by Admiral Blake. The Cavaliers also took command at one time. Almost three hundred years later, another Prince of Wales—the short-lived future King Edward VIII—officiated at Star Castle's opening ceremony as a hotel in 1933.

THE PRESENT 🐚 The name Star Castle perfectly suits this Elizabethan fortress. Its eighteen-foot broad ramparts are in the form of an eight-point star surrounded by a dry moat. Standing high on Garrison Hill on the island of St. Mary's, the castle's view of the sea and islands is stunning. It is just a five-minute walk west of Hugh Town.

You have a choice of two types of accommodation. The guest rooms in the castle are in keeping with the ancient character. Some have ocean views, and two—the King Charles II Room and the Francis Godolphin Room—feature canopy beds, modern bathrooms, and dark wood beams across whitewashed walls. The more modern Garden Apartments have French windows opening onto verandas with spectacular views of the sea.

The restaurant is situated in the former officers' mess. Dinner is a set four-course menu offering traditional fare of local fresh seafood, steak, or poultry. Vegetables are grown in the castle's own gardens.

The Garrison, St. Mary's, Isles of Scilly TR21 0JA. Tel: 011-44-1720-422-317. Fax: 011-44-1720-422-343. Rooms: 30, including 9 rooms in the castle, 3 singles in guardhouses on ramparts, and 18 in garden annex; all with bath, shower, or both. **Rates:** Expensive; doubles from £106; includes dinner, breakfast, and tax; bed and breakfast rate also available. **Dates closed:** Mid-October through mid-March. **Dining facilities:** Restaurant; vegetarian meals available; bar lunches in Dungeon Bar; children younger than age 5 not allowed in dining room for dinner. **Children:** Age 2 and younger, 5 percent of room rate; children taking high tea, 25 percent of room rate; children taking dinner, 50 percent of room rate; baby-listening. **Facilities for disabled:** None. **On-site recreation:** Indoor swimming pool; grass tennis court. **Nearby diversions:** Boating; golf; windsurfing; diving; horseback riding; bicycling. **Proprietors:** John and Mary Nicholls. **Operated as a hotel since:** 1933. **U.S. representative:** None.

Directions: The Isles of Scilly are located several miles off Land's End in Cornwall. They can be reached by plane, helicopter, or boat from Penzance. The hotel provides transfer service for guests arriving by air. For stays of 10 or more days, the hotel offers discounts or free transportation from the mainland.

Thornbury Castle

A Sixteenth-Century Castle

Anyone who thinks a castle is a gloomy, damp, and cheerless place to spend the night is sure to be impressed by the warmth and coziness of Thornbury Castle—the last major fortified manor house built in England. Since the 1500s this castle has hosted some of the most famous names in English history, including Henry VIII, Anne Boleyn, and Mary Tudor.

THE PAST 🐚 A manor house existed here as far back as 925. In 1020 possession passed into the hands of Berthric, who was the ambassador at the court of Baldwin—the count of Flanders. Baldwin's daughter Matilda fell in love with Berthric and sent him many letters proposing marriage. Berthric wasn't interested and hurried back to England. Unfortunately for him, Matilda went on to marry William of Normandy. After he conquered England, Matilda lost no time persuading her new husband to confiscate all of Berthric's lands and imprison him in Winchester, where he later died.

In 1087 Thornbury passed to Robert Fitzhamon for services rendered to the crown. With few lapses, it remained in his family, the Staffords, for twenty-eight generations.

In 1444 the Stafford family became titled, and Humphrey Stafford was named the first duke of Buckingham and a Knight of the Garter. The second duke of Buckingham became a Constable of England after helping Richard III gain the throne. King Richard wanted the duke to visit him, but instead of going to London, the duke went to Wales to gather troops for an invasion of England. The plot failed, and the duke hid in the house of a retainer until a bounty of one thousand pounds convinced the retainer to turn him in. The duke was soon brought to Salisbury and beheaded in the marketplace without trial, but the retainer failed to collect his reward. As King Richard commented, "If he could betray so good a master, he would be false to all others."

The third duke of Buckingham regained his father's lands and titles after helping King Henry VII crush the Perkin Warbeck revolt. In 1508 he received a permit to build a castle—the foundation of today's structure. The duke became a great friend of Henry VIII, and every honor England had to offer was bestowed upon him. He was the king's right-hand man and commanded in his absence. All seemed to be going well until a disgruntled servant repeated to Cardinal Wolsey some gossip about the duke's possibly

having some designs on the royal succession. Henry believed the gossip and arrested Buckingham while he was watching the construction of his castle. Imprisoned in the Tower of London, he was found guilty of high treason and beheaded.

The duke's lands were confiscated and the Tudor family made use of the castle for the next thirty-five years. Henry VIII and Anne Boleyn spent ten days here in 1533. Mary Tudor lived in the castle for several years until she gave the property back to the Stafford family.

Thornbury remained unoccupied for nearly two hundred years and gradually deteriorated. Restoration has continued slowly since the eighteenth century. In 1727 the Staffords sold it to a cousin, Thomas Howard, the eighth duke of Norfolk, in whose family it remained until 1959.

THE PRESENT 🏵 Today Thornbury offers some of the plushest accommodations in England. Originally it opened as a restaurant with a three-fork Michelin rating and an Egon Ronay Restaurant of the Year award. Since then it has become a deluxe hotel and been awarded further honors.

Spacious grounds and a vineyard surround the castle, and it has its own helicopter landing pad. Look closely and you will find an inscription by the duke of Buckingham over the gateway. Badges of his coat of arms are also found over the gatehouse, windows, and fireplaces.

A double brick chimney on the south side is unique in England. The oriel windows on the same side are fine examples of tracery (one has seven hundred and twenty panes of curved glass). The library has a fine view, over hedges and flowers, to the spire of the village church.

No expense has been spared to transform some of the individually furnished guest rooms into ultimate retreats. Four-poster beds, beautifully carved in a sixteenth-century style, were especially commissioned for the rooms. High ceilings and tall mullioned windows looking out over the gardens remind you of the castle's origins. The Tower Room is exceptional. Its walls are covered in silk, deep rose-colored brocades frame the canopy bed, and a sitting area and fireplace provide coziness, not to mention its bathroom has gold-plated fittings.

The paneled walls, heraldic shield, and open fireplaces in the baronial dining room create a cozy atmosphere for sampling the first-rate cuisine. The fine wine selection includes a Thornbury Riesling Sylvaner.

 Thornbury, Nr. Bristol, South Gloucestershire, BS12 1HH. Tel: 011-44-1454-281182. Fax: 011-44-1454-416188. Rooms: 18; all with bath. **Rates:** Expensive to very expensive; doubles from £95 to £220; includes breakfast and tax. **Dates closed:** Open all year. **Dining facilities:** Restaurant (no smoking permitted; jacket and tie required for dinner). **Children:** Not accepted under age 12 unless known. **Facilities for disabled:** None. **On-site recreation:** None. **Nearby diversions:** Golf; horseback riding; fishing; excursions to the Cotswolds, Bristol, Bath, and South Wales. **Proprietor:** Baron and Baroness of Portlethen. **Operated as a hotel since:** 1966. **U.S. representative:** Josephine Barr; Euro-Connection.

Directions: Thornbury is about a 1/2-hour drive north of Bristol. Exit from either the M4 or M5, depending on which direction you're coming from, onto A38. Watch for side road B4061. The castle gate is next to St. Mary's parish church.

MORE HOTELS

St. Briavel's Castle Youth Hostel

This enormous Norman castle lies in the Forest of Dean on the
border between England and Wales, forty-five miles northeast of Cardiff.
King John converted it from a twelfth-century motte and bailey into a
hunting lodge. For eight hundred years the castle has served as a
law court, prison, school, and now as a youth hostel.

**The Castle, St. Briavel, Lydney, Glouscestershire GL15 6RG.
Tel: 011-44-1594-530-272. Fax: 011-44-1594-530-849.**

Scotland

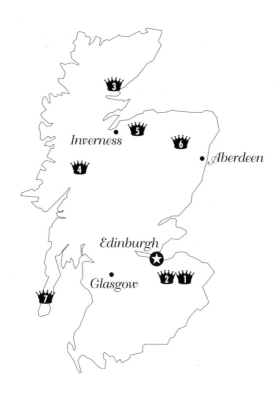

Inverness

Aberdeen

Edinburgh

Glasgow

Borthwick Castle

A Fifteenth-Century Castle

At this very famous castle in Scottish history you can sleep in the bedchamber of Mary Queen of Scots.

THE PAST 🏵 Mary often came here to visit her friend, the fifth Lord Borthwick, and to be near her future third husband, the earl of Bothwell, who was master of Crichton Castle only two miles away. Accused of the murder of Mary's husband Darnley, Bothwell was formally acquitted by the Privy Council. An arrogant sort of fellow, he practically kidnapped Mary to Dunbar Castle, hastened a divorce from his own wife, and married Mary. The populace immediately rebelled. Mary, under suspicion for the murder of her husband and condemned for her new marriage, had to flee from Holyrood Palace in Edinburgh to Borthwick Castle. The mob found its way to Borthwick, but Mary managed to escape disguised as a page. She never saw Bothwell again (he died a prisoner in Denmark) and spent the rest of her life as a prisoner of her cousin Elizabeth I in England.

During the Civil War of 1650, the ninth Lord Borthwick, a Royalist, refused to hand over his castle to Cromwell's forces. Cromwell sent a formal request to surrender:

> I thought fitt to send this trumpett to you to let you know, that if you please to walk away with your company and deliver the house to such as I shall send to receive it, you shall have libertie to carry off your arms and good…if you necessitate me to bend my cannon against you, you must expect what I doubt you will not be pleased with. I expect your present answer and rest. Your servant, O. Cromwell.

Borthwick refused to yield, and Cromwell's cannons opened fire. Although the fourteen-foot-thick walls protected the interior from damage by fire, parts of the battlements were fragmented (you can still see the scars today). Borthwick surrendered, and his great castle was spared.

THE PRESENT 🏵 Reached via a narrow lane under a canopy of trees, this baronial keep, with twin towers measuring one hundred and ten feet high, has been almost continually occupied since it was built in 1430. Its austere exterior belies the warmth and atmosphere found inside. Almost the entire first floor is taken up by a great hall with a high, barreled Gothic ceiling and

minstrels' gallery. At the end of the hall, a twenty-foot-high hooded fireplace provides warmth and comfort. Four narrow, curving stone staircases wind up to the guest rooms and down to the dungeons and cellars. To one side is a small chapel where Mary Queen of Scots prayed. Walls in many rooms are unpainted stone.

Guest rooms are furnished in period style. Both Mary Queen of Scots' bedchamber (which has a blood-red fabric bed cover) and that of the earl of Bothwell have four-poster canopy beds. Bathrooms are small and set in alcoves with thick walls and low doorways—giving the feeling of being enclosed in a cozy cave. Long, narrow windows provide small framed views of the bucolic countryside.

Dining is by candlelight and firelight in the rustic great hall. Dinner is a four-course set menu that changes daily and includes excellent Angus beef, lamb, and seasonal game. Visitors are welcome to stop in for an informal sandwich lunch by the fireplace; if you call ahead, a more elegant spread can be prepared.

Borthwick can be rented for weddings, parties, or a gathering of your clan.

 North Middleton, Midlothian, EH23 4QY. Tel: 011-44-1875 820 514. Fax: 011-44-1875 820 702. **Rooms:** 10, including 5 doubles and 5 twins; all with bath. **Rates:** Expensive; doubles from £90; includes breakfast and tax. **Dates closed:** January 1 through March 15. **Dining facilities:** Restaurant. **Children:** No discounts. **Facilities for disabled:** None. **On-site recreation:** None. **Nearby diversions:** Archery; game and clay pigeon shooting; fishing; falconry; golf; horseback riding; Edinburgh. **Proprietor:** Mr. Loadsman. **Operated as a hotel since:** 1970. **U.S. representative:** None.

Directions: About 12 miles south of Edinburgh on A7 is the small town of North Middleton. Turn left here onto a country lane. In 3/4 mile, after passing a school and Borthwick Church, enter the private roadway leading to the castle gates.

Dalhousie Castle Hotel

A THIRTEENTH-CENTURY CASTLE

It's a shame that when visitors come to Great Britain they generally allow only a few days to "do" Scotland. That usually means just a quick tour of Edinburgh. If you find yourself in this position, you can still squeeze in a Scottish castle experience at Dalhousie Castle. Located only a twenty-minute drive from Edinburgh, this castle is elegant, comfortable, and faithful to its past. It has played host to Edward I, Henry IV, Cromwell, Sir Walter Scott, and Queen Victoria.

THE PAST The history of Dalhousie is synonymous with that of its owners, the Ramsay family, who have held Dalhousie longer than any other family has retained possession of a castle in Scotland. Accounts vary, but the Ramsay family probably came to Scotland in the twelfth century. All that remains of the earliest castle are the walls at the foundation level and the vaulted dungeons.

Edward I of England spent a night at Dalhousie before marching on to defeat the Scots patriot William Wallace at Falkirk, and William Ramsay later joined Robert Bruce's forces at the Battle of Bannockburn in 1314. When the English gained the upper hand in the war against Scotland, many

castles, including Dalhousie, passed into their hands. For years Sir Alexander Ramsay, William's son, led forays against the castle, until the English finally surrendered and returned it to the family. He went on to recapture Roxburgh Castle, which belonged to his friend Sir William Douglas, by scaling the walls and surprising the occupants who were celebrating a holiday. But when Alexander Ramsay won appointments as sheriff and constable from the Scottish King David, this so infuriated Sir William Douglas that he plunged a dagger into Alexander's back and carried him off to Hermitage Castle, where he threw Alexander into a dungeon and left him to starve. The story relates that Alexander survived for seventeen days by eating grain that fell through the cracks in the floor. Four hundred and fifty years later, the remains of Alexander were found by workmen clearing Hermitage Castle.

A charter of 1618 granted the Ramsay family royal recognition with the title of Lord Ramsay of Dalhousie, and the family became favorites of King James VI of Scotland. They later pledged allegiance to the Parliamentarians during the English Civil War and hosted Oliver Cromwell. Members of the family served in the Wars of the Spanish Succession and one was a signatory to the capitulation of Quebec to General Wolfe.

The ninth earl and governor-in-chief to North America founded Dalhousie University in Halifax and was present at the Battle of Waterloo. One of his lifelong friends was Sir Walter Scott. His youngest son, James, became a famous governor-general of India at the age of thirty-five.

Since the turn of the century, the earls of Dalhousie have lived in another home at Brechin. The building we see today at Dalhousie was built in 1450 of red stone quarried from the nearby South Esk River.

THE PRESENT 🌀 If you were a castle guest here in ancient times, you would have crossed a drawbridge over a deep moat to reach the front door. If you had no invitation in hand, the residents might have poured burning oil on you from an opening in an overhead parapet or lowered you by ropes into a ten-foot-square windowless dungeon. (These features can still be seen today.)

Hospitality to the wayfarer at Dalhousie has changed considerably. Completely restored, the castle is an elegant and charming hotel. An Imperial staircase, built around 1840 to resemble a ship's quarter-deck, leads upstairs from the entrance hall. A magnificent oak-paneled library with a molded ceiling makes a fine place to relax with a book in front of a blazing fire. Guests gather here for a pre-dinner drink from the "secret bar" hidden behind a false bookcase door, and to gaze out the window at the river Esk.

Seven recently refurbished guest rooms now carry historical themes.

In the castle tower, the Dalhousie Suite features a sixteenth-century-style reproduction four-poster bed and oak furniture; a private corridor decorated with miniature tapestries leads to an antique-decorated bathroom. The Sir William Wallace Suite blends the castle's natural stone with Gothic-style fittings, while a bright tartan spread covers the canopy bed; oak paneling and tiles with the Wallace crest line its bathroom. The India Suite, named in honor of the young marquise of Dalhousie who became a governor-general of India, has a canopy raffia bed and furniture copied from the period of the Raj. "Ordinary" rooms feature twelve-foot-high ceilings and tall windows framed with heavy brocade drapes.

The ancient barrel-vaulted dungeon serves as an unusual restaurant with candlelight dining. Local game and fish feature prominently on the traditional Scottish and French menu. Vegetarian menus are available on request.

A picturesque crumbling watch tower, used most recently as a wash house, is just a short walk away through a bucolic horse pasture, and large expanses of lawn backed by a thick edge of trees invite exploration.

Bonnyrigg, Edinburgh, EH19 3JB. Tel: 011-44-1875-820-153. Fax: 011-44-1875-821-936. Rooms: 29, including 1 single, 27 doubles, and 1 suite; all with bath. **Rates:** Expensive; doubles from £110; includes breakfast and tax. **Dates closed:** January. **Dining facilities:** Restaurant. **Children:** Inquire about discounts when booking; baby-listening; baby-sitting; children's menus. **Facilities for disabled:** None. **On-site recreation:** Archery; falconry; clay pigeon shooting. **Nearby diversions:** Fishing; horseback riding; golf. **General Manager:** Neville Petts. **Operated as a hotel since:** 1972. **U.S. representative:** Grand Heritage Hotels International.

Directions: Bonnyrigg is just outside of Edinburgh. Take A7 south through Lasswade and Newtongrange. Turn right on B704. The castle is 1/2 mile further on the left. However, to reach it, turn right and go back under the road bridge.

Dornoch Castle Hotel

A FIFTEENTH-CENTURY PALACE

Measuring high on unspoiled scenery and low on population, with sheep outnumbering people twenty to one, the Northern Highlands of Scotland offers many quiet pleasures.

THE PAST 🐚 The first inhabitants of the town of Dornoch arrived three thousand years ago, followed by a Norse settlement. In 1224 Gilbert Murray, Bishop of Caithness, built both the town cathedral—which still exists today—and Dornoch Castle—which he used as his residence. Three hundred years later, a clan feud between the Murrays and the Mackays caused the town to be pillaged and the cathedral and castle to be burned. Dornoch also lays claim to the spot where the last witch in Scotland was burned in 1722 (the town of Fortrose disagrees). Janet Horne was accused of turning her daughter into a pony and riding her to a witches' coven, where her daughter-pony was shod by the Devil.

The castle was rebuilt in the eighteenth century. Before it became a hotel, it served as a garrison, courthouse, jail, and school.

THE PRESENT 🐚 Family-run Dornoch Castle (which officially is referred to as a "bishop's palace") provides an off-beat quality often missing in more luxurious castle hotels. You enter the castle through a turret door and then climb a tiny, winding staircase to reach reception. The tower and staircase are part of the original structure, as are the dungeons, now used ingloriously for storage.

Several stairways and labyrinthine corridors lead to the guest rooms. It is well worth paying a few extra pounds to get one of the nicely decorated rooms in the old section with a view of the garden and countryside.

The original stone-wall kitchen overlooks Dornoch Cathedral and is now the dining room. You can choose from a four-course or à la carte menu offering seafood, Angus beef, or rack of lamb with herb crust.

On most Saturday evenings in summer a pipe band parades in the main square in front of the castle. The Royal Dornoch Golf Club—where golf was first played in 1616 and which now rates as one of the top twenty courses in the world—is a five-minute walk from the hotel. Miles of empty beaches inviting long walks are also nearby.

 **Dornoch, Sutherland, IV25 3SD. Tel: 011-44-1862-810-216. Fax: 011-44-1862-810-81.** **Rooms:** 17, including 13 in new wing and 4 in old section; all with bath or shower. **Rates:** Moderate; doubles from £65; includes breakfast and tax. **Dates closed:** November through March. **Dining facilities:** Restaurant; bar menu; lunch packed upon request. **Children:** Age 14 and younger sharing with parents free. **Facilities for disabled:** None. **On-site recreation:** None. **Nearby diversions:** Pony-trekking; swimming, 2 golf courses; Dornoch Cathedral; Town Jail Craft Center; Dunrobin Castle; distillery in Tain. **Proprietor:** Michael Ketchin. **Operated as a hotel since:** 1947. **U.S. representative:** McFarland; Scots-American Travel.

Directions: Dornoch is 45 miles north of Inverness on A9. Turn right on A949 toward Dornoch, and continue the few miles into town. The castle is in the center of town.

Inverlochy Castle

A Nineteenth-Century Castle

"I never saw a lovelier or a more romantic spot," wrote Queen Victoria in her diary after a week at Inverlochy. Happily, in the hundred years since then the castle has scarcely changed. Ben Nevis, the highest mountain in Great Britain, still rises behind it. As it did then, purple heather carpets the hills, and many beautiful varieties of rhododendron line the path to the castle. Today Inverlochy is universally considered one of the finest hotels in the world. Nearly every guidebook to Britain notes the castle's personalized service, exquisite decor, and beautiful locale.

THE PAST 🌀 Like many Scottish fortresses, the first Inverlochy Castle—which dates back to the thirteenth century—now lies in ruin. Its replacement is a castle-like Victorian baronial mansion completed in 1870 by Lord Abinger. His son James held the title for only eleven years, when he died suddenly without an heir, and the property passed to a second cousin whose family sold the estate in 1944 to Mr. Hobbs of Vancouver, Canada. Grete Hobbs, formerly from Copenhagen and his daughter-in-law, is now the proprietor. All the accolades the hotel receives are the result of her hard work and careful supervision.

THE PRESENT 🌀 Today's castle of gray stone turrets, merlons, and battlements sits in fifty acres of woods and gardens on the shore of Loch Linnhe. Though the outdoors reflects the untamed Highlands with its rugged coastline, stormy seas, and rushing rivers, the inside of Inverlochy is a world of refined elegance and luxury. A lovely frescoed ceiling and crystal chandelier highlight the two-story grand hall. Period furnishings, fine artwork, Oriental rugs, fireplaces, and gorgeous flower arrangements provide beauty and comfort in the public rooms, and a billiard room is available for the indoor sportsman.

All of the guest rooms look out on Ben Nevis. They are furnished with chintz-upholstered chairs and sofas and feature large bathrooms stocked with bath oils and fine soaps.

Dining at Inverlochy is a special experience. There is no set menu. Rather, earlier in the day you tell the staff your preference—whether it is wild salmon, Angus beef, or duck—and it is served to you that evening on silver and crystal in a dining room overlooking the hotel's private loch. After dinner you can take your Madeira or coffee into a drawing room lined with

lovely mirrors and fine paintings and chat with other guests. In the morning, breakfast is brought to your room. When weather permits, lunch and tea are served on the terrace.

Chauffeured sightseeing can be arranged. The hotel prides itself on offering guests total peace and seclusion; for this reason, hotel sightseers are not encouraged.

Torlundy, Fort William, PH33 6SN. Tel: 011-44-1397-702-177. Fax: 011-44-1397-702-953. Rooms: 17, including 1 suite; all with bath. **Rates:** Very expensive; doubles from £240; includes breakfast and tax. **Dates closed:** December through February. **Dining facilities:** Dining room (jacket and tie required); reservations required; under age 12 not permitted. **Children:** Discounts available; baby-sitting. **Facilities for disabled:** None. **On-site recreation:** Tennis. **Nearby diversions:** Golf; fishing; hunting; horseback riding. **Proprietor:** Grete Hobbs. **Operated as a hotel since:** 1969. **U.S. representative:** Relais & Châteaux.

Directions: The castle is 3 miles north of Fort William. With prior notice the staff will arrange for you to be picked up at the Fort William train station, or even at Prestwick, Glasgow, or Edinburgh International airports.

Kilravock Castle

A Fifteenth-Century Castle

Accommodations in Britain where you can experience local family life are rare. A generation ago you could share an occasional meal with the family in most bed and breakfasts, but those places are rapidly disappearing as the demand for *en suite* bathrooms and televisions increases.

At Kilravock you'll feel a part of the everyday events in a castle that's part quirky museum and part personal home. You won't find luxury or doting servants here, but you will experience a truly unique, personal style of accommodation that could soon disappear.

THE PAST 🌸 For over five hundred years, twenty-five generations of the Clan Rose have held command over their ancestral castle. For two hundred of those years they called a tall keep home. When the threat of warfare in this region of Scotland diminished in the seventeenth century, the family attached a manor house.

Over the centuries, famous visitors have included Mary Queen of Scots in 1562, Prince Charles Stuart in 1746, and, soon after, the duke of Cumberland. Poet Robert Burns came calling in 1787.

THE PRESENT 🌸 Elizabeth Rose, the twenty-fifth baroness of Kilravock, is known affectionately as Miss Rose. For twenty years she has presided over her family's castle, operating a non-profit, smoking- and alcohol-free Christian guest house. However, this description should not deter you, even if you are planning to visit the nearby Whiskey Trail. You won't be made to feel guilty for indulging your sins *off* the premises.

Every evening at seven a gong announces dinner. In a high-ceilinged room filled with oil portraits of various Baron Roses from centuries past, you'll share the table with Miss Rose, manager Graham Ford (who might have his kilt on), Ford's wife, other guests, and perhaps a visiting clergyman. Before you can lift your fork, a passage from the Bible is read. But even if the last Bible you laid eyes on was in a motel drawer when you were looking for a phone book, you won't feel uncomfortable. The proceedings are low key and part of Kilravock's charm. Miss Rose also pours tea each afternoon in the drawing room and gives castle tours on Mondays.

Guest rooms are in the castle, in the separate East Wing, and in a bungalow a short walk away. Historic rooms in the castle proper bear names such as the Bee Room, the Moon and Stars Room, and the Slip Room—which has a wash basin and mirror in the turret and holds a former dressing

room used by the Rose daughters of yore. Rooms are decorated with everything from watercolors of Scottish seascapes to oil portraits to circus scenes.

Assorted relics—antlers, spears, a stuffed badger, a tiger skin, chain mail—decorate the castle. The grounds and surrounding woods of ancient trees and ferns invite exploration. (Upon request, the staff will pack a lunch for you.) A working farm is also on the property.

Croy, Inverness, IV1 2PJ. Tel: 011-44-1667-493-258. Fax: 011-44-1667-493-258. **Rooms:** 20; guest rooms are in the castle, in a separate wing 30 yards from the castle, and in the Rose House—a bungalow about 100 yards from the castle; some rooms share bathrooms; smoking not allowed in guest rooms. **Rates:** Moderate; doubles from £54; includes dinner, breakfast, and tax; rooms cannot be booked on bed and breakfast only basis; no credit cards are accepted. **Dates closed:** October through April. **Dining facilities:** Dining room; on Sundays a 3-course lunch and afternoon tea replaces dinner, and an inexpensive optional self-service buffet is also available; no alcohol served. **Children:** Age 2 and younger free; age 3 through 5, 50 percent discount; age 6 through 14, 25 percent discount. **Facilities for disabled:** None. **On-site recreation:** Tennis; squash; putting green; croquet. **Nearby diversions:** Horseback riding; fishing; golf; Cawdor Castle; Culloden Battlefield. **Proprietor:** Baroness Elizabeth Rose. **Operated as a hotel since:** 1967. **U.S. representative:** None.

Directions: The castle is approximately 10 miles east of Inverness. From A96 turn toward the direction of Croy, continue through town and turn left. About 1¹/2 miles farther and before the intersection, look for a sign on the right marked "Mains of Kilravock Farm." Continue down this road for ¹/2 mile. Try to arrive in daylight.

Leslie Castle

A Seventeenth-Century Castle

When Baron David Leslie brought his bride, Leslie, to view the family's fixer-upper castle in 1979, little did she know that ten years later she would preside over one of Scotland's most elegant castle hotels. The baron and baroness were looking at a roofless stone skeleton, far beyond the expertise of anything on TV's *This Old House*. Ten years of meticulous reconstruction have produced stunning results. Leslie Castle has it all—history, good taste, and, especially, personal warmth.

THE PAST The first baron of Leslie was a Hungarian nobleman, Bartholomew, who in 1070 married Princess Beatrix, the sister of the king of Scotland. He built a timber stockade settlement on the site, establishing the seat of the Clan Leslie. He also held the caput of the Barony of Leslie. By the early twelfth century the stockade had grown into a stone castle with all the fashionable defensive outerworks of the time—gatehouse, drawbridge, watchtower, curtain walls, and moat. Today only part of the original keep remains.

By the 1630s the castle had become a ruin and was mortgaged to John Forbes. His son William built a new castle in an L-shaped design. It was one of the last fortified tower houses built in the northeast of Scotland. Within a few years William sold the property to the Leith-Hay family whose descendants held ownership until 1979.

THE PRESENT Situated on the north side of the road beyond the parish church of Leslie, this white castle stands watch over the valley of Gadie Burn. Through a door in the keep and up a winding stone stairway, you enter a baronial hall warmed by a grand fireplace.

The baroness personally designed and decorated the lounges and guest rooms of her lovely castle. A dark wood-beamed ceiling, Oriental carpets on a flagstone floor, and furniture upholstered with beautiful tapestry fabric warm up the stark white walls. Ask the baron and baroness to show you their photo album displaying incredible before-and-after pictures of the castle's reconstruction, and you'll see why they are so proud of their home.

Spacious cream-colored guest rooms with dark wood accents are furnished in a Jacobean style and stocked with fresh flowers and fruit, sweets, and sherry. Two have four-poster beds.

The baroness personally plans and prepares each night's gourmet dinner. Among her specialties are smoked trout and smoked salmon

mousse, Gaelic-style Angus steak filets in a whiskey sauce, and roast duckling with port and cranberry sauce. Dessert choices might include a sticky toffee pudding with fudge and a French apple flan. With advance notice, the baroness can arrange a private dinner party or reception with crystal and silver place settings.

Leslie, by Insch, Aberdeenshire AB52 6NX. Tel: 011-44-1464-820-869. Fax: 011-44-1464-821-076. E-mail: leslie.castle@nest.org.uk. Rooms: 4, including 3 doubles and 1 twin; all with bath; smoking discouraged in guest rooms. **Rates:** Expensive; doubles from £124; includes breakfast and tax. **Dates closed:** 2 weeks in November. **Dining facilities:** Dining room; non-guests must make reservations. **Children:** Age 4 and younger sharing with parents £5; age 5 through 11, £15; age 12 through 15, £20; special children's tea available upon request. **Facilities for disabled:** None. **On-site recreation:** None. **Nearby diversions:** Fishing; shooting; hillwalking; pony trekking; alpine and cross-country skiing; Whiskey and Coastal Trails; excursions to Huntly Falconry Center, Archaeolink, Baxter's Food factory tours, and Leith Hall. **Proprietor:** Baron and Baroness David and Leslie Leslie. **Operated as a hotel since:** 1989. **U.S. representative:** McFarland.

Directions: Follow A96 northwest of Aberdeen. Turn on B9002 to Insch. Look carefully for signpost "Old Leslie 2¹/2 miles" (this is a one-lane road). The castle sits off to the left.

Landmark Trust Properties

The fictional character David Copperfield once said, "It was a wonderfully fine thing to walk about town with the key of my house in my pocket." With a self-catering apartment, you, too, can walk about town with the key of your house in your pocket. You can live in an area like a bonafide resident, shop in the local stores, and observe the small charms of a different culture. Isn't that what travel is all about?

The Landmark Trust is highly recommended to travelers who want to pause and absorb the world around them. This charity "rescues" historic and architecturally stunning buildings in distress and renovates them into self-catering apartments. Landmarks can be cottages, manor houses, railway stations, towers, or, fitting the theme of this book, castles and palaces.

Founded by Sir John Smith in 1965, the Landmark Trust has saved over two hundred unique buildings from probable demolition. The organization does this by making the building a useful entity that generates income for its preservation.

Although the majority of the Landmark properties are in Great Britain, Rudyard Kipling's home in Vermont (known as Naulakha) and the homes of poets Elizabeth Barrett Browning and John Keats in Italy also belong to the association.

The care given in reconstructing a Landmark property should be a model for future preservationists. Craftsmen use original building techniques and materials, keeping the structure's authentic integrity whenever possible. Thanks to Lady Smith, thoughtful considerations such as local maps, paintings of local scenes, and small libraries with information on the area's history, wildlife, and famous residents are provided in each property. Staff members themselves periodically stay at the properties looking for those small irritants that could ruin someone's vacation—the toaster that doesn't toast both sides, the dripping faucet.

The fun of staying in a Landmark has given rise to a new subgroup of vacationers called "Landmarkers," who vow eventually to rent every property on the list.

What to expect in a Landmark Property

Although every Landmark property is unique, they share certain qualities. They are functional, not luxurious. Kitchens are modernized and equipped with everything you'll need—utensils, pots, dishes, and blue and white Old Chelsea crockery; some have dishwashers, none have microwaves. Bathrooms are also modernized and equipped with heated towel racks. Bed linens and towels are provided once a week. Baby cribs are available. Along with the previously mentioned library, a logbook in each property provides guidance to sights in the surrounding area and to where you can obtain provisions. Electricity and gas are included in the rental, but laundry facilities, central heating, and air-conditioning are not. (Fireplaces and stoves provide plenty of heat.)

Nobody will intrude on you. There are no telephones, televisions, or mail delivery. A housekeeper tends to each property, but you won't see her if you don't want to. (In case of emergency, messages can be received through the housekeeper.)

How to book a Landmark Property

To obtain a delightful Landmark Trust guide book, with full descriptions of each property—including background, floor plans, and photos—contact the Landmark Trust at: RR 1, Box 510, Brattleboro, Vermont 05301, Tel: 802-254-6868. It costs $19.50.

To make a reservation, contact the head office in England at: The Landmark Trust, Shottesbrooke, Maidenhead, Berkshire SL6 3SW, United Kingdom, Tel: 011-44-1628-825-925, Fax: 011-44-1628-825-417. Because properties book up far in advance, it is best to call to determine if a particular one is available on the dates you want.

In summer, properties can be rented for a minimum of one week and a maximum of three weeks. During the rest of the year, three- and four-day "short stays" are available.

Along with your booking confirmation, you will receive further information about your chosen property, including a detailed map on how to find it, the housekeeper's phone number, and some useful addresses. Landmarks are not signposted and in many cases are a challenge to locate. You may check in any time after four o'clock on the day of your booking, but to save yourself some frustration, especially if you don't know the area, arrive before dark.

Hampton Court Palace

A SIXTEENTH-CENTURY PALACE

Surely Cardinal Wolsey and King Henry VIII never dreamed that future generations of commoners would walk through the gates of their sumptuous palace carrying a sack or two of groceries from the local Sainsbury market. Yes, now you can rent Hampton Court Palace as your holiday home.

THE PAST 🐚 In the early sixteenth century, Cardinal Thomas Wolsey was Henry VIII's most trusted advisor. He single-handedly managed English foreign diplomacy. Feeling smug with the king's favor, he built himself the most splendid palace in England (it could sleep two hundred and eighty guests). Although he was unpopular with the public for his pro-French policy, which had disrupted the cloth-export trade, as long as he remained in the king's graces he was untouchable politically. However, Wolsey failed in his goal to become pope, and, more significantly, he couldn't do anything to help along Henry's divorce proceedings. Realizing he was on shaky ground, Wolsey presented his palace to the king. In 1529 Wolsey was stripped of his titles and arrested.

The palace has remained in royal hands ever since. Elizabeth I and James I often celebrated Christmas here. Oliver Cromwell used it for getaway weekends. Charles II honeymooned at the palace with his bride and rendez-voused here as well with his mistress. George II was the last monarch to call Hampton Court home. His successor, George III, disliked the place and converted many rooms into apartments for his loyal servants.

Guidebooks available at the palace's gift shop detail dozens of stories about Hampton Court's history, magnificent rooms, artwork, and grounds.

THE PRESENT 🐚 The most exciting feature of staying here is having access to the grounds at any time (the gates close to the public at dusk). Feel like running through the garden by moonlight? It's all yours. But you won't be sleeping in Cardinal Wolsey's bedchamber. On behalf of Historic Royal Palaces—the agency that takes care of Hampton Court for its owner, Queen Elizabeth II—the Landmark Trust oversees only two historic buildings on the grounds: Fish Court and Georgian House.

Fish Court was once part of Henry VIII's huge kitchen complex and provided lodgings for the Officers of the Pastry (or pastry chefs, as we call them today). (One of the kitchens was devoted entirely to baking pies.) Windows look out over the Master Carpenter's Court, where food and

Georgian House

supplies for the palace were once delivered. Storehouses formerly filled with fish gave the building its name.

Georgian House, a former kitchen built in 1719, is north of the palace. Entry is through a wisteria-covered arbor. From the main bedroom you can gaze out on the crenellated walls and decorative spirals and chevrons of the palace roof. Ceilings in the living room are high, and windows run nearly the length of the wall. In the morning you can eat breakfast in your bathrobe as the first visitors of the day pass by wondering just who you might be. Georgian House comes with a private garden.

Location: In England, 13 miles west of London on the Thames. **Rooms:** Fish Court: 4 bedrooms, including 2 singles, 1 twin, and 1 double; 2 baths. Georgian House: 5 bedrooms, including 2 singles, 2 twins, and 1 double; 2 baths. **Rates:** Fish Court: winter short stays £508, summer weekly rental £1276. Georgian House: £553/£1386. **Children:** Suitable. **Nearby diversions:** Golf; horseback riding; boating; Windsor.

Kingswear Castle

A Sixteenth-Century Castle

This dramatic castle sits on precipitous rocks high above the mouth of the Dart River along the South Devon coast. The location is truly spectacular. You can brood, play sentry, or spend your time idly watching the activity on the river.

THE PAST 🦁 Built in 1502, with large guns installed inside and aimed through rectangular windows, Kingswear was the last word in defensive structures for the time. The castle came to life only during times of war and eventually fell into ruin.

In 1855 Charles Seale Hayne bought the property to use as a summer bachelor pad, and during World War II the concrete blockhouse was added.

THE PRESENT 🦁 Staying here is a real adventure. The isolated castle is hard to find and has no neighbors, yet there is so much river activity that it is impossible to feel lonely.

As was typical in castles of the time, living quarters are on the upper floor. From the ground floor, a circular stairway leads up to the living room and kitchen and continues up to a bedroom. You'll find the bathroom on a roof platform with a romantic twin-bedded (push them together) tower room. A few steps away, a concrete blockhouse provides an extra twin-bedded room that is reached by a ladder; it has a shower but no toilet. A guest wrote in the logbook about the blockhouse: "I'd never imagined it could be such an intriguing place. My first impression was of being inside a submarine."

The Landmark Trust warns prospective residents that dampness from the river might bother some people.

Location: In England, across from Dartmouth on the south coast of Devon. **Rooms:** 3 bedrooms, including 1 double and 1 twin; 1 twin in the blockhouse; 1 bath. **Rates:** Winter short stays £407, summer weekly rental £1179. **Children:** Not suitable for young children because of location. **Nearby diversions:** Dartmouth Castle; excursions along South Devon Heritage Coast.

Lundy Castle

A THIRTEENTH-CENTURY CASTLE

Located a few hours' boat ride from the north Devon coast, Lundy Island is a world apart. Rising over four hundred feet from the sea, the three-mile-long island is only one square mile in area. Grass and heather seem virtually the only form of plant life that can survive the sudden gale force winds that occur here. But on closer inspection, you will discover trees growing out of rocky cliffs and, in the early summer, bluebells and rhododendrons. The island is also populated with abundant sea and bird life.

Come to Lundy Island to explore wind-swept fields, cliffs, and coves. The entire island is yours to discover. The voyage from the mainland takes about two and a half hours. A launch takes you from the ship and drops you right on the beach. The island Land Rover is on call to help if you have trouble with the one-mile climb from the beach to the village.

The Landmark Trust operates the entire island on behalf of the National Trust, which acquired it in 1969. It took twenty years of restoration work to prepare the island for visitors. Twenty-three different self-catering accommodations, sleeping from one to fourteen, are available. Among them are a lighthouse, barn, lookout, school, and castle.

THE PAST 🌸 A Norman knight, Henry de Newmarch, became the first known owner of Lundy. He was followed by the Marisco family. Of French origin, they paid allegiance to the king when it suited their interests and eventually became common pirates, giving rise to a long list of complaints by sailors and shipowners. They reached their criminal peak in 1242 when William de Marisco sent an assassin into the bedchamber of King Henry III. Fortunately the king was away, and William was promptly hanged, then drawn and quartered on Tower Hill.

King Henry III built the castle on Lundy as part of his coastal fortifications to ward off the pirates and political enemies infesting the Bristol Channel. The king ordered that construction of the castle be paid for by the sale of rabbits.

Over the centuries a succession of owners held the island. Some used it as a base for piracy and smuggling operations. Others tried improvement projects. One man in charge of transporting convicts landed his charges for use as slave labor. Yet another lost the island in a dice game.

For most of the twentieth century, Martin Coles Harman, known as

Lundy's "Last Great Eccentric," possessed the island. He devoted his time and money to preserving the rare species of flora and fauna found here and to maintaining Lundy's independence from English bureaucracy. Since Lundy never fell under any county administration, he argued, courts, taxes, licenses, and the usual county registrations did not apply. He also asserted his right to mint coins and issue stamps. Though he was not allowed to mint coins, he was permitted to issue stamps, and since 1929 the stamps have been known as "Puffinage" (after the puffins that inhabit the island). Because he didn't want the wealthy building holiday homes, Harman also established a policy that all island tenants must be employed.

Harman's son administered the island until his own death in 1968. His sisters decided to sell, and bids were put in by a gambling consortium, some wealthy Americans looking for tax relief, and the Church of Scientology. The British public urged the National Trust to buy the island, but they didn't have the one-hundred-thousand-pound asking price. A British expatriate living in the Bahamas heard about the situation and donated the money to the National Trust for Lundy's purchase.

THE PRESENT 🌸 Lundy Castle commands a spectacular position on the island's southeast point overlooking the landing harbor. It offers four separate lodging units referred to as "cottages." Living rooms and kitchens are on the ground floor, with the bedrooms above. Three face an inner courtyard and have a few ocean-facing windows. A fourth, which was once the post office and cable station, is on the outside front of the castle; the ocean view from its windows is superb.

Note that the water supply is a real problem on the island and at times water is restricted. Also, generators supplying electricity are usually shut off every night at eleven.

Should you feel lonely, companionship, hot meals, a library, and games are just a short walk away at the Marisco Tavern. Also, a shop sells groceries, souvenirs, and walking guides of the island.

Location: In England, on a small island in the Bristol Channel; accessible by the MS OLDENBURG from the Devon ports of Ilfracombe, Bideford, or Clovelly (depending on the tide). **Rooms:** Castle Cottage: 1 twin (bunk beds) bedroom, 1 single in living room; shower and outside toilet adjoining property. Castle Keep East: 1 twin bedroom; 1 bath. Castle Keep North: 1 twin bedroom; 1 bath. Castle Keep South: 2 twin bedrooms; 1 bath. **Rates:** Castle Cottage: winter daily rate £25, summer weekly rental £425. Castle Keep East: £25/£400. Castle Keep North: £21/£334; Castle Keep South: £31/£514. **Children:** Suitable. **Nearby diversions:** Hiking; bird-watching; diving; rock-climbing.

Morpeth Castle

A FOURTEENTH-CENTURY GATEHOUSE

The pleasant Northumberland town of Morpeth was once an important trading center. It offers no grand tourist attractions but is well located for excursions.

THE PAST Morpeth was never in the path of any marauding armies, so except for an occasional border raid, life here was fairly quiet. The castle's greatest claim to fame in the annals of warfare occurred in 1644, when five hundred lowland Scots on the side of Cromwell's Parliamentarians withstood a twenty-day siege by two thousand and seven hundred Royalists.

Morpeth Castle was built around 1200. A century later, Lord Greystoke added a gatehouse to be used as a court to try those unruly border Scots. The plaintiffs' waiting room is now the kitchen.

THE PRESENT The fortified gatehouse is today's Landmark Trust. It sits on a small hill with great views of the town and distant countryside. Manicured lawns and gardens surround the property. Sharp eyes can spot the bullet holes from the Civil War above the gate.

The living quarters is on three floors connected by a spiral staircase. Narrow arrow-slit windows provide a glimpse of the drive; larger windows look out upon the gardens and woods. Morpeth's well-stocked kitchen includes a dishwasher. Several nearby restaurants are an option when you're not in the mood to cook.

Location: In England, north of Newcastle-Upon-Tyne, Northumberland. **Rooms:** 4 bedrooms, including 1 single, 2 twins, and 1 double; 2 baths. **Rates:** Winter short stays £304; summer weekly rental £1037. **Children:** Suitable. **Nearby diversions:** Beaches; Newcastle; Hadrian's Wall.

Saddell Castle

A Sixteenth-Century Castle

Isolated along the water's edge halfway down the east coast of Scotland's Kintyre Peninsula, Saddell Castle is the ideal place to finish writing that novel or to host a murder mystery dinner. This rugged tower house stands right on the beach, ready to withstand storms of gale-force strength.

The Past 🐚 Somerled, Lord of the Isles, who built nearby Saddell Abbey, is thought to have built a castle on this site in the middle of the twelfth century. The only fact historians know for sure is that in 1508 the Bishop of Argyll built the large square battlemented tower that we see today. The Campbell clan took possession of the property in 1600 and kept it for the next four hundred years.

The Kintyre Peninsula (sometimes called the Mull of Kintyre) was one of the first stepping stones from which Christianity came to Scotland from Ireland.

The Present 🐚 When the Landmark Trust acquired this property, large trees were growing out of the castle's roof and the windows were gone. Now repaired, it is surrounded by the ruins of the outer defenses and outbuildings.

Inside, a circular stairway leads up to four stories of rooms and down to a cellar. Up to eight people can sleep in the bedrooms on the top two floors. Although there is an open log fireplace, you might want to tuck a hot water bottle in your luggage if you plan to sleep on the top floor in winter. Bathrooms are on the top floor and ground floor. Thick walls hold closets and window embrasures. Concerned about privacy? Simply detach the floor inside the front entry so that anyone who comes calling falls into an ancient pit below.

The property also holds some dear little rental cottages.

Should you miss the bright lights of civilization, Campbeltown has plenty of restaurants and activities and is just several miles south. A few miles to the north, Carradale also has a restaurant.

Location: In southwest Scotland on the Kintyre Peninsula. **Rooms:** 5 bedrooms, including 2 singles, 2 twins, and 1 double; 2 baths. **Rates:** Winter short stays £426; summer weekly rental £2002. **Children:** Suitable. **Nearby diversions:** Hiking; ruins of Saddell Abbey; Campbeltown.

Ireland

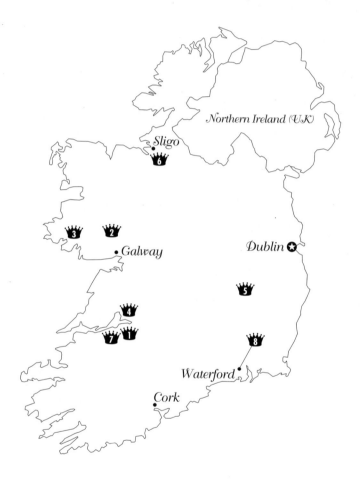

Northern Ireland (U.K.)

Sligo

Galway

Dublin

Waterford

Cork

Castles by the hundreds dominate today's Irish landscape. Because there are so many, it is not surprising that the castle hotels of Ireland offer a range of accommodations to suit every taste. You can experience both exclusive surroundings and a very intimate slice of Irish life.

Ireland has been invaded since the time of the Vikings and Danes, but it was the fateful Norman invasion that permanently changed the face of the countryside and established its devastating link with Britain. The Normans were at first invited to come to Ireland by Dermot MacMurrough, Irish king of Leinster. It seems that Dermot stole the wife of a neighboring king, O'Rourke of Breifne. Outraged, O'Rourke allied himself with Rory O'Connor—high king of Ireland—and other minor kings and ran Dermot out of the area. Dermot, not to be outdone, turned to King Henry II of England for help. It came in the form of the Normans, led by Richard, earl of Pembroke, who was also known as Strongbow. They entered at Waterford and soon established themselves as the dominant power in Ireland. Strongbow married Dermot's daughter and, at Dermot's death, became the first Norman king.

As the Normans captured a district, they built fortresses known as motte and baileys to protect it. These forerunners of stone castles were made of wood on mounds of earth with a fortified enclosure at the base of each mound. During the next four centuries the Normans built castles throughout Ireland, including nine hundred around the Shannon area and two hundred and thirty-five stone castles in Wexford County alone. To the Irish these castles represented oppressive English rule, while the English continued to perceive the Irish as uncivilized barbarians. Today many castles are open for exploration, and some host medieval banquets. All of the hotels in this section are located in the Republic of Ireland. Northern Ireland, which is part of the United Kingdom, has no castle or palace hotels.

For a very different and special castle experience in Ireland, you can rent by the week a castle with full staff and amenities. For further information, contact Elegant Ireland at: 15 Harcourt Street, Dublin 2, Ireland, Tel: 011-353-1-475-1632, Fax: 011-353-1-475-1012.

For further information on Ireland, contact the Irish Tourist Board at: 345 Park Avenue, New York, New York 10154, Tel: 212-418-0800, Fax: 212-980-9475.

Adare Manor

A Nineteenth-Century Manor

Besides offering the usual resort facilities, this fantastic multi-towered and turreted Gothic extravaganza exudes a friendly atmosphere that extends throughout the manor and the surrounding thousand-acre estate.

THE PAST 🦁 A genuine castle existed on this site until 1720, when it was replaced by a Georgian manor house. The second earl of Dunraven, stricken with gout, spent most of his time indoors, bored. His wife, Lady Caroline Wyndham, an heiress in her own right, suggested that designing a grand new home would give him something to do. He embraced her idea with gusto. For years, local artisans and architects labored to create a palace that would rival the magnificent French châteaux. Construction not only kept the earl busy, but it also provided work for villagers during the devastating famine that struck Ireland in the mid-nineteenth century.

The earl spared no expense. Throughout the manor are fifty-two chimneys (commemorating each week of the year), seventy-five ornate fireplaces, three hundred and sixty-five leaded-glass windows, and plenty of arches, gargoyles, bays, and window frames elaborately carved in stone. It also holds a one-hundred-and-thirty-two-foot-long minstrel's gallery—the second longest in Europe—inspired by the Hall of Mirrors in Versailles, and seventeenth-century Flemish choir stalls outfitted with doors imported from a confessional box in Vienna.

Though the earl didn't live to see his dream finished, his son, the third earl of Dunraven, did. The Dunraven family continued living in the manor until they sold it to an investment consortium in 1982. An American from New Jersey, Thomas Kane, bought the property and transformed it into a luxury hotel.

THE PRESENT 🦁 Some ornate hotels can be overwhelming, but good taste reigns throughout Adare Manor. The three-story-high reception hall boasts a magnificent wood staircase, chandeliers hung from wood-coffered ceilings, and stone archways. American and European newspapers are laid out next to inviting tapestry-covered couches. Lovely fabrics in shades of rose and a floral-design carpet accent a large lounge. In the library, you can warm up by the fireplace while daydreaming over garden views, and perhaps choose a book from the outstanding selection to enjoy in your room.

Period reproductions furnish most guest rooms. The enormous state-

rooms feature Gothic ceilings, antique furnishings, and lace curtains. The hotel's premier room, the Dunraven Stateroom, is decorated in shades of pale jade and rose and enjoys a sweeping view across the river.

In the formal restaurant you sit on carved Jacobean chairs while enjoying such tempting entrées as *croustillant* of salmon or grilled guinea fowl. Desserts include a chocolate and blueberry soufflé in a roasted-hazelnut crust and a raspberry crème brûlée. After dinner, you can listen to live music in the warm and friendly Tack Room Bar.

Walking through the grounds reveals many small surprises—pet graveyards, a three-hundred-year-old cedar of Lebanon tree, ruins of a former lodge, and inscribed stones.

Adare, County Limerick. Tel: 011-353-61-396-566. **Fax:** 011-353-61-396-124. **E-mail:** info@adaremanor.ie. **Website:** http://www.adaremanor.ie/. **Rooms:** 64, including 13 staterooms or suites; all with bath. **Rates:** Expensive: doubles from IR£112; includes service and tax. **Dates closed:** Open all year. **Dining facilities:** Restaurant (jacket and tie required for dinner); Tack Room Bar. **Children:** Age 11 and younger sharing with parents free; baby-sitting. **Facilities for disabled:** Yes. **On-site recreation:** 18-hole Robert Trent Jones-designed golf course; year-round swimming pool; sauna; gym; horseback riding; clay pigeon shooting; trout and salmon fishing; walks through the estate. **Nearby diversions:** Walks through village of Adare; Ring of Kerry. **Proprietors:** Tom and Judy Kane. **Operated as a hotel since:** 1986. **U.S. representative:** Adare Manor; Small Luxury Hotels of the World.

Directions: Adare is southwest of Limerick on N21. The castle is signposted.

Ashford Castle

A Fourteenth-Century Castle

Ashford proves that a castle can rank among the finest luxury hotels in the world. Its imposing exterior, elegant interior, and lovely grounds combine to create a memorable and pleasurable vacation experience.

THE PAST 🦋 After crossing the drawbridge and portcullised passageway under a turreted tower, you face an enormous stone building that incorporates architecture from several eras. The oldest section is a thirteenth-century Norman castle that once belonged to the de Burgh family; in the 1500s it became an English fortress after Queen Elizabeth's soldiers attacked. A French château (the original Ashford house) was added in the eighteenth century.

But the major structure was built a little over one hundred years ago. Its story began when Benjamin Guinness, head of the Dublin brewing company, came to County Mayo to pursue his archaeological interests. After falling in love with the beauty of the property and nearby Lough Corrib, he bought Ashford estate, the surrounding land, and other properties in this part of Ireland. His son, Sir Arthur Guinness, inherited twenty-seven thousand acres in County Galway, four thousand acres in County Mayo, and thirty-three islands in Lough Corrib. Choosing his father's beloved property in Cong, Guinness worked with architect Joseph Fuller to build this enormous home incorporating both the castle and the château.

Queen Victoria bestowed a peerage on Sir Arthur and his wife, who became Lord and Lady Ardilaun. After Lord Ardilaun's death in 1915, Lady Ardilaun raised an obelisk on the grounds to his memory and lived in the castle until her death in 1939. The castle and contents were then sold at an auction that lasted two weeks. The government of Ireland bought the property and reforested thirty-five hundred acres. The next owner, Irish-American industrialist John Mulcahy, renovated and enlarged the castle as a hotel.

Over the years the castle has hosted such luminaries as King Edward VII, for whom a special billiard room was built. Oscar Wilde was a frequent guest, and President Ronald Reagan stayed here in 1984.

THE PRESENT 🦋 When the weather outside is stormy, there's not a cozier place to be than in one of the public rooms here. They boast fireplaces, rich wood-coffered ceilings, Waterford chandeliers, enormous Chippendale

mirrors, period furniture, and fine art objects. Guest rooms are also elegantly furnished yet comfortable.

The dining room features both haute and nouvelle cuisine.

The Egon Ronay association gives Ashford Castle an eighty-eight percent rating, and it is the only Irish hotel to win the prestigious Gold Plate award.

You can walk along twenty-five miles of paths or stroll the lovely grounds (scenes from *The Quiet Man*, with John Wayne and Maureen O'Hara, were filmed here). Lough Corrib is famous for its trout and salmon fishing. It's easy to see why this area of Ireland has inspired so many artists and writers.

Cong, County Mayo. Tel: 011-353-92-46003. **Fax:** 011-353-92-46260. **E-mail:** ashford@ashford.ie. **Website:** http://www.commerce.ie/ashford/. **Rooms:** 83, including 5 junior suites (or staterooms), and 6 suites; all with bath. **Rates:** Expensive; doubles from IR£121; includes service and tax; winter specials and 3-day Christmas and 2-day New Year's packages available. **Dates closed:** Open all year. **Dining facilities:** 2 restaurants; bar. **Children:** Age 11 and younger sharing with parents free. **Facilities for disabled:** Yes. **On-site recreation:** Tennis; 9-hole golf course; equestrian center; health center; fishing; clay pigeon shooting. **Nearby diversions:** Hiking; Cong; Ballymagibbon Cairn at the Plain of Moytura; Ballintubber Abbey. **General Manager:** Rory Murphy. **Operated as a hotel since:** 1939. **U.S. representative:** Dromoland/Ashford Castles; Relais & Châteaux.

Directions: Cong is about 30 miles north of Galway on L101, which runs between Lough Mask and Lough Corrib.

Ballynahinch Castle

AN EIGHTEENTH-CENTURY CASTLE

Located in the remote, starkly beautiful region of Connemara, this castle abounds with stories of the swashbuckling pirates, eccentrics, and even maharajas who once stayed here. Now you, too, can come to relax and get away from it all at this peaceful country hotel.

THE PAST 🐚 The history of Ballynahinch is the history of Connemara.

In the sixteenth century the O'Flaherty family reigned over Connemara and the larger region of Connaught from their many castles, including Ballynahinch. Young Donal O'Flaherty, heir-apparent to the family fortunes, took as a bride sixteen-year-old Grace O'Malley, daughter of another powerful family. Grace proved to be as manly as any Irishman and gallantly fought at the side of her husband. She even helped defend one of her in-laws' castles on nearby Lough Corrib—Hen's Castle (named after a witch's gift hen that laid enough eggs during times of siege to feed a garrison). When her husband Donal died (most probably he was murdered), Grace became the head of the family and took to piracy. Her exploits took her far from Ireland. She eventually met Queen Elizabeth I on equal terms.

Ballynahinch soon passed into the hands of the Martin family. The most colorful member of this family was Richard Martin, also known as Humanity Dick. He served for several years as minister of Parliament, introducing the Cruelty to Animals bill in the House of Commons, which later established the Society for the Prevention of Cruelty to Animals. Martin was also famed for his dueling skills. Before each duel, he enjoyed showing an old wound to his opponent while commenting, "Let this be your target, Sir." When he lost his seat in Parliament, Martin fled Ireland for France with creditors at his heels. He was asked on his deathbed why he preferred animals over humans and replied, "Did you ever see an ox with a pistol?" Martin's son, Tom, stayed on at Ballynahinch and died from famine fever. Tom's daughter, Mary, unable to cope with the castle's debts, fled the country. Soon after arriving in New York at the Union Palace Hotel, she died from the effects of giving birth aboard ship.

The Encumbered Estates Court sold the estate to the Berridge family who did much to restore the present-day castle. They sold the property in 1922 to His Highness the Maharaja Jam Sahib of Nawanagar, India. Known as Ranji—the Prince of Cricketeers (he still holds two cricket records in the

Guinness Book of Records), the maharaja used to come to Connemara every summer to fish. When he arrived each June, he bought five new cars, including two limousines, and gave them away to whichever local citizen caught his fancy before he left for India in October. Ranji landscaped the castle grounds, gardens, and woods and built fishing piers and shelters along the river. Each year on his birthday he held a grand party for his staff and served the drinks himself. He kept trucks waiting outside to take his inebriated guests home. When he died in 1932, his nephew sold the estate.

Famous guests who have enjoyed Ballynahinch's hospitality include writer Liam O'Flaherty, actor Sir Alec Guinness, and former president Gerald Ford.

THE PRESENT 🐚 When you step through the door at Ballynahinch, you enter a charming world of faded glory. Wherever you look, you see old photographs, oil paintings of fishing scenes, and souvenirs of the castle's former owners. Burnished wood paneling, wooden floors covered with Oriental-style carpets, and deep, comfortable chairs give a homey feel to public rooms warmed by crackling log fires. An earthy atmosphere prevails, with fishermen feeling comfortable enough to walk into the bar with their fishing gear. Antiques and period furniture lend an elegant air.

In addition to good fishing in the rapidly moving Owenmore River, you can hike on miles of delightful nature trails that wind through the dense woods of the estate's three hundred and fifty acres.

The best guest rooms are in a new ground-floor wing that blends flawlessly with the old architecture. Four-poster beds and Georgian-style mahogany furniture decorate these deluxe rooms, and floor-to-ceiling windows overlook the river. A few even have fireplaces. Rooms bear names such as Salmon Leap, Elephant Walk, and Grace O'Malley.

The dining room overlooks the river and gardens. As befits a fishing haven, lunch and dinner menus here feature the catch of the day and several kinds of salmon accompanied by special sauces. Grilled lobster, lamb, steak, and several vegetarian main courses are also on the menu. The Fisherman's Bar is a popular meeting spot for locals, and during the summer musicians entertain.

Recess, Connemara, County Galway. Tel: 011-353-95-31006. **Fax:** 011-353-95-31085. **E-mail:** bhinch@iol.ie. **Website:** http://www.commerce.ie/ballynahinch/.   **Rooms:** 28, including 8 in a new wing; all with bath. **Rates:** Moderate; doubles from IR£80; includes breakfast and tax; service is an additional 10 percent. **Dates closed:** 1 week at Christmas and the month of February. **Dining facilities:** Restaurant; bar. **Children:** Age 2 and younger free; age 3 and older IR£15-20. **Facilities for disabled:** None. **On-site recreation:** Salmon and trout fishing; shooting; croquet; bicycling. **Nearby diversions:** Tennis; golf; pony-trekking; drives through Connemara National Park; Connemara Pony Show in Clifden in August. **General Manager:** John O'Connor. **Operated as a hotel since:** 1946. **U.S. representative:** Consort Hotels Ltd.

Directions: Along N59, watch for a small signpost that reads "Ballynahinch." Drive carefully; sheep wander freely on the road. After a few miles, another signpost guides you onto the estate.

Dromoland Castle

A NINETEENTH-CENTURY CASTLE

Located just eight miles from the Shannon airport, Dromoland Castle offers some of the finest accommodations in Ireland. Here you will live in the style of an Irish baron and experience Irish hospitality on a grand scale. The castle is the ideal base for excursions into County Clare or Limerick.

THE PAST Dromoland had long been the home of the Royal Clan O'Brien. A thirty-six-foot-long genealogy traces the family directly to Brian Boru, high king of Ireland in the eleventh century. His firstborn son, Donough O'Brien, inherited the land called Drum-Olain (the Hill of Olan), later changed to Dromoland. Not until 1543, when clan chief Morrough O'Brien pledged his loyalty to King Henry VIII of England, did the O'Briens receive the title of barons of Inchiquin and earls of Thomond. The family's ancestral home was destroyed during the wars with Cromwell, but Sir Donough O'Brien went on to build Dromoland Castle.

In 1826 Sir Edmund O'Brien updated his home by tearing down a Queen Anne-period building and, for eighty thousand pounds had new stone quarried and transported for the present structure.

Several times during its history, Dromoland had been marked for demolition. The O'Briens were members of the British House of Lords and a target for members of the I.R.A. Twice, sabotage plans were thwarted by local I.R.A. members who persuaded their leaders that the O'Briens were always fair with their tenant farmers. Also, Dromoland was the birthplace of a famous Irish revolutionary, William Smith O'Brien, who fought for the rights of Irish Catholic farmers. His brother, Lucius, thirteenth baron of Inchiquin, was respected for his famine relief work in the 1840s.

Despite the standing of the family, their fortunes diminished after the Land Acts of 1880 to 1921 forced them to sell their tenant farms, which had been their major source of income. For another twenty-five years the O'Briens managed to keep their ancestral home, even attempting to support themselves by running a dairy farm. In 1948 finances were so low that they accepted tourists as paying guests.

Lord Inchiquin finally sold the castle and four hundred acres of land, including hunting and fishing rights, to Bernard McDonough, an American industrialist whose grandparents had emigrated from Ireland. Mr. McDonough wanted to use his property to help the economically depressed area and, after considerable expense and effort, opened Dromoland as a luxury hotel.

Dromoland is very popular among Americans, who often return to enjoy its beauty and tranquillity. Famous guests have ranged from Richard Nixon to the Beatles.

THE PRESENT 🦪 Although substantial changes have been made, many touches from the past remain. O'Brien ancestral portraits line the walls of the formal public rooms. Comfortable sofas and chairs by the fireplace create a cozy spot to enjoy a cup of tea while relaxing with a good book.

Some guest rooms are done in floral patterns, others in subdued colors. Eight are built into turrets, and room 206 has an exceptional view of the grounds.

Well-prepared traditional cuisine, such as roast lamb and Irish smoked salmon, is served in a dining room looking out onto a lake. Lunch is served in the tower bar that was once Lord Inchiquin's study.

The grounds are ideal for strolling, golf, or riding (horses can be rented nearby), and the flower gardens, lily ponds, and woods are fun to explore. A particularly interesting spot on the grounds is a domed gazebo holding a statue of Mercury, the god of speed. It seems that in the eighteenth century Sir Edward O'Brien buried his favorite racehorse here. A fanatical horse breeder and bettor (usually unsuccessful), he once bet his entire estate, including Dromoland, on his favorite horse, Sean Buidlhe. Fortunately, the horse won and Sir Edward, undoubtedly relieved, later built this monument.

Newmarket-on-Fergus, County Clare. Tel: 011-353-61-368144. Fax: 011-353-61-363355. E-mail: dromolan@dromoland.ie. Website: http://www.commerce.ie/dromoland/. **Rooms:** 74, including 12 junior suites (or staterooms), and 6 suites; all with bath. **Rates:** Expensive; doubles from IR£121; includes service and tax; winter specials and 3-day Christmas and 2-day New Year packages available. **Dates closed:** Open all year. **Dining facilities:** Restaurant; bar. **Children:** Age 11 and younger sharing with parents free. **Facilities for disabled:** Yes. **On-site recreation:** Tennis; 18-hole golf course. **Nearby diversions:** Bunratty Castle and Folk Park; Cliffs of Moher. **General Manager:** Mark Nolan. **Operated as a hotel since:** 1973. **U.S. representative:** Dromoland/Ashford Castles; Relais & Châteaux.

Directions: From Shannon Airport, follow N18 (T11) north toward Ennis.

Kilkea Castle

A TWELFTH-CENTURY CASTLE

The heart of the Irish countryside begins less than an hour from the center of Dublin. North of Dublin is the fascinating town of Drogheda, settled by the Vikings almost a thousand years ago, and to the southwest, in gentle farmland, is the oldest continually inhabited castle in Ireland—Kilkea Castle.

THE PAST 🌀 Kilkea was the scene for eight hundred years of periodic local wars and, at times, larger national ones. Sir Walter de Riddlesford, a young Anglo-Saxon knight, invaded Ireland at Wexford with the second party of Normans in 1170. Within ten years he had built Kilkea Castle under the order of Hugh de Lacy, the Norman military governor. He selected its low-lying position along the river Griese to protect the communication between Wexford and the new capital at Dublin.

Within three generations no male heirs were around to keep the castle in the family, but a granddaughter married a Fitzgerald, in whose family it remained for the next seven hundred years. Like any other family, the powerful Fitzgeralds had their ups and downs—and their occasional eccentric personalities.

During the Tudor era, Gerald Fitzgerald, the eleventh earl—better known as the Wizard Earl—was such a character. To protect his estates, he changed his religion repeatedly to curry favor with the English crown. Born in an age when fortified castles were impractical and traditional feudal aristocracy was powerless to declare war, he spent many years in London and Italy where he learned astrology, alchemy, and magic. At Kilkea he spent many nights in the turret observing the heavens. Not surprisingly, legends grew around him. The most famous dates from 1718, one hundred and thirty-three years after his death. It relates that a crew of workmen encountered several horsemen when returning home at night across the Curragh Plain. The leader asked one of the workmen, a blacksmith, to examine his horse's shoes, which were made of very worn silver. Later the blacksmith realized this leader was the Wizard Earl, who is believed to be lying in an enchanted sleep since his death in 1585, making a nighttime journey every seven years across the Curragh to Kilkea to haunt the castle tower and free Ireland from its foes, or, at the very least, to scare the wits out of any tourists who happen to cross his path. The Wizard Earl was probably astounded the last time he came by to haunt the castle tower—and found a new bathroom inside!

In the seventeenth century a widow of another earl gave Kilkea Castle to the Jesuits so she could live by the seaside for her remaining fifty-three years. After twelve years the Jesuits gave it away, and the new owners surrendered the castle to Cromwell, who, for some unknown reason, didn't destroy it.

The Fitzgeralds again regained control of the castle, but then leased it out. One tenant, Thomas Reynolds, a cousin of the famous painter, was related by marriage to the Irish patriot Wolfe Theobald Tone. With great enthusiasm, he joined Tone's Society of United Irishmen. After a night of drinking and bragging about his part in the coming fight, Reynolds had second thoughts, squealed on his comrades, concealed his cash and valuables in a secret hole in the walls of his study, and fled to France with a thousand pounds a year for life as payment for his testimony. He later became a prosperous consul general in Paris. His wife collected an additional reward of five thousand pounds, while her sister became a widow upon the suicide of Wolfe Tone. The castle was looted, and the next tenants, the Caulfields, spent their time with sledgehammers and mallets looking for Reynolds' hidden treasure.

During the time of the Great Potato Famine, the Fitzgeralds had the castle restored on a grand scale—as a make-work project for the local unemployed and so that members of the family would have a spare place to live should the need arise. But in the ensuing years even the Fitzgeralds had a hard time hanging on, and in 1960 the Marquess of Kildare moved permanently to England.

The Land Commission took over the castle and sold it. In 1965 William Cade, a French-American businessman, bought the property and, with the help of Dublin architect Niall Montgomery, renovated the castle and opened it as a luxury hotel.

THE PRESENT 🌀 Today, Kilkea looks much the same as it has for several centuries. Its gray granite walls, towers, and battlements remain intact. Although the property is not as extensive as it once was, one hundred acres of grounds provide ample area to fish and hunt.

The castle is full of interesting things to look for. About seventeen feet above the former guardroom is an evil-eye stone, a common feature in Ireland and in some other countries of northern Europe (the idea was to attract evil to evil, much like a lightning rod attracts lightning). Kilkea's stone features monster forms of wolf and gargoyle heads on human bodies ripping each other apart. Another point of interest is a carving of a monkey with paws outstretched and a collar and chain around its neck. This piece is high up on a bracket that supports the chimney on the haunted tower. From room 121 you can put your head out the window and see it.

Recently, the castle has undergone a complete renovation, and the guest rooms—many of which have high ceilings and Gothic windows—are all updated.

In the great hall you can dine on dishes based on fresh regional produce. A comfortable lounge presents traditional entertainment on weekends.

Castledermot, County Kildare. Tel: 011-353-503-45156. Fax: 011-353-503-45187. **Rooms:** 51, including 11 rooms in the castle and the rest in an annex across an adjacent courtyard; all with bath. **Rates:** Very expensive; doubles from IR£140; includes tax. **Dates closed:** December 22 through December 27. **Dining facilities:** Restaurant; bar. **Children:** Age 11 and younger sharing with parents free; age 12 and older 50 percent room discount. **Facilities for disabled:** Yes. **On-site recreation:** 18-hole golf course; tennis; archery; clay pigeon shooting; fishing; indoor swimming pool; exercise room and saunas. **Nearby diversions:** Horse racing; Irish Horse Museum in Kildare; ruins of a Franciscan friary at Castledermot; granite crosses scattered throughout the countryside. **Proprietor:** Shane Cassidy. **Hotel since:** 1965. **U.S. representative:** None.

Directions: Castledermot is located on N9 about 43 miles southwest of Dublin, and 7 miles northeast of Carlow. Kilkea Castle is 3 miles northwest of Castledermot on the road to Athy.

Markree Castle

AN EIGHTEENTH-CENTURY CASTLE

It's easy to see why Nobel Laureate William Butler Yeats found inspiration in the charming countryside of County Sligo. The sparkling watered woodlands and stately mountains here abound with myths and fairy tales, and this great Irish poet used many of these mystical legends in his works. He brought to his audience the soul of Celtic Ireland.

Throughout the county ancient burial mounds hide tales of bravery in heroic battles between the warriors of Connacht and Ulster. An easy walk to the top of Knocknarea hill leads to a cairn and the ancient grave of the Celtic Queen Maeve. Yeats spent his boyhood summers discovering this magical corner of Ireland and often stayed in the county's great homes, including Markree Castle.

THE PAST 🕸 The castle's history is closely associated with that of the Cooper family. Coronet Cooper came to Ireland with Cromwell's army in the seventeenth century and acquired Markree Castle as payment for services. (Cromwell chronically had trouble meeting his payroll.) After the siege of Limerick, Cooper married the widow of the chief of the defending garrison, Maire Rua (Red Mary), adopted her two sons, and together they had a third son. This son inherited Markree, and today's proprietor, Mr. Charles Cooper, is his direct descendant.

Except for a short time in the late seventeenth century, the Cooper family has remained at Markree, involving themselves in Irish politics. In 1922 Brian Cooper, Charles Cooper's grandfather, was elected to the first Irish parliament. This is noteworthy in that he and only one other had been Unionist members of the English parliament.

Although Markree has remained as the estate of the Cooper family since the time of Cromwell, nothing remains of the original castle. The present castle dates from the eighteenth century, with additions designed in 1802 by Francis Johnston, architect of many grand buildings in Dublin. After World War II, the main house was too big to maintain as a private residence and was closed off. It lay in sad ruins until recent years. Charles Cooper bought the property several years ago from his brother with the intention of transforming it into a hotel.

THE PRESENT 🕸 Lord Clark of the television series *Civilization* called Markree one of Ireland's finest castles of its age. After driving through the

arched stone gatehouse, and then on in via the narrow road leading past sheep and horses grazing on the castle's thousand-acre estate, you confront an imposing five-story gray stone mansion. Despite its immense size, when you walk through the double wooden doors and up a stone stairway to the main hall, you know you're in someone's home. Charles Cooper—the tenth generation of Coopers to live at Markree—or his wife, Mary, will welcome you.

When the weather is chilly, fires blaze in cozy lounges that include a library—which once held fifty thousand books and is now decorated in pretty shades of yellow and blue—and a sitting area—which features old paintings of the Cooper forebears hung on pale raspberry-colored walls as well as a marble fireplace topped with Aynsley vases. An unusual hanging oak staircase leads from the front hall past a stained-glass window depicting the Cooper family tree back to the era of King John of England.

Guest rooms have views overlooking the garden or countryside and are decorated with rich mahogany furniture from the Victorian and Edwardian ages. Bathrooms are tiled and completely modernized. Tower room 15 is ideal for families: Rooms are stacked on top of each other, with a perfect room for kids on the bottom, topped by a room for the parents, topped by a bath accessible by a tower stairway.

Markree is now the home of the Knockmuldowney Restaurant, famed throughout County Sligo for its fine cuisine. Once located several miles away, the restaurant was moved by the Coopers when they acquired the castle. Sparkling gold chandeliers hang down from a high Louis XIV plaster ceiling over an ornate dining room surrounded by mirrors hung on pale green walls. Three- and four-course set menus offer entrées of fresh bass or salmon, sautéed stuffed quail, and roast rack of lamb, finished with a dessert of plum and orange brûlée.

Collooney, County Sligo. Tel: 011-353-71-67800. Fax: 011-353-71-67840. E-mail: Markree@iol.ie. Rooms: 30; all with bath. **Rates:** Expensive; doubles from IR£93; includes breakfast, service, and tax; weekend, 3-day, and weekly rates available. **Dates closed:** Christmas. **Dining facilities:** Restaurant; reservations essential; smoking not permitted. **Children:** Age 4 and younger sharing with parents free; age 5 through 12 sharing with parents IR£12; baby-listening. **Facilities for disabled:** Yes. **On-site recreation:** Horseback riding center with cross-country course. **Nearby diversions:** Trout and salmon fishing; golf; hiking; County Sligo Museum and Yeats Art Gallery in Sligo; drives through "Yeats Country"; hiking on Knocknarea. **Proprietor:** Charles Cooper. **Operated as a hotel since:** 1989. **U.S. representative:** BTH; Utell International.

Directions: Collooney is several miles south of Sligo on N4. The road to the castle is on the south side of town and is signposted. The castle gate is about 1/2 mile farther.

Castle Matrix

A Fifteenth-Century Castle

The eighty-foot-high castellated square tower that is Castle Matrix commands views over the countryside to Shannon. This small, intimate family-run castle takes you back in time to medieval Ireland.

THE PAST The story of Castle Matrix begins in the fifteenth century with the earl of Desmond (related to the Fitzgeralds of Kilkea Castle), who was murdered in the tower. A century later, the Desmonds rebelled against Queen Elizabeth I and lost their fortress to the crown.

The queen installed Sir Walter Raleigh in the castle when he was twenty-eight. His friend, Edmund Spenser, wrote part of the *Faerie Queene* while staying at the castle.

The queen soon granted the castle to Lord Southwell from Suffolk, who desired to seek his fortune in the Irish colony. He planted the fields around the castle with the "Virginia tubers" Raleigh had brought back from the New World, beginning the first cultivation of the potato in Europe. The Irish later seized the castle during the Rebellion of 1641, but Cromwell's troops soon recaptured it.

In the eighteenth century another Lord Southwell invited two hundred Lutheran families to settle on his land to avoid persecution in Germany. The colony thrived and produced a good income. Fifty years later John Wesley from England came to visit and converted the tiny colony to Methodism. One German convert emigrated to New York, where he founded the first Methodist church.

THE PRESENT 🌀 The castle eventually fell into ruin until Colonel O'Driscoll, the late husband of the current proprietress, bought the property. On the second floor, you will find his personal library of medieval books—one of the finest in the British Isles—as well as tapestries, armor, antiques, and a Celtic harp. Seminar groups often come here to study. A long spiral staircase leads to the ramparts, where you can see how the sentries and archers defended the castle behind the crenellations and also enjoy a wonderful view.

Each guest room is uniquely furnished. A favorite holds a carved antique canopy bed dating back to 1624. One room has a private sauna, several have wood-burning fireplaces, and one opens onto a terrace with parapets.

Castle Matrix is operated like a bed and breakfast rather than a full-service hotel. There are several restaurants in the area, but if you wish to eat in, let Mrs. O'Driscoll know early in the day. Banquets and weddings can be arranged during those months when the castle is closed.

Rathkeale, County Limerick. Tel: 011-353-69-64284. Fax: 011-353-69-63242. **Rooms:** 5, including 3 twins and 2 doubles; all with bath. **Rates:** Moderate; doubles from IR£60; includes breakfast, service, and tax; credit cards not accepted. **Dates closed:** September 16 through May 14. **Dining facilities:** Guests welcome to join in family meals. **Children:** Age 14 and younger 20 percent discount; cribs available. **Facilities for disabled:** None. **On-site recreation:** None. **Nearby diversions:** Adare; Ring of Kerry. **Proprietor:** Elizabeth O'Driscoll. **Operated as a hotel since:** 1970. **U.S. representative:** Erin Driscoll (Mrs. O'Driscoll's step-daughter); Tel: 770-428-5021.

Directions: Rathkeale is located on N21, about 18 miles southwest of Limerick. In town, signposts direct you to the castle.

Waterford Castle

A Seventeenth-Century Castle

Located in the "sunny southeast," between Dublin and Cork, Waterford County offers activities of every kind for the history, nature, and sports enthusiast. The often overlooked city of Waterford deserves a few days on your itinerary.

Waterford Castle sits on its very own three-hundred-and-ten-acre island, ensuring exclusivity and peaceful accommodations. Crossing the River Suir on a chain-driven ferry to reach the castle tips you to the fact that you're in for a treat.

THE PAST 🐚 The strategic position of this island—in the middle of a river outside Waterford City—guaranteed a long and colorful history. According to legend, monks first settled the island between the sixth and eighth centuries. (A couple of carvings found on the property validate the story: a monk's head from the sixth century and a winged angel from the eighth century.) After frequent attacks, the monks had to flee to safer ground. The Danes eventually built two castles to guard the river, and the island was named "Dane's Island," or "Island Vryk."

During the Norman invasion of Ireland, Maurice Fitzgerald, the

cousin of Strongbow, the English earl of Pembroke, was captured and imprisoned on the island. After the Norman victory, Fitzgerald took possession of the island, beginning an eight-hundred-year stewardship.

The Fitzgeralds first built a Norman keep with typical thick walls and narrow arrow-slit windows. In the fifteenth-century a tower replaced this structure and was enlarged over the centuries with additional stone wings.

In the eighteenth century socialite Mary Frances Fitzgerald made Waterford Castle her home. She broke off her engagement to the Duke of Wellington, hero of the Battle of Waterloo, to marry her cousin. Whenever she returned to her family home, twenty-four musicians entertained her as she was rowed across the river on a barge. Her son, Edward Fitzgerald, found world fame as the translator of the *Rubaiyat* of Omar Khayyam. Several generations later, another Mary Fitzgerald married Italian Prince Caracciolo. They sold the island and castle in 1958, thereby ending eight centuries of Fitzgerald ownership.

The next series of owners established greenhouses, from which fruits and flowers supplied local and world markets, and a "disease-free" dairy farm. Eddie Kearns, the present proprietor, bought the island in 1987 and invested millions of pounds to establish a lovely and exclusive luxury resort.

THE PRESENT ❁ Mullioned windows, gargoyles, turrets, towers, and battlements embellish this castle built entirely of stone. Antiques filling the grand public rooms include an Aubusson tapestry, a settee and chairs with carved eagles and swan heads, and George III and Victorian mahogany and oak cabinets. Portland stone walls rise to meet ornate plaster ceilings; burgundy-colored, Irish-crafted carpets cover the floors; and a large stone fireplace welcomes you on cold evenings.

Antique-filled guest rooms range from standard size to deluxe and have views of the river, woodlands, or landscaped grounds. A carved four-poster bed dominates the enormous Presidential Suite. Many bathrooms retain their original one-hundred-and-fifty-year-old tile and feature freestanding bathtubs; all have lovely floral-design sinks.

Considered one of the finest rooms of its kind in Ireland, the Munster Dining Room features Elizabethan oak paneling, a carved oak mantelpiece, and an ornate plaster ceiling. Fresh seafood, traditional steaks with cognac sauce, and roast lamb with Dijon mustard, rosemary, and garlic are served on Wedgwood dinnerware bearing the Fitzgerald crest. Stemware is, of course, Waterford crystal. All fruits and vegetables served are grown organically on the estate.

The Island, Ballinakill, Waterford, County Waterford. Tel: 011-353-51-878-203. Fax: 011-353-51-879-316. E-mail: wdcastle@iol.ie. Website: http://homepages.iol.ie/~wdcastle/. Rooms: 18, including 1 single, 13 doubles, and 4 suites; all with bath. **Rates:** Expensive; doubles from IR£100; includes tax. **Dates closed:** Open all year. **Dining facilities:** Dining room; reservations essential. **Children:** Inquire about discounts when booking. **Facilities for disabled:** None. **On-site recreation:** 18-hole golf course; indoor swimming pool; tennis; clay pigeon shooting; croquet. **Nearby diversions:** Horseback riding; seaside resorts; Reginald's Tower Museum; Waterford Crystal Factory; harbor and river cruises. **Proprietor:** E. J. Kearns. **Operated as a hotel since:** 1988. **U.S. representative:** BTH Hotels.

Directions: The Island is east of Waterford City off R683. Follow signposts to the river, where the castle's own ferry transports guests and their cars across the river.

Italy

Almost every city and town in Italy has a villa that once belonged to an old patrician family, and in which now you can lodge for the night. Palaces abound, and though you might not associate Italy with castles, they, too, exist. Hillside castles are positioned throughout the Dolomites and the Aosta Valley, especially near the passes they once guarded—the Saint Bernard Pass near the French border and the Brenner Pass near the Austrian border. The castles in Merano listed here are German in origin and identified with Tyrolean history (this area was ceded to Italy only after World War I).

The expansion of commerce during the Renaissance gave people more money to lavish on private residences. Outside the cities, they built splendid villas that became famous throughout Europe not only for their design, but also for the beauty of their gardens.

Every art style from Romanesque to Baroque is reflected in the architecture of the city palaces. The typical palace is three storys high and rectangular, with windows set in symmetrical rows. Pilasters, pillars, and cornices provide decorative touches.

With such an overwhelming number to choose from, the hotels for this guide were selected for the beauty of their locale and for personalities in keeping with their historic background. You'll find them in such spectacularly scenic areas as the Dolomites, Lake Como, and the Amalfi Coast. More than those in any other country, these hotels offer food for the romantic soul.

Although a car gives you the flexibility of setting your own schedule, excellent public transportation serves all of these areas.

For further information on historic hotels in Italy, contact the Italian Government Travel Office at: 630 Fifth Avenue, Suite 1565, New York, New York 10111, Tel: 212-245-4961, Fax: 212-586-9249; or 500 North Michigan Avenue, Suite 1046, Chicago, Illinois 60611, Tel: 312-644-0990, Fax: 312-644-3019; or 12400 Wilshire Boulevard, Suite 550, Los Angeles, California 90025, Tel: 310-820-0098.

Hotel Cappuccini Convento

A THIRTEENTH-CENTURY MONASTERY

The drive along the Amalfi Coast is one of the most spectacular in the world. The twisting road climbs over deep gorges, caverns, inlets, and precipitous cliffs that plunge straight down to the sea. Enchanting white-washed villages and sumptuous villas hide among the colorful flowers and groves of citrus, olives, and almonds. The highlight of any visit to southern Italy, this region has attracted travelers for centuries with its charm and fantastic views.

THE PAST 🦋 Appreciating the beauty of the countryside, the Phoenicians, Greeks, and Romans built their palatial resort homes here. Successive Spanish, Austrian, and Bourbon rulers also enjoyed their pleasures on this strip of coastline. In addition to making cultural contributions, especially in the field of architecture, the foreign courts attracted many artists, writers, and musicians who drew inspiration from the lovely setting.

The popular coastal town of Amalfi was once an independent state ruled by self-proclaimed dukes. It was also a great sea power whose trade with the East rivaled that of Pisa and Genoa. The Amalfi Navigation Tables—the oldest maritime code in the world—is still preserved in the town hall. A citizen of Amalfi, Flavio Gioia, was said to have invented the mariner's compass in 1302.

The sea that gave Amalfi so much of its power also played a part in its downfall. In the eleventh and fourteenth centuries, tidal waves lashed the coastline and destroyed the town and its oceangoing fleet.

Perched on a cliff high above town, the Hotel Cappuccini Convento has remained virtually intact through the centuries. Foundations of the original monastery date back to the eleventh century. Capuchin monks lived here peacefully for almost three hundred years. In 1826 the Vozzi family took possession of the property and transformed it into a small guest hotel, hosting European royal families and such notables as William Gladstone, Henry Wadsworth Longfellow, and Teddy Roosevelt. A great-grandson, Giuseppe Aielli, Count of Vallefiorita, inherited the property and his family continues to operate the hotel today.

THE PRESENT 🐚 An elevator carries you up the hillside to the hotel, where a pretty vine-covered arbor leads to the reception area. Collections of fine paintings, antiques, Oriental carpets, and art objects decorate the public rooms.

A long whitewashed corridor leads to the simply furnished, immaculate guest rooms. Many have views looking out to the Mediterranean.

The main dining room retains its original vaulted ceilings and pillars, and breakfast and snacks are served on an outside terrace. The hotel is the headquarters of the Academy of Medieval Convent Cuisine, an association that recreates the cuisine of medieval times in Amalfi as well as its culture and traditions.

By request you can explore the old cloisters and the chapel — built in 1212 by Cardinal Pietro Capuano and still used for wed-

View from hotel

dings and Mass. You can also explore the peaceful gardens, lemon grove, and woods surrounding the grounds and bask on the hotel's private beach. The staff can arrange excursions to the beautiful Emerald Grotto or to the Isle of Capri and its famed Blue Grotto.

Via Annunziatella 46, 84011 Amalfi (Salerno). Tel: 011-39-89-871-877. Fax: 011-39-89-871-886. Rooms: 53, including 5 singles, 43 doubles, and 6 suites; all with bath. **Rates:** Expensive; doubles from L200,000; includes breakfast, service, and tax. **Dates closed:** Open all year. **Dining facilities:** Restaurant; outside terrace. **Children:** Age 1 and younger free; age 2 through 6 sharing with parents 30 percent discount. **Facilities for disabled:** None. **On-site recreation:** None. **Nearby diversions:** Water sports; Isle of Capri; town of Ravello. **Proprietor:** Dr. A. Aielli. **Operated as a hotel since:** 1826. **U.S. representative:** None.

Directions: Amalfi is located on the Gulf of Salerno about 63 kilometers south of Naples and 24 kilometers west of Salerno. Bus service is available from Sorrento and Salerno. The closest train station is in Salerno.

Hotel Danieli

A Fourteenth-Century Palace

One hundred years older and of a different architectural style than the nearby Gritti Palace, the Hotel Danieli is every bit as sumptuous. Located adjacent to the stately Doge's Palace and the Bridge of Sighs, the hotel commands a magnificent view across the lagoon to the Church of San Giorgio Maggiore.

THE PAST 🌸 Built at the end of the fourteenth century by order of the Dandolo family, the Danieli housed family members as well as visiting royalty, cardinals, and ambassadors. Over two centuries, four members of this extremely wealthy and respected Venetian family were doges. The first, Enrico Dandolo, promoted the Fourth Crusade that overthrew the Greek Byzantine empire and further enhanced Venetian prestige. Two doges in the thirteenth and fourteenth centuries expanded Venice's sphere of influence, especially over Genoa, the rival maritime power. The fourth doge, Andrea Dandolo (1307–1354), was a friend of the poet Petrarch. He carried on a highly criticized war with Genoa, but history remembers him more for his learning and patronage of the arts. He added a new wing to the Doge's Palace and did much to beautify Venice. As procurator of Saint Mark's, he altered the fabric of the chapel and ordered the restoration of the famous Pala d'Oro altarpiece. These accomplishments are particularly noteworthy since during this era an earthquake devastated the city, leaving the Grand Canal dry for fifteen days, and the infamous Black Death ravaged Venice, claiming three-fifths of its population.

The Dandolo Palace survived through the centuries in good condition. Marriages and successions passed the property into the hands of the Gritti, Mocenigo, and Bernardo families.

With the fading of Venice's glory, the floors of the palace were divided among several owners. In the nineteenth century Giuseppe Dal Niel (Danieli) bought the second floor from the widow of Alvise Bernardo, and Giuseppe's adoptive daughter bought the first floor from the Mocenigo family.

In 1822 Dal Niel transformed the property into a deluxe hotel where Venetian society could hold receptions and ceremonies. The hotel has hosted kings and princes as well as Wagner, Charles Dickens, and George Sand together with the twenty-four-year-old Alfred de Musset (they had the corner room overlooking the lagoon).

THE PRESENT 🐚 A private canal runs between the hotel's two four-story buildings. The lobby has silk-covered walls that glow in golden tones and a magnificent staircase with Venetian arches and balustrades. Public lounges are ornately decorated with gilt furniture, mirrors, painted ceilings, Oriental carpets, chandeliers, marble columns, and stained-glass windows. A new wing connects to the original palace.

Guest rooms are located in two wings—the original Dandolo Palace and the Casa Danielino. Empire-style rooms are decorated in shades of pale blue, yellow, and pink, while the gilt-accented Doge's Suite boasts fifteenth-century murals, antiques, paintings, and original Murano chandeliers. All rooms have marble bathrooms, and the most costly overlook a lagoon.

During the warm months the rooftop Danieli Terrace restaurant features regional dishes. Special diets can be accommodated with advance notice. You can also enjoy drinks on the outside terrace bar while looking out at the gondolas passing by in the canal.

Note: An elegant guest room sitting area is depicted on the back cover.

Riva Schiavoni 4196, 30122 Venice. Tel: 011-39-41-52-26-480. Fax: 011-39-41-52-00-208. Website: http://www.venere.it/venezia/danieli.html. **Rooms:** 231, including 44 singles, 178 doubles, and 9 suites; all with bath. **Rates:** Very expensive; doubles from L814,000; includes breakfast and tax. **Dates closed:** Open all year. **Dining facilities:** Restaurant; outside terrace; bar; afternoon tea. **Children:** Age 5 and younger sharing with parents free. **Facilities for disabled:** None. **On-site recreation:** None. **Nearby diversions:** St. Mark's Square and Basilica; the Accademia Museum; the Church of Santa Maria della Pietà; excursions to the islands of the lagoon; at Venice Lido: water sports, tennis, horseback riding, golf. **General Manager:** Giuliano Corsi. **Operated as a hotel since:** 1822. **U.S. representative:** The Luxury Collection-ITT Sheraton; Utell International; Euro-Connection.

Directions: The Danieli Hotel is just a few steps away from the heart of Venice on the Canale di San Marco. Private parking is provided at the Piazzale Roma.

Hotel Gritti Palace

A FIFTEENTH-CENTURY PALACE

Somerset Maugham described this lovely hotel well: "There are few things in life more pleasant than to sit on the terrace of the Gritti." This fifteenth-century Venetian doge's palace has also charmed the likes of Queen Elizabeth II, the Aga Khan, Winston Churchill, and Ernest Hemingway. Its refined graciousness creates a rare atmosphere—that of a private world in which you are treated with every consideration imaginable. Of course, the price for this is dear, but if you're seeking a stylish romantic hideaway in one of the world's most romantic cities, this is it.

THE PAST 🌸 No expense was spared in building this beautiful palazzo on the Grand Canal. It was once the home of Andrea Gritti, the seventy-seventh doge of Venice. Born in 1455 to a noble Venetian family, Gritti had a long, productive life at the height of Venice's fortunes.

Not only was Venice commercially powerful at this time, controlling the trade of the eastern Mediterranean, but its cultural flowering produced some of the world's finest artists—Bellini, Giorgione, and Titian. If Venice reached the zenith of its wealth during this era, it also began its decline, as the Turkish advance, the discovery of America, and the new sea routes to India began to shift the focus away from Venetian sailors.

Gritti played an important role in the events of the day. Known for his intelligence and wit, he commanded Venetian troops against the emperor Maximilian at Padova. He was later captured and sent to Milan and Paris as a prisoner of Louis XII. The French king and Gritti became friends and negotiated a common pact. In 1523 Gritti returned to Venice after the Council of the Republic nominated him as doge.

When the Spanish Habsburg emperor Charles V invaded Italy and threatened the Vatican, Gritti sent his troops to help defend the Pope. A peace treaty was signed at Bologna, and the following period of prosperity was devoted to beautifying Venice. The Church of San Giovanni Elemosinario, the Palazzo dei Camerlenghi at Rialto, and the Palazzo Gritti were all built at this time. Before his death at age eighty-four, Gritti negotiated a treaty with the Turks that brought a temporary peace.

THE PRESENT 🌸 As with many old Italian city palaces, the outside façade of the Gritti is not of great consequence, but upon stepping inside you enter a regal world of fine antiques, gold chandeliers, and Oriental carpets.

Guest rooms are a real treat, and suites are incredible. You have a choice between a room overlooking the Grand Canal, which provides a continual show, or a more serene room set back in the building. Each room is uniquely furnished with rich fabrics and chandeliers, and your bed might be a four-poster or one that sits in a curtained alcove.

Dining takes place either on an outside terrace overlooking the Grand Canal or in a candlelit restaurant serving regional and Italian dishes. Throughout the year famous guest chefs teach gourmet cooking classes here.

Campo Santa Maria del Giglio, 2467; 30124 Venice. Tel: 011-39-41-79-46-11. Fax: 011-39-41-52-00-942. Rooms: 93, including 6 singles, 81 doubles, and 6 suites; all with bath. **Rates:** Very expensive; doubles from L493,000; includes breakfast; does not include 10 percent tax. **Dates closed:** Open all year. **Dining facilities:** Restaurant; outside terrace. **Children:** Age 12 and younger sharing with parents free. **Facilities for disabled:** None. **On-site recreation:** None. **Nearby diversions:** St. Mark's Square and Basilica; the Accademia Museum; the Church of Santa Maria della Pietà; access to facilities at the Golf Club Venezia on the Lido: tennis; 18-hole golf course; water sports; swimming pool; horseback riding. **General Manager:** Francesco Sinisi. **Operated as a hotel since:** 1948. **U.S. representative:** The Luxury Collection-ITT Sheraton; Utell International; Euro-Connection.

Directions: The hotel is located on the Grand Canal, 15 minutes away from the road and train station by launch. Parking facilities for guests are at the Mattiazo Garage in the Piazzale Roma.

Hotel Schloss Labers

AN ELEVENTH-CENTURY CASTLE

This fine old castle, with its unusual "black tower," sits on a hillside surrounded by vineyards against a spectacular backdrop of mountains. It is in a region of the Tyrol that has been a part of Italy only since 1919. Until that time it belonged to the Austrian Habsburgs and, before them, to the counts of Tyrol and the duke of Carinthia. The German language and customs are as dominant here as the Italian.

THE PAST 🐚 The entire region around the Brenner Pass, which separates Italy from Austria, is thick with castles, but unfortunately the documents that could tell us about their past have not survived. So all that is known about Schloss Labers is that the great-grandfather of the present owner, Mr. Neubert, came from Copenhagen in 1885, when he bought this castle and opened it as a hotel.

THE PRESENT  The Neubert family has succeeded in retaining Schloss Laber's character and charm. Public lounges are comfortably furnished in keeping with their medieval ambiance. A stone staircase with fine wrought-iron railings leads upstairs to the guest rooms, which have wooden floors and goose feather duvets. Many also have views of the surrounding mountains.

The kitchen offers Tyrolean, Italian, and international cuisine served outside in the gardens at lunch, and either on the veranda or in the wood-paneled, vaulted-ceiling dining room at dinner. The hotel's own vineyards provide the wine. Concerts are scheduled each month.

Via Labers 25, 39012 Merano. Tel: 011-39-473-234-484. Fax: 011-39-473-234-146. Rooms: 32, including 10 singles, 20 doubles, and 2 suites; all with bath or shower. **Rates:** Moderate; doubles from L115,000; includes service and tax. **Dates closed:** November 1 through March 31. **Dining facilities:** Restaurant open to hotel guests only. **Children:** Age 5 and younger sharing with parents 50 percent discount; age 6 through 11 sharing with parents 30 percent discount; age 12 and older sharing with parents 20 percent discount; crib L30,000. **Facilities for disabled:** None. **On-site recreation:** Tennis; swimming pool. **Nearby diversions:** Hiking; Tirolo Castle; the Dolomites. **Proprietor:** J. Stapf-Neubert. **Operated as a hotel since:** 1885. **U.S. representative:** Schlosshotels; Euro-Connection.

Directions: From the center of Merano, drive east up the hill on Via Scena following signposts. Merano can be reached by train from Bolzano.

Hotel Palumbo

A Twelfth-Century Palace

Suspended one thousand and two hundred feet above the sea, Ravello is a picturesque and charming little village offering stunning views of the entire Amalfi Coast. A short drive uphill from the coast road—through the Valley of the Dragon with its hills, ravines, fruit trees, and whitewashed houses—takes you to Ravello, hidden from view until the moment of arrival. The town is filled with ancient palazzos and gardens, making it an idyllic spot for strolling and relaxing.

THE PAST 🐚 Once a prosperous town of thirty thousand inhabitants under the reign of the French Anjou rulers in the thirteenth century, Ravello declined due to human and natural disasters. Throughout its history, noble families visited for the same reason we do today—to enjoy its spectacular location. Fortunately, they left their luxurious villas for us to explore.

The town's most famous home is the Villa Rufolo, built in Moorish and Norman style and once the residence of several popes and Charles of Anjou. During the nineteenth century, German composer Richard Wagner, who was orchestrating "Parsifal" at the time, visited Rufolo and found his setting for the garden of Klingsor. Wagner enthusiastically wrote in the guest book of the Hotel Palumbo: "The magic garden of Klingsor has been found!" Today the Villa Rufolo is in ruins, but what a beauty it must have been. Happily, the villa's gardens, used by Boccaccio as the background for many of his tales in the *Decameron,* are still full of pine trees and cypresses and bright with colorful and exotic flowers and plants.

Formerly known as the Palazzo Confalone, the Hotel Palumbo was a twelfth-century episcopal residence. It has been owned by the Vuilleumier family since 1875.

In addition to Wagner, the hotel has hosted such notables as Henry Wadsworth Longfellow, the Norwegian composer Edvard Grieg, the Kennedys, Tennessee Williams, and D.H. Lawrence, who wrote part of *Lady Chatterley's Lover* here. Hollywood has left its mark with visits by Humphrey Bogart, Greta Garbo, and Ingrid Bergman.

THE PRESENT 🦋 You reach this absolute jewel of a hotel through a high gateway with bougainvillea-covered walls, then enter a charming reception room with inlaid tile floors, columns, stone staircases, white walls, and vaulted ceilings. Colorful flowers, green plants, and family antiques fill the public rooms. A series of beautiful vine-covered terraces outside allow you to gaze out at magnificent views and dream the day away.

Guest rooms boast the same tile floors and white vaulted ceilings as the main public rooms. Some rooms are in an annex across the street.

Meals are served in an attractive dining room and on a terrace. The cuisine features regional Italian dishes such as semolina gnocchi, spaghetti with Gorgonzola, and shrimps in puff pastry, as well as some Swiss entrées that call attention to the Vuilleumier family background. (*Gourmet* magazine has done a feature on the Palumbo's cuisine.) Of special note is the wine the family produces under the Episcopio label.

Via S. Giovani del Toro 16, 84010 Ravello. Tel: 011-39-89-85-72-44. Fax: 011-39-89-85-81-33. E-mail: palumbo@amalfinet.it. Website: http://www.hotel-palumbo.it/. **Rooms:** 23, including 7 in annex; all with bath. **Rates:** Expensive; doubles from L270,000; includes breakfast, service, and tax. **Dates closed:** Open all year. **Dining facilities:** Restaurant; bar. **Children:** Age 8 and younger sharing with parents 30 percent discount. **Facilities for disabled:** None. **On-site recreation:** None. **Nearby diversions:** Swimming pool; beach (accessible by hotel mini-bus). **Proprietor:** Mark Vuilleumier. **Operated as a hotel since:** 1875. **U.S. representative:** E & M Associates.

Directions: Ravello is 7 kilometers uphill from Amalfi. Signposts mark the way to the hotel. Bus service is available from Amalfi.

Hotel Schloss Rundegg

A Twelfth-Century Castle

Needing no hyperbole, the Italian Dolomites is one of the most spectacular destinations in Italy. Exquisite sapphire-blue lakes nestle in isolated alpine valleys, and myriad medieval castles stand sentry in the mountain passes. Famed for magnificent walking trails and drives, the Dolomites have captivated travelers for centuries. You'll find the spa town of Merano a great base for daily explorations.

THE PAST On first glance this castle looks like a white candy confection. The smooth white walls with red and white shuttered windows topped by a steep tile roof hardly look like a threat to marauding invaders. Nevertheless, Rundegg was indeed built as a castle around 1100, although written records don't exist before 1580.

A long line of wealthy families lived in the castle, among them the Talbackers, who were judges in the Tyrolean county of Merano. In 1625 the Grand Duke Leopold received the right to bear the name of his newly acquired castle. ("Rundegg" is a German word meaning "by the round corner," referring to the characteristic round wing on the castle.)

The widow of Ferdinand von Kiebach zu Ried sold the castle to the famous Baron Parovicini. The baron was expelled from the French army for

dueling with a personal enemy and went on to marry four times and father ten children. He lived to the age of one hundred and four, attributing this good fortune to his regimen of taking two-hour walks every day of his life. His granddaughter, widow of the mayor of Innsbruck, lived at Rundegg un-

til 1878. By the next generation, the castle was in ruins and in desperate need of repairs.

The south Tyrolean industrialist Paul Sinn bought the property in 1976 with the aim of transforming the castle into a luxury hotel. Modernization was accomplished without disturbing the ancient wall structures or the original architecture.

THE PRESENT 🦋 In the public rooms exquisite furnishings, antiques, and Oriental carpets are displayed to advantage against white Gothic vaulted ceilings, timberwork, and wooden floors.

The large guest rooms are decorated in the same style. All have either Gothic vaulting, beamed ceilings, or bay windows. The Tower Room has beams dating from the twelfth century and a three-hundred-and-sixty-degree view from eight windows.

The restaurant has a stone-vaulted ceiling and some interesting alcove rooms. The menu features local and Italian specialties.

Schloss Rundegg is conveniently located within walking distance of the center of Merano.

Via Scena 2, 39012 Merano. Tel: 011-39-473-23-41-00. Fax: 011-39-473-23-72-00. **Rooms:** 30, including 6 singles, 21 doubles, 2 suites, and 1 appartment; all with bath or shower. **Rates:** Very expensive; doubles from L400,000; includes dinner, breakfast, service, and tax. **Dates closed:** Last 3 weeks of January through first 2 weeks of February. **Dining facilities:** Restaurant. **Children:** Age 2 and younger free; age 3 through 8 sharing with parents 30 percent discount; age 9 through 12 sharing with parents 20 percent discount. **Facilities for disabled:** None. **On-site recreation:** Indoor swimming pool; health and beauty center. **Nearby diversions:** Walks along the Passirio valley and river; the Dolomites. **Proprietors:** Sinn family. **Operated as a hotel since:** 1978. **U.S. representative:** Schlosshotels.

Directions: The castle is on the main road leading east and uphill from the center of town. Merano can be reached by train from Bolzano.

Villa d'Este

A SIXTEENTH-CENTURY PALACE

This elegant hotel well deserves its international reputation as one of the best resorts in the world. With its enchanting location on the shore of Lake Como, Villa d'Este leaves you wanting to return year after year.

THE PAST 🦪 In 1568 Cardinal Tolomeo Gallio began to plan a sumptuous villa on the shore of Lake Como. The famous architect Pellegrino Pellegrini of Valsoldo designed the building (named Villa Garrovo after a nearby stream) and landscaping to attract high society. No expense was spared. The cardinal's nephew inherited the property and continued building in the Renaissance style. For almost two hundred years the villa housed party-goers from all over Europe, including the sultan of Morocco and his royal entourage. Though it is hard to believe, the Gallio family gradually grew bored with the villa and moved to Naples, leaving a sad and neglected property to the Jesuits.

An old, wealthy aristocrat from Milan finally bought the estate and handed it over to his new wife, Vittoria Peluso, a ballerina at La Scala. At first she was disliked by the old society, so she spent incredible sums renovating the villa's interior and gardens, and, when it was completed, she gave lavish parties. Soon the snobs were clamoring for her attention. The moment her husband died, she married a handsome young general under Napoleon, Count Domenico Pino. Afraid of losing him to the greater attraction of battle, she built some imitation fortresses and towers overlooking the gardens in the hope of keeping him with her. Domenico was so happy that he brought a special group of cadets to play war games in the gardens and to gorge afterward on Roman-style feasts.

The next woman to arrive on the scene was Caroline of Brunswick-Wolfenbüttel, Princess of Wales. Married to the future King George IV of England, who disliked her and treated her poorly, she was unhappy and left him to travel about Europe in search of happiness. She considered Lake Como paradise on earth and settled here with the intention of buying the famous villa. The Countess Pino, who must have been about fifty at the time, grudgingly sold the property to her on the condition that it was a royal demand and recorded as such in the deed of sale. Caroline renamed it the "New Villa d'Este" after the famous estate in Tivoli, near Rome. For five years she poured money into the palace, and, with the help of Chamberlain Bartolomeo Pergami (another handsome young man who served as her official escort), she threw scandalous parties.

Caroline was well liked among the local people, and her generosity did much to improve the area. A road from Como was built, a library maintained, and a theater supported. But in 1820 she ran out of money and returned to England to take her place beside George as the new queen of England. Her husband, not too keen on that idea, filed an action against her. She died the following year before her divorce was complete. Her will stated that Vittorina, the daughter of Caroline's lover, should inherit the villa, but her banker, who possessed the deed of sale, laid claim to it. The estate was completely abandoned, and the banker's heirs eventually sold the property.

THE PRESENT 🌸 Villa d'Este's elegant public rooms feature marble columns, vaulted ceilings, crystal chandeliers, a grand staircase, and silk brocade draperies and upholstery. An interesting frescoed ceiling and silk wall draperies, made especially for Napoleon's visit, decorate the Salon Napoleone, while Queen Caroline's Salon has become a cozy reading room.

Most guest rooms are in the main building. A nearby annex, built in 1856 and called the Queen's Building in honor of Caroline, houses more. The best rooms overlook Lake Como, but all feature Italian provincial antiques, period furniture, and marble bathrooms.

You have two dining rooms to choose from. The formal Veranda features continental and northern Italian cuisine and has enormous electronically controlled windows with views of the garden. The less formal Sporting Grill serves seafood and haute Italian dishes. On occasion, an Italian orchestra adds a special touch to the romantic setting. Breakfast is served buffet-style on an outdoor terrace.

Serene and tranquil Romanesque gardens have been tended here for four hundred years. Lovely paths wander past cypress trees, flowers, statuary, and an imposing mosaic colonnade. With a careful eye, you can discover many reminders of the hotel's colorful past.

Via Regina 40, Lake Como, 22012 Cernobbio. Tel: 011-39-31-34-81. Fax: 011-39-31-348-844. E-mail: info@villadeste.it. Website: http://www.villadeste.it/. **Rooms:** 156, including 8 singles, 77 doubles, and 37 suites; 34 rooms in the Queen's Building; all with bath. **Rates:** Very expensive; doubles from L650,000; includes breakfast, service, and tax. **Dates closed:** November through February. **Dining facilities:** 3 restaurants; jacket and tie required for dinner in the Veranda and Empire Room; the Sporting Grill is open only for dinner and is closed on Mondays; 3 bars serve light snacks. **Children:** Extra bed L115,000; children's swimming pool. **Facilities for disabled:** Yes. **On-site recreation:** Tennis; squash; indoor swimming pool, and unique outdoor swimming pool that extends into the lake giving the appearance that it is floating; fitness room; water sports. **Nearby diversions:** Golf; horseback riding; boat tours of Lake Como; casino. **General Manager:** Jean-Marc Droulers. **Operated as a hotel since:** 1873. **U.S. representative:** Leading Hotels of the World.

Directions: Cernobbio is on the western shore of Lake Como, just a few kilometers from the town of Como. The A-9 autostrada passes by Cernobbio. Como has a train station, and buses and boats depart from there for Cernobbio.

Grand Hotel Villa Serbelloni

A Seventeenth-Century Palace

It's hard to imagine a setting more lovely than Bellagio. Nicknamed the Pearl of the Lake, this unspoiled old-world village sits out on a promontory that divides Lake Como and Lake Lecco. A backdrop of hills descends to the lake, and the uphill streets of the village are actually stairways leading by villas, gardens, and sidewalk cafés. Before World War I, many of Europe's royalty came here to visit.

THE PAST 🐚 Originally, the Grand Villa Serbelloni was a private home built by the Milanese architect Sfrondati on commission from a wealthy patrician family. The Serbelloni family acquired the property and added two new wings from 1869 to 1872; shortly after, the property opened as a hotel. The luxury hotel's lovely setting continues to attract famous guests, who in the past have included Franz Liszt, the queen of Sweden, King Faisal, John F. Kennedy, and German Prime Minister Helmut Schmidt.

THE PRESENT 🐚 Retaining its former elegance, today's hotel is proud of its calm repose. Its motto reads: "Far from the noisy street."

With its painted vaulted ceilings and fluted classic columns, the Grand Hotel Villa Serbelloni is indeed a grand structure. Its drawing room is lushly decorated with gilt furniture, chandeliers, marble columns, Oriental carpets, and an intricately painted ceiling. Elsewhere murals, a baronial fireplace, and a gorgeous marble staircase add to the dramatic effect of the Baroque style.

Guest rooms are priced according to the view, with lake views commanding the highest rate. They vary in size and decor from the large and ornate to the small and simple. Special touches include oversize down pillows, linen sheets, eiderdown spreads, carved Florentine headboards, and antique-style telephones.

The evening meal is often a formal affair, with an orchestra for dancing. When the weather is pleasant, you can dine on an outside terrace overlooking the lake. The menu offers regional, national, and international selections. A lovely view of the garden and lake from the inviting breakfast room starts each day off right.

The hotel is surrounded by sub-tropical gardens, and the charming town of Bellagio is just outside the gates. Ferry service links Bellagio with Cadenabbia and Menaggio to the west and Varenna to the east, permitting car-free day trips to visit the area's famous villas and gardens.

22021 Bellagio, Como. Tel: 011-39-31-950-216. Fax: 011-39-31-951-529. **Rooms:** 85, including 2 singles and 83 doubles; all with bath; 13 self-catering apartments apart from main building. **Rates:** Very expensive; doubles from L440,000; includes breakfast, service, and tax. **Dates closed:** November 1 through March 31; apartments open all year. **Dining facilities:** Restaurant; outside terrace. **Children:** Cribs L25,000; age 2 through 14 sharing with parents L40,000; age 15 and older sharing with parents L60,000; baby-listening; playground. **Facilities for disabled:** None. **On-site recreation:** Tennis; squash court; swimming pool; sandy lakefront beach; health spa. **Nearby diversions:** Golf; water-skiing; boating; ferry rides to see villas and gardens. **Proprietors:** Bucher family. **Operated as a hotel since:** 1870. **U.S. representative:** Premier World Marketing.

Directions: Como has a train station. Buses and boats depart from there for Bellagio.

More Hotels

Ansitz Heufler

Situated in a forested valley, this fourteenth-century castle offers
rustic, yet elegant, accommodations in the northern Dolomites.
39030 Rasun di Sopra, (Bolzano). Tel: 011-39-474-496-288. Fax: 011-39-474-498-199.

Hotel Caruso Belvedere

Spectacularly positioned on a cliff above the Gulf of Salerno,
this Renaissance palace was once known as the d'Afflito Palace.
The Caruso family has operated a hotel here for four generations.
Via Toro 52, 84010 Ravello, (Salerno). Tel: 011-39-89-857-111. Fax: 011-39-89-857-372.

Hotel Castel Freiburg

This fourteenth-century castle once guarded the area's mountain
passes. A hotel since 1973, it now provides an enchanting view of
valleys and snowcapped peaks. Its interiors retain medieval touches
such as vaulted ceilings and wood paneling.
Via Labers, 39012 Merano. Tel: 011-39-473-44196.

Castello di Gargonza

Located in Tuscany, Gargonza is a walled, medieval hilltop village dating from the thirteenth century. Count Roberto Guicciardini, whose family has owned Gargonza for nearly four hundred years, restored the entire village into twenty self-catering cottages. No cars or shops are permitted, and music festivals are often held here.

52048 Monte San Savino, (Arezzo). Tel: 011-39-575-847-021. Fax: 011-39-575-847-054.

Castel Pergine

Just east of Trento in northern Italy, this thirteenth-century hilltop castle offers inexpensive accommodations. Michelin awards a two-fork rating to the cuisine.

38057 Pergine, (Trento). Tel: 011-39-461-531-158.

Castel San Gregorio

Located near Assisi in central Italy, this small, intimate castle dates from the twelfth century. Its medieval ambiance is well preserved.

Via San Gregorio 16, 06081 San Gregorio, (Perugia). Tel: 011-39-75-80-38-009. Fax: 011-39-75-80-38-904.

Schloss Korb

Surrounded by vineyards and orchards, this family-run castle hotel dates back to the eleventh century. Stone walls, beamed ceilings, and antique furnishings add to the atmosphere.

Missiano, 39050 San Paolo Appiano, (Bolzano). Tel: 011-39-471-636-000. Fax: 011-39-471-636-033.

Portugal

Portugal is one of the few countries in Europe that remains unspoiled by mass tourism. It is not, as some people think, a western extension of Spain, but a country with its own distinctive traditions and culture. Hospitable people, a beautiful five-hundred-and-fifty-mile coastline, a long and fascinating history, and some of the lowest prices in Europe make it strongly appealing to the traveler looking for new experiences.

Dotting the landscape along the major routes of commerce, Portugal's castles were first built in defense against the Moors during the period known as the Reconquista from 717 until 1259, then against the Spanish from the thirteenth to the seventeenth centuries. Most of these castles have double perimeter walls surrounding a massive square tower. The pyramid-shaped merlons suggest the Moorish influence. Although royal palaces were scattered around the country, the court was without a formal established capital and thus roamed from town to town, lodging at the host's expense in castles and monasteries.

European styles such as Gothic, Renaissance, and Baroque eventually reached Portugal and left their mark. A unique Portuguese style also developed. Known as Manueline—from the reign of Manuel I (1495–1521), which was noted for its prosperity and cultural advancement—it is essentially Late Gothic with influences borrowed from the Moors, India, and the Orient. Ornamentation, especially with themes regarding the sea, is its main feature. One of the best examples of Late-Manueline style is the Palace Hotel at Buçaco.

Another characteristic of Portuguese architecture is the widespread use of *azulejos*. These glazed ornamental earthenware tiles, which originated with the Moors, come in shades of blue, yellow, green, and brown. In the seventeenth century artists created great murals with these tiles, depicting outdoor scenes and landscapes. In later years, flowers, birds, and simpler designs became the fashion.

Like Spain, Portugal has a series of excellent government-owned hotels called "pousadas." In 1940 Antonio Ferro conceived the idea of the pousadas as modestly priced accommodations providing good regional cooking. He began with three pousadas in 1942. Today over thirty operate throughout Portugal in buildings of historic interest such as castles or convents, or in unique geographical settings. All have been designed to give you a better knowledge of the culture and traditions of the area through displays of local handicrafts and the presentation of local cuisine and wine.

The maintenance of high standards is assured by the state's Directorate-General of National Buildings and Monuments. Some pousadas limit stays to five days; check when making reservations.

If you plan to do any driving in Portugal, a good road map is essential and can save you countless hours of confusion on roads that are not always marked in ways a tourist is likely to understand.

For further information on Portugal, contact the Portuguese National Tourist Office at: 590 Fifth Avenue, 4th floor, New York, New York 10036, Tel: 800-767-8842, 212-354-4403, Fax: 212-764-6137. Website for Portuguese pousadas: http://www.pousadas.pt/.

Palace Hotel do Buçaco

Palace Hotel do Buçaco

A Nineteenth-Century Palace

Located in the hills of northern Portugal, the national park of Buçaco is a lesser-known treasure of Europe. It is one of the best places in Portugal to enjoy peace, quiet, and long tranquil walks on forest footpaths. Its two hundred and fifty acres contain four hundred native species and three hundred exotic species of trees, including giant cedars of Lebanon, cypresses, sequoias, and palms. Flowers are brilliant in the springtime and include hydrangeas, camellias, and lilies of the valley. In the middle of this forest, amid moss and vine-covered trees, sits the Palace Hotel.

THE PAST 🌸 As far back as the sixth century, Benedictine monks from Lovrão established a hermitage in the Buçaco Forest. Later, the priests of Coimbra maintained the forest. In 1622 Pope Gregory XV forbade women even to enter the area, and six years later a Carmelite convent was built where the present hotel now stands. In 1834, when all religious orders were secularized, the land became the property of the Crown.

In 1810 Buçaco was the scene of a battle between the British and Portuguese armies (under the command of the Duke of Wellington) and the French army in its third attempt to invade Portugal. An obelisk just outside the park and a military museum containing various mementos of the period commemorate another Wellington victory over Napoleon.

Built between 1888 and 1907, the current palace was designed by the Italian architect Luigi Manini as a summer residence and hunting lodge for King Carlos I. The unfortunate king didn't have much of a chance to use it, since he was shot in 1908 when the Republic of Portugal was proclaimed. The property has been a five-star hotel since that time.

THE PRESENT 🌸 A wonderful example of neo-Manueline and Renaissance architecture, this palace features a tower, a gallery of double arches, and some interesting stone carving. Inside, the hotel is warm and comfortable. A large sitting room, full of antique furniture, is the perfect place to sip an apéritif while warming yourself in front of a large fireplace. A grand staircase leads up to another sitting area filled with carved rosewood furniture from India and China. One corridor is hung with fascinating vintage-framed photos from the palace's royal days.

Guest rooms come in all sizes from small to enormous. All are comfortable, with antique furnishings, modern bathrooms, and views of the forest. The President's Suite is extra-special, with a terrace, silver tea service, and marble bath; British Prime Minister Anthony Eden and his wife honeymooned here.

Lunch and dinner are served elegantly in the formal dining room where pastel-colored paintings illustrate scenes from the *Lusiads,* and needlepoint work covers the chair seats. Overhead is a ceiling in the Mudéjar style with crystal chandeliers. The cuisine is excellent, and the wine cellar holds an impressive collection, including local vintages.

The lovely grounds hold an arcade covered with lavender flowers, a pool with resident swan, a maze garden, and several walking paths. An outstanding series of *azulejos* by Jorge Colaço is displayed beneath the outside arches. These blue-tiled panels depict more scenes from the *Lusiads* of Luis Van de Camöes, one of Portugal's greatest writers. (Written in the 1500s, the *Lusiads* is a great epic poem honoring the achievements of the Portuguese nation.) One panel shows a beautiful goddess-like figure pointing the way to new worlds and discoveries to a Portuguese explorer. The next panel promises that when he returns, all the world will be at peace and full of love. Another set of *azulejos* illustrates the Battle of Buçaco.

Mata do Buçaco, 3050 Mealhada. Tel: 011-351-31-930-101. Fax: 011-351-31-930-509   **Rooms:** 66, including 6 suites; all with bath. **Rates:** Expensive; doubles from 30,000Esc; includes breakfast, service, and tax. **Dates closed:** Open all year. **Dining facilities:** Restaurant. **Children:** Under age 2 free; age 3 through 12 sharing with parents 50 percent of extra bed price. **Facilities for disabled:** None. **On-site recreation:** Tennis. **Nearby diversions:** Seasonal swimming pool; mini-golf; walks through Buçaco forest. **Operated as a hotel since:** 1908. **U.S. representative:** Marketing Ahead; Pinto Basto.

Directions: You'll need a good map. Buçaco is 30 kilometers northeast of Coimbra and just off National Road 234. From Coimbra, go north on N-1. Do not take the road marked España. Go east on NR-234 toward Luso. Luso has bus and train stops and is 1 kilometer away from Buçaco.

Pousada do Castelo

A THIRTEENTH-CENTURY CASTLE

Portugal has declared the well-preserved medieval town of Óbidos a national monument. Afonso Henriques captured the town from the Moors in 1148 and proceeded to fortify it with massive walls and towers that still stand in a commanding position on the hill. Óbidos once looked over the sea, but years of silt buildup on the bay to the south created a lagoon, and the town is now located several miles inland.

Óbidos has always been known primarily for the charm of its narrow streets, whitewashed walls, and ironwork. As in other Portuguese towns, potted flowers and birdcages abound.

Entry into the old town is through a narrow double gate, lined by eighteenth-century *azulejos*. One long main street, bordered by Renaissance and Baroque houses and bright with flowers, enters the old city. Craftsmen sit outside weaving carpets, a local handicraft specialty.

THE PAST 🌀 Santa Isabel, the wife of King Dinis, was so enchanted with Óbidos during a visit in 1278 that the king gave it to her for her dowry. (The tradition of presenting this town as a bridal gift continued until 1833.)

Queen Leonor, wife of João II, lived here for several years mourning her only son and heir, who died in 1491 following a riding accident.

The castle was built in the twelfth century as a defensive fortress against the Moors. Converted into a royal palace in the sixteenth century, it later became a governor's quarters.

THE PRESENT 🐚 During cold weather a big granite fireplace warms the castle's lounge, which is furnished with eighteenth-century antiques (including a suit of armor), carved furniture, and leather high-back chairs.

Charming handcarved and restored antiques fill the six small guest rooms and three suites located in the rampart's towers.

The dining room is attractively decorated in brown on beige with hand-painted tiles, ceramics, and copper and brass plates. It features regional specialties such as baked fish and veal steaks, and the house white wine comes from local vineyards.

Note: Guest room with canopy bed is depicted on back cover.

2510 Óbidos. Tel: 011-351-62-95-91-05. Fax: 011-351-62-95-91-48. Rooms: 9, including 3 suites; all with bath. **Rates:** Expensive; doubles from 23,500Esc; includes breakfast, service, and tax. **Dates closed:** Open all year. **Dining facilities:** Restaurant. **Children:** Under age 2 free; age 3 through 12 sharing with parents 50 percent of the extra bed price. **Facilities for disabled:** None. **On-site recreation:** None. **Nearby diversions:** Walking tours of Óbidos. **Operated as a hotel since:** 1950. **U.S. representative:** Marketing Ahead; Pinto Basto.

Directions: Óbidos is 94 kilometers north of Lisbon. It is accessible by train and bus. The pousada is at the end of the main street inside the old town.

Pousada de Dom Dinis

A Fourteenth-Century Castle

The Portuguese were serious about keeping the Spaniards on the Spanish side of the border. Along the northern frontier, four small towns retain signs of ancient fortifications. Fortunately for the medieval fortress lover, the government has built a pousada in the middle of one of them.

THE PAST ☯ The Minho River, which separates Portugal and Spain, flows so serenely at Vila Nova de Cerveira that invading armies could simply paddle across. The Portuguese had to build a fortress to protect themselves. Records don't exist about when the first fortress appeared, but during the reign of Dom Sancho II (1223–1246) the property was presented as a bridal gift to his wife. In the following years, maintenance records indicate that local citizens were obliged to provide labor and material.

Dom Dinis, the pousada's namesake, enclosed the entire township within the castle walls and granted a charter in 1321. His work paid off when in 1643 Philip IV of Spain failed in an attempt to take the castle. In the following years, when threats to Portuguese sovereignty subsided, the fortifications gradually fell apart due to neglect. When the government took over the property in 1975, people were living in the ruins.

THE PRESENT ☯ Reception is in an old mansion on the town square. This appealing pousada is reached from there by walking up a cobblestone path and then through an enormous double-walled gate. Rooms are spread out in seven buildings, all within the ancient crenellated ramparts.

Many of the spacious guest rooms have private courtyards and views looking out over the town's cobblestone streets. Period furnishings include carved beds and brocade-upholstered chairs. Some rooms are inside reproductions of village houses.

The dining room, which specializes in regional cuisine, is in a separate building with views of the Minho River. The breakfast room below it faces the ramparts.

One of the best features of this pousada is the many outdoor places where you can just sit and relax, or perhaps have a drink, and enjoy the view.

Praça da Liberdade, 4920 Vila Nova de Cerveira. Tel: 011-351-51-795-601. Fax: 011-351-51-795-604. **Rooms:** 29, including 3 suites; all with bath. **Rates:** Moderate; doubles from 12,500Esc; includes breakfast, service, and tax. **Dates closed:** Open all year. **Dining facilities:** Restaurant. **Children:** Under age 2 free; age 3 through 12 sharing with parents 50 percent of extra bed price. **Facilities for disabled:** None. **On-site recreation:** None. **Nearby diversions:** Fishing; water sports; excursions in Minho district and across river to historic town of Tuy, Spain. **Operated as a hotel since:** 1982. **U.S. representative:** Marketing Ahead; Pinto Basto.

Directions: Vila Nova de Cerveira is in the north of Portugal along the Rio Minho, bordering Spain. The town has a train station.

Pousada dos Lóios

A Fifteenth-Century Monastery

Évora is one of the most charming towns in Portugal. It is deserving of its nickname "the Museum City" and is classified as a World Heritage site. The remains of a Roman temple, Visigothic walls, Moorish archways, and Romanesque, Gothic, Renaissance, and Baroque architecture are all found here, and palaces, mansions, and churches seem to be around every corner. You'll delight in exploring the narrow, twisting streets with their balconies, whitewashed walls inset with beautiful colored tile façades, and grillwork hung with bird cages and flowerpots.

The Past 🌸 The Pousada dos Lóios sits on a cobblestone square that also holds a museum, cathedral, and second-century Roman temple sometimes called the Temple of Diana. During the Middle Ages Évora was the favored capital of the Portuguese kings, who brought artists and men of learning to establish a political and cultural center here. When the court shifted to Lisbon, the university closed, and the town's wealth declined. Today it is a market town for the produce of the province of Alentejo.

Saint John the Evangelist built and consecrated this monastery in the late fifteenth century. Over the centuries it was enlarged and restored by donations, and you can still see the various time periods reflected in its architecture. The monks, who wore a sky-blue habit, taught the sons of the Portuguese kings and offered hospitality and charity to anyone who requested it.

The Present 🌸 Though the pousada is just a few steps away from the Roman temple, it is hardly noticeable from the square. From the doorway you enter long white corridors surrounding cloistered gardens. High vaulted ceilings, marble and stone columns, and a grand staircase with a pink marble balustrade remind us of the building's origins. One Gothic-Moorish doorway leads to a

chapter house that once held records from the Inquisition. Small sitting rooms throughout the hotel contain charming hand-painted frescoes on the walls and ceilings, as well as crystal chandeliers and period furniture.

Guest rooms leading off an upstairs arched gallery contain hand-carved armoires, canopy beds, and headboards with the eagle emblem of the monks. Bathrooms are lined with gray marble. You have to duck to pass through the tiny doorways, and some of the rooms are on the small side. Rear rooms are quietest, and rooms 1 and 2 are the best.

The dining room stretches around the courtyard and features regional Alentejo fish and lamb specialties. Breakfast is served in the former refectory.

 Largo Conde de Vila Flor, 7000 Évora. Tel: 011-351-66-240-51. Fax: 011-351-66-272-48. Rooms: 32, including 2 suites; all with bath. **Rates:** Expensive; doubles from 23,500Esc; includes breakfast, service, and tax. **Dates closed:** Open all year. **Dining facilities:** Restaurant. **Children:** Under age 2 free; age 3 through 12 sharing with parents 50 percent of extra bed price. **Facilities for disabled:** None. **On-site recreation:** Swimming pool. **Nearby diversions:** Walking tours of Évora. **Operated as a hotel since:** 1965. **U.S. representative:** Marketing Ahead; Pinto Basto.

Directions: Évora is about 140 kilometers east of Lisbon where N-114 and N-18 intersect. From Lisbon, take E-4 east and turn south on N-114. There are 8 buses and 3 trains a day from Lisbon; the train station is about 1 mile from town.

Pousada do Castelo da Palmela

A FIFTEENTH-CENTURY CASTLE-MONASTERY

The little village of Palmela, with its steep cobblestone streets lined with whitewashed houses, is almost overwhelmed by this imposing complex above it that is part castle and part monastery. From the castle's ramparts, a three-hundred-and-sixty-degree view looks out over hills and sea, windmills and vineyards. On especially clear days, you can see all the way to Lisbon.

During September the region gives itself over to the wine harvest, in which you can actively take part.

THE PAST 🌀 Like the nearby castle of São Filipe at Setúbal, Palmela sits high on a hilltop with views extending for miles in every direction. It was an obvious location for warriors in the past to erect a lookout post from which to protect their territory. Archaeological discoveries have revealed man's presence here since Neolithic times.

The Moors captured Palmela in the eighth century and built a castle on the site of what might have been a Celtic settlement. In 1147 they surrendered to Afonso Henriques, the first king of Portugal, who founded a

monastery next to the castle in honor of the Knights of Santiago. He also allowed those Moors who had not fled to remain.

The Knights finally completed the monastery in 1482. Two years later the castle played a part in a conspiracy against King João II. While out overseeing his realm, the king decided to return overland to Lisbon instead of by the usual river route, thereby avoiding a waiting ambush. Considering João's first act upon taking the throne was imposing a detailed and drastic oath of allegiance on his vassals, the conspirators were doomed. The king demanded the presence of the duke of Viseu, who was visiting his mother at Palmela, and personally stabbed him in his bedchamber. He next imprisoned the bishop of Évora in Palmela's dungeon, where in a matter of days the bishop then died by suspected poisoning.

The great earthquake of 1755 that leveled much of Lisbon also damaged Palmela, but monks continued living in the monastery until the dissolution of religious orders in 1834. The Portuguese government designated the castle-monastery a national monument in 1940.

THE PRESENT 🐚 The pousada is installed in part of the old monastery, where public rooms are centered around the original cloisters—now with glassed-in arches. Tapestries and a plethora of potted plants soften the austerity. Long marble-floored hallways with vaulted ceilings lead to comfortable lounge areas furnished with leather sofas and armchairs.

Upstairs, the spacious guest rooms have red tile floors and hand-painted tile baths. Rough-woven fabrics and leather and carved furnishings contrast pleasantly with the whitewashed and natural stone walls. All but two rooms have views looking out toward Setúbal.

Operating in the former refectory (the pulpit from where prayers were once read still stands), the dining room is extremely popular with locals who come from as far away as Lisbon. Venison, wild boar, and a good selection of seafood are on the traditional Portuguese menu.

2950 Palmela. Tel: 011-351-1-235-12-26. Fax: 011-351-1-233-04-40. Rooms: 28, including 2 suites; all with bath. **Rates:** Moderate; doubles from 18,000Esc; includes breakfast, service, and tax. **Dates closed:** Open all year. **Dining facilities:** Restaurant. **Children:** Under age 2 free; age 3 through 12 sharing with parents 50 percent of extra bed price; play area. **Facilities for disabled:** None. **On-site recreation:** Swimming pool. **Nearby diversions:** Excursions to Setúbal, Troia Peninsula, and fishing village of Sesimbra; wine tours of Azeitão; golf. **Operated as a hotel since:** 1979. **U.S. representative:** Marketing Ahead; Pinto Basto.

Directions: Palmela is 8 kilometers north of Setúbal on N-379. Buses make the trip from Setúbal every 20 minutes.

Pousada da Rainha Santa Isabel

A Fourteenth-Century Castle

Not far from the Spanish border, on the way to Lisbon, is the picturesque whitewashed town of Estremoz. The government-run Pousada makes a convenient spot for eating lunch or spending the night.

A drive through the narrow, winding streets up the hill into the old town, with its Gothic and Manueline houses, is a trip into the Middle Ages. At the top of the hill, the castle of Estremoz is adjacent to a great keep—a thirteenth-century marble tower some ninety feet high.

The town of Estremoz can be seen in an afternoon. Saturday is market day on the main square, when you can see displays of the well-known Alentejo pottery.

THE PAST 🐚 Built during the reigns of three kings—Sancho, Afonso III, and Dinis—the castle served as a frontier post against Spanish encroachment.

Perhaps it is the namesake of the castle that deserves the most attention. Santa Isabel, who died at Estremoz in 1336, was fifteen years old when she came to Portugal from Spanish Aragon as the bride of King Dinis. Shy and modest throughout the wedding festivities, she unexpectedly announced that she had invited all the poor of the town to be her guests, and moreover, that she would wash their feet and feed them bread with her own hands. She continued doing this every Friday during Lent for her entire life—as well as fasting, performing every religious ritual imaginable, and

giving away most of her money to the poor. And she also managed to produce two heirs for the king.

Dinis, who was not as interested in such intense devotion, produced seven illegitimate children by seven different women. Isabel welcomed all of them into her household, educating and caring for them.

One legend, depicted in blue *azulejos* in the chapel, is of the Miracle of the Roses. This occurred when Dinis suddenly stopped the queen on her way out of the palace by a side door. He thought she was carrying gold coins for the poor, but when she opened her cloak, red roses fell out. Isabel was considered a saint in her lifetime because of the miraculous cures the sick attributed to her blessing. In the fifteenth century she was formally canonized Santa Isabel.

King Dinis was no slouch himself. He was nicknamed "the Farmer" for his establishment of agricultural schools and encouragement for cultivating new acreage. He was also called "the Poet," with over a hundred poems attributed to him. He sponsored men of letters who wrote in Portuguese, thereby making it the official language, and during his reign the first Portuguese university was founded.

At the end of the nineteenth century, the palace at Estremoz was used as a military installation until an explosion destroyed much of the structure. The government restored a great deal of the building.

THE PRESENT 🌀 Just inside the entrance is a stunning white marble staircase with blue-tiled sides. The public lounge resembles a small museum of Portuguese furniture and art from the seventeenth and eighteenth centuries, with paintings, tapestries, and ceramics valued at two million dollars.

Guest rooms have period furniture, embroidered or painted decorations, and either four-poster canopy beds or elaborate carved headboards.

The dining room is in a great baronial hall featuring heavy wooden chandeliers and high-backed chairs. Its high vaulted ceiling is supported by several marble columns. Local specialties and lamb dishes are featured.

Largo D. Dinis, 7100 Estremoz. Tel: 011-351-68-332-075. Fax: 011-351-68-332-079. **Rooms:** 33, including 3 suites; all with bath. **Rates:** Moderate; doubles from 18,000Esc; includes breakfast, service, and tax. **Dates closed:** Open all year. **Dining facilities:** Restaurant. **Children:** Under age 2 free; age 3 through 12 sharing with parents 50 percent of extra bed price. **Facilities for disabled:** None. **On-site recreation:** Swimming pool. **Nearby diversions:** Walking tour of Estremoz. **Operated as a hotel since:** 1970. **U.S. representative:** Marketing Ahead; Pinto Basto.

Directions: Estremoz is 60 kilometers west of Badajoz, Spain, on E-4. Bus service is available from Évora and Lisbon. Trains go to Estremoz on the Portalegre and Évora line, but there is no train service between Estremoz and Spain. Signs marked "Pousada" lead up the hill to the castle.

Pousada de São Filipe

A 16TH-CENTURY CASTLE

If you're on the way to the Algarve, Setúbal is worth a day's stopover. It's an active city where you can observe segments of Portuguese life. Harbor scenes are vibrant with noisy fish auctions, boats unloading their catches, and fishermen mending nets.

THE PAST In 1590 Philip II of Spain commanded the Italian architect, Terzo, to design this castle on the site of an ancient fortress. The Spanish king's concern was to guard his maritime frontier from pirates and to keep an eye on the rebellious inhabitants of Setúbal. He also suspected the British of setting up a military installation on the Troia Peninsula. In 1766 the castle became a prison.

THE PRESENT This star-shaped fortress features several corner sentry towers and massive battlements, and it commands stunning views of the harbor and town of Setúbal.

After winding up the steep hill and passing through a stone archway, you must leave your car outside the castle walls (to avoid theft, don't leave anything in the car). An underground passageway, with floor stones worn

smooth from centuries of footsteps, leads up to the reception area. On the way, you pass a charming little 1736 chapel that is completely lined with blue and white *azulejos*. The pousada operates in a stone manor built into the castle (it once housed the governor and his soldiers).

From the reception area, more steps lead up to the guest rooms. Although they vary in size, all have whitewashed walls, red tile floors, tile baths, and carved wood furnishings. The best rooms have a superb view of the city and harbor.

The second-floor dining room features whitewashed walls and a wood ceiling and also has a great view. In good weather you can dine outside on a sunny terrace. The pousada's proximity to a seaport ensures fresh fish on the menu, but delicious roast kid and suckling pig are also options. The cozy bar retains a medieval ambiance, with copper lanterns hanging from a vaulted ceiling and tile work brightening the walls.

This castle has lots of nooks and crannies to explore. From atop the ramparts you can see windmills on the hillsides. On the lower levels you can see the large former barrack rooms, cisterns, and casemates. Tunnels and underground prison cells now serve as storage areas.

 2900 Setúbal. Tel: 011-351-65-523-844. Fax: 011-351-65-532-538. **Rooms:** 14, including 1 suite; all with bath. **Rates:** Moderate; doubles from 18,000Esc; includes breakfast, service, and tax. **Dates closed:** Open all year. **Dining facilities:** Restaurant; bar. **Children:** Under age 2 free; age 3 through 12 sharing with parents 50 percent of extra bed price. **Facilities for disabled:** None. **On-site recreation:** None. **Nearby diversions:** Beaches; fishing; water sports; golf; excursions to Troia Peninsula. **Operated as a hotel since:** 1965. **U.S. representative:** Marketing Ahead; Pinto Basto.

Directions: Setúbal is 1 hour south of Lisbon on A-2. Bus service from Lisbon is every half hour. The castle is visible to the west of town. Follow signposts up the hill.

Hotel Palácio dos Seteais

AN EIGHTEENTH-CENTURY PALACE

Lo! Cintra's glorious Eden intervenes
In variegated maze of mount and glen...

In "Childe Harold's Pilgrimage," Lord Byron wrote that the setting of Sintra was one of the most delightful in Europe, with its "palaces and gardens rising in the midst of rocks, cataracts, and precipices; convents on stupendous heights—a distant view of the sea and the Tagus." This beautiful setting and its cool climate made Sintra the favorite summer residence of Portuguese kings for six centuries.

Besides the natural beauty of ocean vistas seen from seventeen hundred feet, the area is rich with tropical and subtropical trees and flowers. Several outstanding hillside palaces make fascinating sightseeing destinations.

On the second and fourth Sundays of each month a lively fair is held in Sintra with antiques, secondhand goods, and food displays.

THE PAST 🕸 Originally built in the eighteenth century by a Gildermeester, this Italian Renaissance-style palace is the site of the signing of the Convention of Sintra treaty. After the Duke of Wellington defeated the French army at the Battle of Vimeiro in 1808, this agreement created a public uproar in England when troops of the French army were transported with their booty back to France on British ships. The name Seteais means "seven sighs" in Portuguese; one theory claims the palace acquired the name because of this treaty.

THE PRESENT 🕸 The Seteais Palace has a triumphal arch connecting the two wings of the building. It is said to commemorate a visit by the prince and princess of Brazil in 1802. Though the outside of the palace looks a little weather-worn, the interiors remain elegant. Paintings, Flemish tapestries, and rosewood and mahogany antiques—including some nice grandfather clocks—fill the public rooms. The spacious halls have high ceilings and marble or wood floors, and flowers, vines, and murals are painted on many of the walls.

Each of the large and comfortable guest rooms is decorated with upholstered furniture, antiques, and big mirrors. Three have hand-painted wall murals.

The Cozina Velha dining room has gold-painted walls and crystal light sconces and is considered one of the best restaurants in Portugal. It offers complete four-course meals. You can also dine on an outdoor terrace.

The hotel sits on spacious grounds. A labyrinthine garden in back overlooks the valley below.

Rua Barbosa do Bocage 8, 2710 Sintra. Tel: 011-351-1-923-32-00. Fax: 011-351-1-923-42-77. Rooms: 30, including 1 suite; all with bath. **Rates:** Very expensive; doubles from 42,000Esc; includes breakfast, service, and tax. **Dates closed:** Open all year. **Dining facilities:** Restaurant (jacket and tie required); outside terrace; bar. **Children:** Inquire about discounts when booking. **Facilities for disabled:** Yes. **On-site recreation:** Swimming pool; tennis; horseback riding. **Nearby diversions:** Pera Palace, Royal Palace, walks through Sintra; excursions to fashionable resort towns of Cascais and Estoril. **Operated as a hotel since:** 1963. **U.S. representative:** Marketing Ahead; Pinto Basto; Utell International.

Directions: Sintra is about 20 kilometers northwest of Lisbon. The hotel is about 1 kilometer west of Sintra on the Colares road. Bus connections are available from Lisbon, Cascais, and Estoril, and trains leave every 20 minutes from the Rossio Station in Lisbon.

More Hotels

Pousada do Alvito

Turrets mark the corners of this square fourteenth-century
castle encompassing several architectural styles.

7920 Alvito, (Beja). Tel: 011-351-84-48-343. Fax: 011-351-84-48-383.

Spain

S pain offers more than two thousand *castillos* (or castles) to explore. In Castile they are so common that the entire region is named for them. Although most of these fortified structures are now little more than roofless skeletons overgrown with weeds, some are perfectly preserved architectural and historical treasures.

For eight hundred years Spain was ravaged by war—from the Arab invasions of the eighth century through the period of the reconquest completed in 1492. This period was the age of castle-building by both Christians and Muslims.

Alcazabas were a major part of the Moorish defense system. For the time, they were more advanced than their counterparts elsewhere in Europe. Erected on mounds and incorporated into the town walls, they featured pointed merlons and massive square towers that guarded the gates. The *alcázar*, developed from the earlier *alcazaba*, was more of a castle-palace; the Alhambra at Granada is an outstanding example. Usually built around courtyards, *alcázars* were decorated with fountains and gardens.

The castles of Christian Spain were built in strategic and usually isolated areas. Many are atop imposing hills surrounded by sheer cliffs and deep ravines and appear impregnable. Amazing engineering feats, these *grandes buques* (or "great ships") look abandoned high and dry on land. Their massive keeps and sentry turrets were built of stone or brick. Like their Moorish counterparts, the first Spanish castles had the purely military function of protecting the lines of the reconquest advance.

Time and the elements alone did not bring on the decline of the great Spanish castles. To consolidate her power after the fall of Moorish Granada, Queen Isabel declared that fortified castles owned by the nobility be destroyed. As it happened, the influences of the Italian Renaissance interested the Spanish nobility more than maintaining such enormous behemoths, and they gladly abandoned the castles and went on to build civilian palaces. The War of the Spanish Succession (1700–1713) and the Napoleonic invasion (1808–1814) further ravaged the castles.

Not until the last century—when increasing numbers of travelers, historians, and writers visited Spain with romantic eyes—did the castles and palaces come to be considered national treasures.

In 1905 the Spanish government set up a commission to improve transportation and hotel facilities throughout the country. The Marqués de la Vega Inclán instigated opening the first "parador" (or inn) in 1926 at Gredos, a site chosen by **King Alfonso XIII** in the mountains near Ávila.

Before that time, lodging in Spain consisted mostly of an area to tie up the animals and a place on the floor to sleep. Highways were practically nonexistent.

The parador at Gredos was such a success that a royal commission—Junta de Paradores y Hosterías del Reino—was founded with the intention of promoting Spanish tourism. Since then, the government has opened more than eighty three- and four-star hotels in castles, palaces, monasteries, and some contemporary buildings throughout Spain, the Canary Islands, and the Spanish colony of Melilla in North Africa.

The parador system now makes traveling in Spain a real pleasure. Not only do the paradores help preserve Spanish history, they enable the traveler to visit a different Spain outside of the big cities. Car rentals in Spain are inexpensive, and when cheap transportation is combined with consistently good lodging, exploring the Spanish countryside and towns adds up to a delightful experience.

Although no two paradores are exactly alike, they have certain things in common: They are easy to find and well signposted; they are spacious and very clean; bathrooms are modern and supplied with the biggest bath-towels in Europe; decorations and furnishings are tasteful; meals are reasonably priced, well prepared, and reflect the local cuisine and wine.

In Spain, many convents, monasteries, royal hospices, and the like were once connected to royalty or nobility. Often they lived in them. These places can be spectacular, and so some that have been converted to hotels are added in here among the castles and palaces.

With the exception of Hostal del Cardenal in Toledo, all hotels mentioned here belong to the government parador system. (Reservations for Hostal del Cardenal cannot be made through the parador system.) If you travel during the summer or fall tourist season or on holidays, especially to popular areas like Granada, you absolutely must make reservations in advance. At other times, just showing up at the door often works if you are flexible. The staff at any parador can call ahead to make a reservation for you at your next stop; you pay just for the call.

For further information on Spain, contact the Spanish National Tourist Office at: 666 Fifth Avenue, New York, New York 10103, Tel: 212-265-8822, Fax: 212-265-8864; or 8383 Wilshire Boulevard, Suite 960, Beverly Hills, California 90211, Tel: 213-658-7188, Fax: 213-658-1061; or 845 North Michigan Avenue, Suite 915, Chicago, Illinois 60611, Tel: 312-642-1992, Fax: 312-642-9817; or 1221 Brickell Avenue, Suite 1850, Miami, Florida 33131, Tel: 305-358-1992, Fax: 305-358-8223. Website for Spanish paradores: http://www.parador.es/.

Parador de Alarcón

AN EIGHTH-CENTURY CASTLE

If any Spanish castle can be described as charming, the Parador de Alarcón is that place. Everything a castle buff might look for is here: ramparts, gateways, a keep, a great hall, and slender crenellated watchtowers. Its setting on the plains of La Mancha, just a few miles from the main Madrid-Valencia highway, is spectacular, and the approach from the valley up a narrow,

winding road through stone archways is unforgettable. With its imposing presence atop a rocky crag surrounded by the Júcar River, you wonder how an army could ever have laid siege to it. Today's parador maintains the aura of an ancient fortress and is the best-preserved in the province of Cuenca.

Coveted by conquerors since Roman times, the village of Alarcón takes its name from the Visigothic king Alarico. During more illustrious times it was home to twelve thousand inhabitants. Now its cobblestone streets lined with whitewashed houses seem almost deserted. Its four churches are locked, but can be visited with permission (inquire at the hotel).

THE PAST 🌸 In the eighth century the Moors were the first to erect an impregnable fortress on the castle site (portions of this structure still exist in the ramparts). It was one of the principal strongholds in the rebellion of Umar ibn Hafsun, a descendant of a Visigothic count who for nearly forty years was a thorn in the side of the Arab caliphate at Córdoba. Throughout Murcia and Andalusia, ibn Hafsun and his band of brigands engaged in Robin Hood-style exploits. Expeditions would be sent out against him, but luck would always go his way. During the middle of one all-out siege in 888, the Córdoban amir was poisoned by his own brother and successor. Within three years, ibn Hafsun was at the gates of Córdoba, using Alarcón castle as a recruiting center for his forces. Though a Moor himself, ibn Hafsun became the champion of Christians and malcontents against the established Moors and even adopted Christianity himself.

Not until three hundred years later, during the reign of Alfonso VIII, did the castle fall wholly from Moorish hands, and then only after a nine-month siege. The Christian commander, Fernán Martin de Ceballos, finally scaled the walls alpine-style by sticking two swords into spaces between the stones. The castle was then given to the Order of Saint James and used as a gathering point for further battles against the Moors. (At one time the castle was even ceded to one new owner in ransom for a prisoner.)

The parador used to be called the Marqués de Villena, the title of Juan Pacheco, a favorite of Henry IV of Castile who rebuilt the castle into its present form. Through conspiracy and other devious means, Pacheco was made Master of the Order of James and given property throughout La Mancha. Because he had supported Juana la Beltraneja, Henry IV's illegitimate daughter, everything but the castle of Alarcón was later taken away from him after the rise of Isabel the Catholic to the throne of Castile.

With the passage of time, the castle fell into ruins. Its final role was during the Civil War of 1833–1840, when it was again restored.

THE PRESENT 🐚 Today, thanks to the outstanding efforts of the Spanish government, the castle's glory has been brought back yet again. The main keep, which houses the guest rooms and reception, forms one side of a central stone courtyard bearing an ancient well and fig tree.

Each guest room is simply furnished, yet unique. A special tower room has one tiny window peeking through very thick walls. Bathrooms, like those in other Spanish paradores, are modern.

The original great hall now holds the dining room and an adjacent lounge with a fireplace, beautiful stonework, tapestries, and medieval paintings. Waitresses wearing traditional costumes serve cuisine typical of the region.

Avenida Amigos de los Castillos 3, 16213 Alarcón (Cuenca). Tel: 011-34-969-33-03-15. Fax: 011-34-969-33-03-03. **Rooms:** 13, including 12 twins and 1 double; all with bath. **Rates:** Expensive; doubles from 18,500Ptas; tax not included. **Dates closed:** Open all year. **Dining facilities:** Restaurant; bar. **Children:** Under age 2 free; discounts for age 2 through 14 sharing with parents; play area. **Facilities for disabled:** None. **On-site recreation:** None. **Nearby diversions:** Horseback riding; visits to Cuenca, where 14th-century houses "hang" over a cliff. **Operated as a hotel since:** 1970. **U.S. representative:** Marketing Ahead.

Directions: Alarcón is at the halfway point on the main Madrid-Valencia highway—National Road III. A signpost marks the exit. The town is not practical to reach by public transportation.

Parador de Alcañiz

A Twelfth-Century Castle

Spain's rapid economic development in the last ten years has scarcely touched the eastern province of Aragon. In fact, the area appears little changed since the last century. Tiny medieval villages seem to be connected to the outside world only by power lines. Aragon also boasts some of the most extreme weather in Spain. Winters are freezing, with subzero temperatures, while summers are absolutely scorching.

The remote Maestrazgo region has some of the most rugged and wild scenery in Spain. You can't go anywhere in a hurry here, because the roads twist through deep gorges and alongside rocky crags and precipices. However, for the undaunted traveler who seeks to discover the many facets of Spain, there is not a corner less traveled or less spoiled by modern civilization.

THE PAST 🌸 The earliest mention of the castle here dates back to 1179, when the Order of Calatrava (a military order founded to wage battle against the Moors) acquired the property.

In the Middle Ages the castle played an important role in the setting of dynasties. For two years the Aragonese parliament met with representatives from the Vatican, Sicily, France, and Castile to determine a new king of Aragon. Ferdinand I, who was the grandfather of the more famous Ferdinand of "Ferdinand and Isabel" fame, was the bastard half-brother of Pedro the Cruel. A meeting was held to determine if Ferdinand I was worthy of the throne. His chief rival was Count James of Urgel, who didn't stand a chance since Ferdinand had the more powerful allies and influential friends. Back in those days, losers of political campaigns were not allowed to retire gracefully. Count James was captured and imprisoned for the remainder of his life in a subterranean dungeon at Xátiva, near Valencia.

The castle was added on to over the years. In 1728 Prince Philip incorporated part of it into an Aragonese-style palace. This section is now the parador, while the rest of the building stands as a national monument.

THE PRESENT 🌸 Two huge, imposing square towers flank each side of this castle's façade. The parador sits unassumingly off to one side. The castle ambiance is carried throughout the public rooms, where Aragonese heraldic banners hang from thick stone walls. Leather couches and chairs sit on woven throw rugs in front of a big fireplace, inviting cozy repose during those brutal winters. A small cloister holds several sarcophagi of the knights of the Order of Calatrava and is open for viewing.

An enormous stone stairway leads to spacious guest rooms decorated with pretty striped curtains and throw rugs atop red tile floors. Small windows overlook the steep streets of the town.

The especially inviting dining room is lined with tapestries depicting the coat of arms of several knights of Calatrava. Overhead, wrought-iron chandeliers hang from a wood-beamed ceiling, and an impressive stone fireplace anchors one end of the room. Here you can sample typical Aragonese cuisine such as *pollo al chilindrón* (chicken cooked in red peppers, onions, and garlic) and *ternasco asado* (a roasted lamb dish).

 **Castillo Calatravos s/n, 44600 Alcañiz (Teruel). Tel: 011-34-978-83-04-00. Fax: 011-34-978-83-03-66.** **Rooms:** 12, including 2 singles, 9 twins, and 1 double; all with bath. **Rates:** Moderate; doubles from 14,500Ptas; tax not included. **Dates closed:** Open all year. **Dining facilities:** Restaurant; bar. **Children:** Under age 2 free; discounts for age 2 through 14 sharing with parents. **Facilities for disabled:** None. **On-site recreation:** None. **Nearby diversions:** Hiking; swimming. **Operated as a hotel since:** 1968. **U.S. representative:** Marketing Ahead.

Directions: Alcañiz lies in the eastern part of the province of Aragon, 105 kilometers southeast of Zaragoza on N-232. The parador is on the hill in the middle of town. Follow the signposts. Bus and train transportation is available to Alcañiz, but it is very slow.

Parador de Ávila

A Sixteenth-Century Palace

Few cities in the world attract visitors with their walls, but Ávila, like Carcassonne in France, is one that does. Declared a Spanish National Monument, this ancient city is like a survivor from a medieval fairy tale. It is encircled by a magnificent mile-and-a-half-long eleventh-century wall that is reinforced with eighty-eight semicircular towers, twenty-five hundred merlons, and eight gateways. When the sun shines on the battlements and towers, the stones glow in golden tones. The parador adjoins this impressive wall.

At three thousand and six hundred feet, Ávila is the highest city in Spain. It is also the city of Santa Teresa—one of the greatest mystics of the Catholic church, a reformer of the monastic orders, and an important figure in the defeat of the Reformation in Spain. Her influences are found throughout the city, where convents dedicated to her are as numerous as churches and palaces.

THE PAST The parador was once named after a medieval knight, Raimundo de Borgoña, who was responsible for rebuilding the wall from material taken from other ancient buildings. It required nine years—from 1090 to 1099—to complete the stonework designed by Casandro, a master

of geometry, and Forin de Pituenga, a French master mason. Muslim captives probably did the actual construction, as Moorish influences are evident in the northern section.

Raimundo de Borgoña came to Spain in 1087 to help in the reconquest of Spain from the Moors. He recaptured Ávila and married the daughter of King Alfonso VI. Raimundo repopulated the city with his followers from Borgoña, Leon, Galicia, and Asturias, and the town became known as Ávilade los Caballeros. Baronial palaces were built for all of Raimundo's aristocratic friends. Among them was the present-day parador, formerly called El Palacio de los Benavides and El Palacio de Piedras Albas (the Palace of White Stones).

Ávila reached its peak in the fifteenth century but lost its prestige a hundred years later when

the nobility moved to Toledo to join the court of Charles V. In 1609, with the expulsion of the Moorish population that had worked as Ávila's craftsmen and merchants, the city declined even further.

THE PRESENT The parador was rebuilt about seventy years ago using as much of the old stone, timbers, and pillars as possible. The main stairway is original. Inside, a small courtyard is surrounded by old columns and doorways leading to the public rooms, which were recently redecorated in a style suggestive of the city's medieval origins.

Guest rooms in the square tower face the gardens and part of the famous wall. They are furnished in a rustic style. Rooms are booked early for summer by residents of Madrid who come here to take advantage of Ávila's cool climate.

The dining room looks onto a terraced garden and features Castilian dishes such as roast suckling pig, veal, and roast lamb. Nearby rivers supply fresh trout.

Marqués de Chozas 2, 05001 Ávila Tel: 011-34-920-21-13-40. Fax: 011-34-920-22-61-66. Rooms: 61, including 45 twins, 12 doubles, and 4 suites; all with bath. **Rates:** Moderate; doubles from 12,500Ptas; tax not included. **Dates closed:** Open all year. **Dining facilities:** Restaurant; bar. **Children:** Under age 2 free; discounts for age 2 through 14 sharing with parents. **Facilities for disabled:** None. **On-site recreation:** None. **Nearby diversions:** Walks along city wall; visits to cathedral, museums, and convent of St. Teresa. **Operated as a hotel since:** 1966. **U.S. representative:** Marketing Ahead.

Directions: Ávila is 115 kilometers northwest of Madrid on N-501. Trains leave from Madrid's Atocha station and take about 2 hours. Buses make the same trip. The parador is on the north side of town along the wall. Look for signposts.

Hostal del Cardenal

AN EIGHTEENTH-CENTURY PALACE

If you have only one day to travel outside Madrid, that day should be spent in the walled city of Toledo. Today's city offers a taste of Spanish history and civilization. A blend of East and West, Toledo is a combination of narrow streets, houses with flowered courtyards, churches, monasteries, and convents. Not the least of the city's charms is its incomparable setting. From miles away Toledo seems to rise from a granite hill surrounded on three sides by the deep gorge of the Río Tajo. Granted, Toledo can be crowded with tourists and souvenir shops are plentiful, but the charm of its maze of winding alleyways and cobblestone lanes and the sense of history imparted from visits to its monuments make it an important destination.

Today the former residence of the archbishop of Toledo, Cardenal Lorenzana, is a charming three-star hotel. Though not a government parador, Hostal del Cardenal should definitely not be overlooked. Built right into the Moorish city walls, it is adjacent to the famous Puerta Antigua de Bisagra—the gateway through which Alfonso VI rode in 1085 to claim the city from the Moors, fulfilling a long-held goal of the Christian reconquest. From the hotel, you can reach any point in the city on foot.

THE PAST 🌸 Called Toletum by the Romans, Toledo has been an important strategic and cultural center for successive Visigothic, Moorish, and Christian kingdoms. In the Middle Ages Christian, Jewish, and Moorish cultures coexisted peacefully, and intellectual life and artistic endeavors flourished.

When Philip II moved the royal court to Madrid in 1561, Toledo, then the seat of the Primate of Spain, remained the nation's religious center.

THE PRESENT 🌸 Built during the eighteenth century, the palace was restored several years ago into a clean and peaceful hotel with antique furnishings and paintings decorating its sturdy interior. Unfortunately, there is no elevator, and the stairs can be a drawback for some. A terraced, Moorish-style garden, with a fountain reminiscent of the Alhambra, greets you each time you return.

The charming guest rooms have whitewashed walls, tile accents, handmade rugs, and heavy carved antique furniture. Some rooms have balconies with views of the garden and city walls.

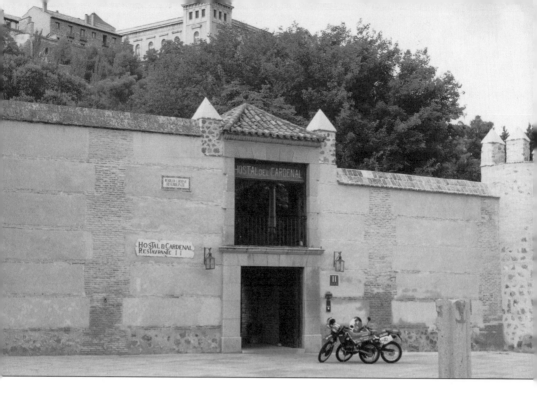

Across the garden, the hotel's excellent restaurant features wood-beamed ceilings and fireplaces in keeping with an Old World ambiance. Its most famous dish is roast suckling pig, prepared in the traditional Castilian manner and cooked in a huge oven. Roast lamb, venison, and partridge are also on the menu. Desserts sometimes include the famous Toledan marzipan. In good weather, meals are served outside on a patio by the garden.

Paseo de Recaredo 24, 45004 Toledo. Tel: 011-34-925-22-49-00. Fax: 011-34-925-22-29-91. Rooms: 27, including 22 doubles, 3 singles, and 2 suites; all with bath. **Rates:** Moderate; doubles from 13,000Ptas; tax not included. **Dates closed:** Open all year. **Dining facilities:** Restaurant. **Children:** No charge for cribs. **Facilities for disabled:** None. **On-site recreation:** None. **Nearby diversions:** Walks through the old town to the cathedral, El Greco house and museum, and El Transito Synagogue. **General Manager:** Luis Gonzalez Gozalbo. **Operated as a hotel since:** 1972. **U.S. representative:** None.

Directions: By car, Toledo is 70 kilometers south of Madrid. Bus and train service from Madrid is available. The Moorish-style train station features gorgeous tile work; it lies outside the main part of town, requiring a taxi ride in. Paseo de Recaredo (some maps mark it as "Paseo de la Ronda Nueva") is on the north side of town and parallels the Arab walls.

Parador de Cardona

A NINTH-CENTURY CASTLE

If the Catalan region of Spain is your destination, you can make an interesting excursion from Barcelona to Montserrat, overnighting at Cardona and then continuing on to the tiny principality of Andorra.

THE PAST 🦪 This massive fortress in the foothills of the Pyrenees was built by King Louis the Pious in 789 as a central strongpoint for securing territories reconquered from the Moors. The counts of Cardona began work on the present structure in 1020. A nephew of the Emperor Charlemagne, Count Ramón Folch, took over the governorship of Cardona, and his descendants were elevated to the rank of duke.

Cardona was always highly desired for its salt beds. A constitution dating from 986 allowed the inhabitants personal use of the salt one day a week if they, in turn, donated a day's work to the castle's upkeep and pledged fidelity to its protection.

Standing on a conical hill fifteen hundred feet above the walled village, the castle was never conquered through a long history of wars. French and Spanish troops failed in their attempt to overtake it during the War of the Spanish Succession in 1711. A hundred years later the castle remained standing after a long siege during the Peninsular War, and the Carlists failed to take it during the Spanish Civil War.

A legend relates that the beautiful daughter of Ramón Folch was imprisoned in the tower by her brothers after she fell in love with a Moor and converted to Islam. She died within the year.

THE PRESENT 🦪 Cardona is now a Spanish National Monument, with its Gothic court and chapel preserved as a museum. Like the other paradores, it is meticulously cared for. The red tile floors are shined to a high gloss. Wood beams cover arched ceilings, heraldic tapestries and wrought-iron torches decorate the walls, and many Catalan antiques fill the rooms.

An elevator carries you to six floors of guest rooms. Many have canopy beds, hand-painted headboards, and woven bedspreads. Room 712 is reputed to be haunted by a ghost dressed in a leotard and period costume. (When the castle underwent restoration, a security dog stood outside the room and barked almost nonstop for over a month.)

The restaurant is in an ancient stone vaulted room. The menu offers typical Catalan dishes such as salmon in red pepper sauce and wild boar

with chocolate. On special occasions medieval banquets and classical music concerts are held.

08261 Cardona (Barcelona). Tel: 011-34-93-869-12-75. Fax: 011-34-93-869-16-36. **Rooms:** 57, including 7 singles, 48 twins, 1 double, and 1 suite; all with bath. **Rates:** Moderate; doubles from 14,500Ptas; tax not included. **Dates closed:** Open all year. **Dining facilities:** Restaurant; bar; medieval banquets. **Children:** Under age 2 free; discounts for age 2 through 14 sharing with parents. **Facilities for disabled:** None. **On-site recreation:** None. **Nearby diversions:** Horseback riding; golf; fishing; canoeing walking tours through old quarter of Cardona; salt museum; Montserrat monastery. **Operated as a hotel since:** 1976. **U.S. representative:** Marketing Ahead.

Directions: Cardona is 97 kilometers northwest of Barcelona on C-1410.

Parador de Chinchón

A SEVENTEENTH-CENTURY CONVENT

The traveler to Spain can all too easily overlook its small, quaint villages in favor of the more famous destinations of Madrid and Toledo. That is a shame, because you miss places like Chinchón—a small medieval village that has just recently begun to promote its historic sights. The hills surrounding the village are cool, and its atmosphere is peaceful—unless it's a weekend during the summer bullfight season, when people pour into town. The Plaza Mayor in the town's center, which is surrounded by three-story-tall covered galleries and arcades, has hosted these bullfights since 1502.

Chinchón can serve as a convenient base for exploring the countryside surrounding Madrid. Located twenty kilometers away, through hills covered with olive trees and grapevines, Aranjuez is the spring and fall home of the Bourbon kings and their famous royal gardens and palaces.

THE PAST 🌸 Once a mighty fortress of the counts of Chinchón, the town's fifteenth-century castle now houses an anisette distillery—a fate the counts undoubtedly never imagined. Another town claim to fame dates back to the seventeenth century, when the countess of Chinchón was married to the viceroy of Peru. She came down with malaria while living in Peru and was cured by an Indian there who used tree bark as medicine. She brought back quinine from South America, and the tree it was derived from was later named *chinchona* in her honor.

The first lords of Chinchón (a title granted by Queen Isabel in 1480) established an Augustinian convent off the main square. The present brick and masonry building dates back to the seventeenth century, when the friars taught Latin studies here. When the state secularized church property, the

thirtieth count of Chinchón, Luis María de Borbón, gave the convent to the town. It served as the town courthouse and jail until it was returned to the government for use as a parador.

THE PRESENT 🌸 Ten years of restoration resulted in this charming hotel. Glassed-in cloisters look out onto courtyards with fountains, fig trees, pomegranate trees, and rose gardens. Modern tapestries by the Spanish artist Rosa Cubero hang on the walls.

A lovely gold-and-pink, high-domed ceiling above the staircase marks the way to the guest rooms, which are found along low, round-arched whitewashed corridors. The furnishings are few but well chosen: handwoven tapestries depicting archangels, white rugs on pale floor tiles, a ceramic art piece here and there, lacy bedspreads. Some windows look out over the courtyard and gardens.

You can sample the local anisette in a lounge decorated with beautiful blue Moorish-style tiles. Decorated in the same style, the adjacent dining room draws crowds from Madrid for weekend brunches. Steaks are a popular menu item.

Avenida Generalísimo 1, 28370 Chinchón (Madrid). Tel: 011-34-91-894-08-36. Fax: 011-34-91-894-09-08. **Rooms:** 38, including 36 twins and 2 suites; all with bath. **Rates:** Moderate; doubles from 17,000Ptas; tax not included. **Dates closed:** Open all year. **Dining facilities:** Restaurant; bar. **Children:** Under age 2 free; discounts for age 2 through 14 sharing with parents. **Facilities for disabled:** None. **On-site recreation:** Seasonal swimming pool. **Nearby diversions:** Horseback riding; bullfights; royal palaces and gardens at Aranjuez; town of Alcalá de Henares. **Operated as a hotel since:** 1982. **U.S. representative:** Marketing Ahead.

Directions: Chinchón is located 46 kilometers southeast of Madrid. Take National Road III (the main Madrid-Valencia highway) and exit at the Arganda bridge. Go south on regional road C-300 to Chinchón. A car is the best way to get around, although buses service the town.

Parador de Ciudad Rodrigo

A Fourteenth-Century Castle

Ciudad Rodrigo is a charming, well-preserved medieval town strategically placed on the Agueda River. An ancient Roman bridge crosses the river toward the Portuguese border, which is only a few miles away. Situated on a small hill, the town was once defended by the square tower dominating the fourteenth-century *alcázar* and by the ramparts surrounding the town.

The government has declared the entire town a Spanish National Monument. Its charm is found chiefly in its narrow streets and in the courtyards of the old baronial mansions. You can circle the town by walking on the ramparts.

THE PAST 🦋 The name Ciudad Rodrigo honors Count Rodrigo González, who established the town in the twelfth century after a Moorish invasion. In time, the town also served as a fortress to launch various expeditions against Portugal.

It was not until the early nineteenth century that Ciudad Rodrigo's greatest moment arrived. The castle was a battle site between the armies of Napoleon and the Duke of Wellington in the Peninsular War, which raged on for five years and left much of the country in ruins. In 1810 the French Marshal Ney besieged the castle and finally captured it. Wellington's armies retreated to Lisbon where, in turn, the French forces were defeated. In 1812 the Duke of Wellington moved an offensive counterattack on Spain. Ciudad Rodrigo was one of the first towns to be secured by the British and became a turning point in the war. For his efforts, the titles of duke of Ciudad Rodrigo and grandee of Spain were conferred on Wellington by the grateful Spanish.

THE PRESENT 🦋 Although devastated by time, the castle is now expertly restored. With its square keep and crenellated walls—which remained intact through the years—the outside of the parador looks somewhat austere, but flowers and ivy growing over the building soften that effect. In the entrance you pass by the royal coat of arms and a plaque that reads:

This *alcázar* was built by order of the Most Grand and Most Noble King Don Enrique II, son of the Most Grand and Most Noble King Don Alfonso, who vanquished Alboacen, King of Benamarin, with all his Might of Africa and took Algeciras. It was on the first day of the month of June in the year of the Lord 1410.

Inside, the atmosphere is warm and charming. Tile floors are highly polished, and regional handicrafts decorate the hallways and public rooms. Dark-stained furniture and brightly colored bedspreads and rugs fill the cozy guest rooms.

An attractive dining room provides views of the river and surrounding countryside. The menu includes such regional specialties as cured hams and sausages, pork filets, and trout.

 Plaza Castillo 1, 37500 Ciudad Rodrigo (Salamanca). Tel: 011-34-923-46-01-50. Fax: 011-34-923-46-04-04. **Rooms:** 27, including 1 single, 20 twins, 5 doubles, and 1 suite; all with bath. **Rates:** Moderate; doubles from 12,500Ptas; tax not included. **Dates closed:** Open all year. **Dining facilities:** Restaurant; bar. **Children:** Under age 2 free; discounts for age 2 through 14 sharing with parents. **Facilities for disabled:** None. **On-site recreation:** None. **Diversions:** Horseback riding; exploring town's ramparts, cathedral, and main plaza. **Operated as a hotel since:** 1931. **U.S. representative:** Marketing Ahead.

Directions: Ciudad Rodrigo is just over the Portuguese border on N-620. Buses and trains stop here. Salamanca is 86 kilometers to the east.

Parador de Granada

A Fifteenth-Century Convent

One of Spain's best-kept secrets is that tourists can spend the night on the grounds of the Alhambra. Parador de Granada operates in a former convent on the main grounds of the famous Moorish palace. The lovely gardens are peaceful in the early morning or evening when the tourists have gone. Close your eyes then and listen to the soft sounds of the birds and fountains; smell the roses and be carried back to the enchantment of Washington Irving's *Tales of the Alhambra*. Perhaps it was in one of the fragrant rose gardens of the Alhambra that Manuel de Falla found inspiration for his beautiful piano composition "Nights in the Gardens of Spain." From here, views of the red-roofed houses of Granada and of the snowcapped Sierra Nevada are unsurpassed.

THE PAST 🌸 For seven hundred and eighty years the Moors ruled Granada —the wealthiest city in Spain. New ideas in philosophy, mathematics, medicine, art, architecture, and poetry were introduced. Europe's first paper-making industry, an import from China, was begun here by the Moors around the twelfth century. One of their greatest legacies is the Alhambra (the name means "red" in Arabic, taken from the red stucco used in its construction), now one of the country's architectural treasures and a highlight of any visit to Spain.

Nearly five hundred years have gone by since the fall of Granada. In 1492, the same year that Columbus reached the New World, the Moorish king handed over the keys of the Alhambra to the Catholic monarchs Ferdinand and Isabel, who had played on the jealousies and rivalries of the last ruling Moorish family of Granada to complete the reconquest of Spain. Abdullah, the son of the amir, overthrew his father at the urging of his mother, who was jealous of her husband's Christian concubine. Abdullah, whose name was corrupted into the Spanish "Boabdil," was later taken captive by Ferdinand and Isabel, supplied with men and money, and sent out to retake Granada again, this time from his uncle. The Christian armies advanced to the city gates and demanded that Abdullah surrender the city to them. When he refused, the Christians destroyed all the crops and orchards surrounding the city, planning to starve the Moors out in the winter months. Abdullah was allowed to ride off after the surrender while his mother turned on him with: "Thou dost well to weep like a woman for what thou

couldst not defend like a man." Within ten years the Inquisition had managed to burn entire libraries of Arabic books and manuscripts; persecution of Moslems and Jews soon followed.

Before the fall of Granada, Isabel made a vow that if she were successful in retaking the city, she would build a convent at the Alhambra. Today this convent is the Parador de Granada. Isabel chose the site of a mosque and palace built by the Nasrid amir Yusuf I for her convent. The High Chapel of the convent was established in the center using some existing Moorish arches and plasterwork, and then surrounded by living quarters. The bodies of Isabel and Ferdinand were temporarily buried here until the completion of the cathedral of Granada in 1521; a small chapel marks the site.

Reconstructed at various times, the convent eventually fell into disrepair and was variously used as a barracks, storehouse, retirement home, and school for landscape artists. Finally, the government rebuilt it as a parador in 1944.

THE PRESENT ❧ Today this parador is the most popular in Spain. The curator of the Alhambra was called in to oversee its renovation. Unfortunately, because the Alhambra is Spain's greatest tourist attraction, the overflow of people can affect the parador during certain times of the day. Its lobby and public rooms—which are filled with antique wood *santos* (carved figures of saints), carved tables, copper pieces, El Greco reproductions, and works by modern regional artists—can be very busy places.

Long corridors lead to the guest rooms framed with carved doorways. Rooms are furnished with vintage carved furniture, romantic lantern lights, and handwoven rugs. Windows look out over views of the gardens and paths at the Generalife Palace located across a ravine.

Tapestries, embroidered piecework, and copper and iron craftwork decorate the restaurant. The menu offers Andalusian cuisine such as *gazpacho* (a delicious cold garlic soup) and *zarzuela de pescado* (a fish stew) as well as veal, ham, and other traditional fare.

Real de la Alhambra s/n, 18009 Granada. Tel: 011-34-958-22-14-40. Fax: 011-34-958-22-22-64. Rooms: 36, including 33 twins, 1 double, 1 suite, and 1 duplex; all with bath. **Rates:** Expensive; doubles from 27,000Ptas; tax not included. **Dates closed:** Open all year. **Dining facilities:** Restaurant; bar. **Children:** Under age 2 free; discounts for age 2 through 14 sharing with parents. **Facilities for disabled:** None. **On-site recreation:** None. **Nearby diversions:** The Alhambra and Generalife palaces. **Operated as a hotel since:** 1945. **U.S. representative:** Marketing Ahead.

Directions: Granada is linked by all means of transportation to the major cities. If driving, follow the signposts around the city. The parador is to one side of the Alhambra.

Parador de Hondarribia

A TENTH-CENTURY CASTLE

Located right on the border with France, this parador makes both a great introduction and a fitting farewell to Spain. Never in the last thousand years would anyone have imagined that this site of constant assaults would someday provide comfortable accommodation to vacationers.

Both the old and new sections of the town of Hondarribia are charming. Moats, ramparts, and Gothic-Baroque churches are all open for exploration. For a wonderful view at sunset, follow the road to the *faro* (lighthouse).

THE PAST 🦪 Founded during the reign of Sancho Abarca, King of Navarre (970–994), enlarged by Sancho el Fuerte (1194–1234), strengthened by Ferdinand and Isabel (1474–1516), and rebuilt in its present form by Charles V (1516–1556), this impressive castle was supposed to guard the frontier from French marauders.

French king François I captured the fortress in 1521 but soon lost it. The French again assaulted the castle for sixty-four days in 1638, but, thanks to the help of Our Lady of Guadalupe, the Spanish took the exhausted French troops by surprise and defeated them. (The citizens of Hondarribia still celebrate this victory every year on September 8.) The French bombarded the fortress yet again in 1794, causing substantial damage that was not repaired until the late nineteenth century.

THE PRESENT 🦪 Completely restored today, the castle looks ready for a siege. Its bullet-pocked, ten-meter-thick walls are massive and severe. Only five windows break up the stonework of its forbidding façade. (In contrast to such austerity, delightful baronial houses, with overhanging balconies filled with bright flowers, are just across the medieval plaza.)

The castle's interior features enormous Gothic arches, winding stairways, and galleries hung with heraldic flags, tapestries, lances, wrought-iron chandeliers, wall sconces, and escutcheons. Outside, the flagstone courtyard holds an ancient well that provided the castle with water during its era of constant siege warfare, and a terrace permits gazing at the vast coastline extending into France.

Comfortable guest rooms are located in the former palace section of the castle.

 Plaza de Armas, 14, 20280 Hondarribia (Guipúzcoa). Tel: 011-34-943-64-55-00. Fax: 011-34-943-64-21-53. Rooms: 36, including 4 singles, 30 twins, and 2 doubles; all with bath. **Rates:** Moderate; doubles from 14,500Ptas; tax not included. **Dates closed:** Open all year. **Dining facilities:** No restaurant; bar; breakfast available. **Children:** Under age 2 free; discounts for age 2 through 14 sharing with parents. **Facilities for disabled:** None. **On-site recreation:** None. **Nearby diversions:** Horseback riding; golf; sea fishing; mountain biking; drives to French Basque country and San Sebastián. **Operated as a hotel since:** 1968. **U.S. representative:** Marketing Ahead.

Directions: Hondarribia (also known as Fuenterrabía) is 21 kilometers east of San Sebastián, and a few kilometers from Irún on the French border. As you near the town, you see an *Aeropuerto* sign. At a large traffic circle with a statue in the middle, turn left up the hill. Look for the castle on the plaza. The nearest train station is in Irún.

Parador de Jarandilla de la Vera

A Fifteenth-Century Castle-Palace

Secluded Jarandilla de la Vera sits on the southern slope of the Sierra de Gredos mountains in Extremadura—far from any large city. A beautiful view extends from the valley below to the mountains in the north. Pine trees, lakes, valleys with apple and pear orchards, and other small villages sporting their own castles dot the landscape. People come here not for grand monuments, but rather for a peaceful atmosphere and to enjoy the rugged beauty of Spain without the interference of tourist buses.

THE PAST At the end of 1555, a visitor came to stay at an isolated castle on the southern slopes of the Sierra de Gredos—a chain of mountains cutting through central Spain. He traveled by ship from Brussels to the Cantabrian coast and then was carried by litter over the mountains to the place where he would spend the final years of his life. Only fifty-five, King Carlos V had ruled half of Europe, established Spanish dominance in Italy, and kept the German princes in line after his victory at Mühlberg. But he failed to overcome France, stop the Ottoman Turks, catholicize Germany, or

end the corsair domination of the Mediterranean. Tired and disappointed, he surrendered his throne to his son Philip II. In his famous abdication speech, he declared:

> I have been nine times in Germany, six in Spain, seven in Italy, ten in Flanders. In peace and war I have been four times in France, two in England and two in Africa for a total of forty expeditions, without counting the voyages to my kingdoms. Eight times I have crossed the Mediterranean and three times the Ocean [to England]. I am at peace with all and from all ask pardon if I have offended anyone.

Carlos stayed at Jarandilla—built at the end of the fourteenth century by order of the counts of Oropesa and the marquises of Jarandilla—until the final touches were added to his monastery at Yuste, twelve kilometers to the west. Despite the remoteness of the area, he never lacked for any creature comforts. Nor was he ever out of touch with his son and the workings of the empire.

THE PRESENT 🐚 This castle's square and round towers stand at the corners of its rectangular grounds. The original walls and drawbridge remain, as do the shields on the walls. Made of local stone, the castle has a rugged quality that is softened by a peaceful surrounding garden featuring climbing roses, lemon trees, and a pond. A small gateway leads to a stone courtyard adorned with Carlos V's coat of arms and beautiful glazed tilework. Wall tapestries, paintings, ceramics, and armor decorate the interior.

Several of the comfortable guest rooms feature simple four-poster beds. Charles de Gaulle once stayed in the Royal Suite.

The medieval-style dining room has wood-beamed ceilings, leather-backed chairs, and wrought-iron chandeliers. The menu offers typical dishes of the region: *caldereta de cordero* (lamb stew) and *perdiz estofada con salsa* (stewed partridge).

Avenida García Prieto 1, 10450 Jarandilla de la Vera (Cáceres). Tel: 011-34-927-56-01-17. Fax: 011-34-927-56-00-88. **Rooms:** 53, including 10 singles, and 43 twins; all with bath. **Rates:** Moderate; doubles from 14,500Ptas; tax not included. **Dates closed:** Open all year. **Dining facilities:** Restaurant; bar. **Children:** Under age 2 free; discounts for age 2 through 14 sharing with parents; play area. **Facilities for disabled:** None. **On-site recreation:** Tennis; seasonal swimming pool. **Nearby diversions:** Horseback riding; trekking; swimming holes; Yuste monastery. **Operated as a hotel since:** 1966. **U.S. representative:** Marketing Ahead.

Directions: To reach the town of Jarandilla, follow C-501 between Plasencia and Arenas de San Pedro. Bus connections can be made from both towns.

Parador de Olite

A Fifteenth-Century Castle

Navarre is a delightful province to visit fifty-one weeks of the year. But from July 6 through 14, when the "Running of the Bulls" occurs in nearby Pamplona, it is filled with the spillover of party-animal tourists. When they leave, the streets and towns empty, and once again you can peacefully explore this area in the lush Pyrenees Mountains that is dotted with unspoiled, charming little villages.

THE PAST 🔅 The history of Navarre begins during the Spanish Reconquest. After the Moors were defeated, various Christian kings argued over what to do with the new territory. Some wanted to maintain the land as a buffer kingdom against the Moslems, others, including Sancho the Great, wanted to include it in a greater Christian kingdom. Sancho the Great won out, but upon his death his kingdom was divided between his four sons. Navarre often changed rulers until the French annexation from 1234 to 1512.

Charles III (1387-1425) took the throne of Navarre and promoted a policy of peace between France and Castile while building churches and castles throughout the land. In Olite, Charles spent ten years building this

castle as his summer residence. One of the largest Gothic castles in Spain at the time, it boasted fifteen towers surrounding hanging gardens, corridors, and three hundred and sixty-five chambers (one for each day of the year), as well as interiors with beautiful marquetry ceilings, painted plasterwork, and Moorish *azulejos*.

One of the first recorded instances of bullfighting is preserved at Olite. In 1387 Charles III commanded that ninety pounds be paid to three matadors who valiantly fought some "brave bulls" in the castle's courtyard.

Ironically, it was Charles III's grandson who was responsible for the demise of Olite and Navarre's independence. Left out of the royal succession, he invaded Navarre in 1512 and stormed the castle at Olite. Spanish Navarre became part of Castile while the territory beyond the Pyrenees went to France.

The following centuries were also unkind to the castle. After suffering severe damage in the seventeenth century, it was nearly destroyed during the Napoleonic Wars by a guerrilla leader who preferred to burn it rather than let it fall into the hands of the French.

THE PRESENT 🌀 The parador sits under the three towers that remain from the castle's original fifteen. Inside a massive stone façade devoid of windows, you find welcoming tapestries, wrought-iron chandeliers, red tile floors, an enormous fireplace, and a suit of armor—alas, without the knight.

The best guest rooms are in the historic castle. Balconies look out over part of the castle, a pine grove, or the rolling mountains of Navarre. Two have huge stone fireplaces, wood floors, and four-poster beds. The newer rooms are larger and also nicely furnished.

The dining room features regional dishes such as *cordonices con alubias* (quail cooked with white beans) and *pimientos rellenos* (stuffed red peppers).

Plaza Teobaldos 2, 31390 Olite (Navarra). Tel: 011-34-948-74-00-00. Fax: 011-34-948-74-02-01. **Rooms:** 43, including 1 single, 33 twins, 2 doubles, and 7 suites; all with bath; 16 rooms are in historic castle. **Rates:** Moderate; doubles from 14,500Ptas; tax not included. **Dates closed:** Open all year. **Dining facilities:** Restaurant; bar. **Children:** Under age 2 free; discounts for age 2 through 14 sharing with parents. **Facilities for disabled:** None. **On-site recreation:** None. **Nearby diversions:** Hiking; Pamplona. **Operated as a hotel since:** 1966. **U.S. representative:** Marketing Ahead.

Directions: Olite is 45 kilometers south of Pamplona off A-15. After entering Olite, continue into the old town through the stone archway. The parador is off the main plaza near the train station.

Parador de Oropesa

A Fourteenth-Century Castle-Palace

Sitting in the foothills of the Sierra de Gredos, this majestic castle is one of the oldest paradores in Spain. It commands an extensive view encompassing snowcapped peaks, olive trees, and the whitewashed village of Oropesa.

The region around Oropesa is known for its handicrafts. The neighboring village of Lagartera is famous for its centuries-old tradition of embroidery work, and to the east in Talavera de la Reina, *azulejos* colored in blue and yellow designs are manufactured.

THE PAST This castle is constructed on the site of an earlier fortress said to have been originally built in 1716 B.C. by the soldiers of Hercules. A little more plausible is another legend recounting that the name "Oropesa" is from *"peso de oro"* (peso of gold)—the ransom for a Christian princess.

Whatever structure existed on the site in those early centuries was destroyed during the Christian reconquest. The present square layout of the castle and massive town walls survive from 1366, when Don García de Toledo took command of the castle. In 1402 he added the palace and plaza.

A century later Oropesa became one of the main bases of rebellion

against King Carlos V during the *comunero* revolt, one of the largest uprisings in Spanish history. The Spanish aristocracy and town communes bitterly opposed the ascendancy of the new king, who had never before set foot on Spanish soil and was making demands on the traditional privileges of the nobility. Juan Padilla, leader of the revolt, was supported by Don García Alvarez de Toledo, count of Oropesa, and used the castle for his soldiers. The rebellion was finally put down, Padilla was executed, and the count, threatened with the destruction of his property, swore allegiance to Carlos V. Many years later, after his abdication, the king stayed at the castle on his way to Jarandilla and Yuste.

The parador is housed in the former palace of the counts of Oropesa and the dukes of Ferias. It was formerly known as the "Virrey Toledo," named after a count of Oropesa, Francisco de Toledo, viceroy of Peru from 1569 to 1581. He was renowned for his liberal laws favoring the Peruvian Indians and for the establishment of the famous University of San Marcos in Lima, Peru. In the castle's stairwell, a tile plaque commemorates his career.

THE PRESENT 🦑 After driving through a stone archway, you enter a large parking lot planted with ivy, roses, and cacti. The parador is to one side of the castle and offers a sharp contrast. Its large reception rooms and outdoor corridors remain cool even in the summer heat. Whitewashed walls, tilework, wrought-iron furniture, and potted flowers provide a peaceful and pleasant atmosphere.

Guest rooms are simply decorated, with dark wood furniture and woven drapes and bedspreads, and the spacious bathrooms have marble floors.

The dining room is painted white and accented with dark-beamed ceilings. Since fish and game are abundant in the area, trout, partridge, and quail are on the menu.

The castle ruins can be explored on request.

Plaza Palacio 1, 45560 Oropesa (Toledo). Tel: 011-34-925-43-00-00. Fax: 011-34-925-43-07-77. **Rooms:** 45, including 2 singles, 34 twins, 5 doubles, and 4 suites; all with bath. **Rates:** Moderate; doubles from 14,500Ptas; tax not included. **Dates closed:** Open all year. **Dining facilities:** Restaurant; bar. **Children:** Under age 2 free; discounts for age 2 through 14 sharing with parents. **Facilities for disabled:** None. **On-site recreation:** Seasonal swimming pool. **Nearby diversions:** Walking tour of Oropesa's old town; drives along "embroidery route" and "pottery route." **Operated as a hotel since:** 1930. **U.S. representative:** Marketing Ahead.

Directions: Oropesa is 117 kilometers west of Toledo off National Road V. The 4-lane highway is good, but driving through Talavera de la Reina is slow. Oropesa has train service.

Parador Hotel de los Reyes Católicos

A FIFTEENTH-CENTURY ROYAL HOSPITAL

Nine hundred years ago Santiago de Compostela was the third most holy city of Christendom, after Jerusalem and Rome. The faithful medieval pilgrim risked life and property to journey the way of Saint James ("Santiago" in Spanish) and pay homage to him—the patron saint of Spain.

The dignified and stately Hotel de los Reyes Católicos is a local monument in this historic, romantic city. Excellent restoration efforts have preserved not just the building, but the solemn and mysterious atmosphere of a long-ago era.

THE PAST Tradition claims that Saint James came to Spain to preach Christianity. After seven years he returned to the Holy Land, only to be beheaded by Herod. His followers smuggled his body back to Spain and buried it near his original landing site at the Ulla River. The site was forgotten for several hundred years until a bright star appeared above his grave. During the reconquest soldiers claimed they recognized Saint James as a knight on horseback charging the Moors at a battle near Logroño. Since that time he has been the patron saint of Spain.

Thereafter, nearly a million pilgrims a year streamed over the Pyrenees and made their way across the northern roads of Spain, giving rise to the first tourist guide ever written. In 1130 the Poiton monk Aimeri Picaud described interesting routes, sights, and inhabitants, and advised readers about where the water was safe to drink and which town had the most skillful thieves.

Pilgrims usually took shelter along the in sanctuaries, hospitals, and hospices that were built for this purpose with donations and legacies from wealthy patrons. Not to be outdone, the Catholic monarchs, Ferdinand and Isabel, made a pilgrimage to Santiago and, dismayed at the condition of the ancient hospital next to the cathedral, resolved to "build a Hospital at our expense, which we intend to back with our own income, to receive and shelter the poor, the sick, and the pilgrims." Actually, the money came from contributions and taxes from the land of Granada after the defeat of the Moors. To their credit, Ferdinand and Isabel took a keen interest in every step of the design and construction. Over a period of ten years they commissioned the greatest architects and masters of their time to plan every detail. Although the building was not quite finished, the doors finally opened to pilgrims in 1509. They opened again in 1958 to modern-day guests as the five-star Hotel de los Reyes Católicos.

THE PRESENT ❦ Located on Santiago's main plaza, the hotel faces the cathedral, which can be seen from miles away. The spectacular structure looks more like a monument than a hotel. Its façade features a magnificent Plateresque doorway extending the full height of the building, and four large, open-air patios inside have gardens, fountains, and covered walkways. A gorgeous dome has supporting columns and sixteenth-century gilded wrought-iron grillwork. Paintings by El Greco and Goya grace the walls, while antiques fill every room. Art exhibitions are sometimes held in the public areas.

Accommodations range from simple rooms to lavish suites. One suite—which has been occupied by General Franco and various members of European nobility—features a coffered ceiling, oil paintings on the walls, and a fireplace. It is furnished with an ornate canopy bed, carved chests, and gilt mirrors, and the large, modern green marble bathroom is equipped with heated towel racks. At the other end of the scale are two ten-bed dormitories separated by curtains. In general, the rooms on the third and fourth floors are choice.

The restaurant is in a large stone vaulted room and offers a fine selection of well-prepared regional cuisine. Lighter meals are served in a cafeteria.

One of the Gothic chapels is the setting for weekly concerts. Each year master classes are taught here by an impressive list of international musicians, including the late classical guitarist Andrés Segovia. An interesting story about the maestro relates that he was searching for the perfect room in which to give his classes. He entered the Room of the Dying—which once held the seriously ill and those with contagious diseases so they could attend Mass apart from the other patients—and declared: "This room has almost perfect acoustics. The only thing I need is a mattress to cover that window." So each year a mattress was brought out to cover the window for him.

Plaza del Obradoiro, 15705 Santiago de Compostela (La Coruña). Tel: 011-34-981-58-22-00. Fax: 011-34-981-56-30-94. Rooms: 136, including 12 singles, 104 twins, 14 doubles, and 6 suites; all with bath. **Rates:** Expensive; doubles from 25,000Ptas; tax not included. **Dates closed:** Open all year. **Dining facilities:** Restaurant; cafeteria; bar. **Children:** Under age 2 free; discounts for age 2 through 14 sharing with parents. **Facilities for disabled:** None. **On-site recreation:** None. **Nearby diversions:** The cathedral; walking tour of the old town; horseback riding; golf; tennis. **Operated as a hotel since:** 1958. **U.S. representative:** Marketing Ahead.

Directions: Santiago de Compostela is in the far northwest corner of Spain and is accessible by all forms of transportation. The hotel is in the center of town on the main plaza.

Parador Hotel San Marcos

A SIXTEENTH-CENTURY MONASTERY-HOSPITAL

The medieval city center of León and the dynamic modern city surrounding it combine to offer a cross-cut of Spanish history. Formerly the seat of the ancient kingdom of Asturias and populated by Mozarabs (Christian refugees from the Moslem south), the city reached its peak in the eleventh century. It features three distinct styles of architecture—Romanesque, Gothic, and Renaissance.

León is two hundred miles from the French border and today's starting point for the popular Pilgrim's Route to Santiago. The stalwart medieval pilgrim traditionally began the pilgrimage in Paris, Vezelay, Le Puy, or Arles in France and certainly did not have a luxurious five-star hotel waiting for them in León.

THE PAST 🌸 The pilgrim traveling to Santiago de Compostela during the Middle Ages not only encountered physical hazards but faced bandits and exploitation by dishonest local residents. During the twelfth century the Knights of Santiago, one of the most noble orders of Europe, took charge of protecting pilgrims along the road while at the same time fighting the Moors and serving the king. The archbishop of Santiago de Compostela, impressed by their good works, made their leader an honorary canon of the cathedral. Originally headquartered in Cáceres, the knights relocated to León and founded the hospice of San Marcos.

The original building was razed in the sixteenth century by order of Ferdinand the Catholic, who planned a magnificent edifice worthy of the fame and wealth of the heroic Knights of Santiago after the reconquest. His pledge was finally realized by his grandson, Charles V, who commissioned the architect that created El Escorial. Through the years his glorious building served as a military barracks, a military prison, a veterinary college, and even as a stables.

THE PRESENT 🌸 A stay at the Hotel San Marcos now offers every twentieth-century comfort. (If you're walking or biking the Pilgrim's Route, it can provide you the splurge you'll be dreaming about.) This outstanding Renaissance building ranks as León's third most popular tourist site after the cathedral and the Basilica of St. Isidore. The Plateresque façade measures three-hundred-and-twenty-eight feet long and two stories high. The friezes, columns, and pilasters are amazing. Medallions in relief depict famous personalities from the Bible and Roman and Spanish history—including Judith and Lucretia on either side of Isabel the Catholic, Hercules, David, Julius Caesar, El Cid, and Philip II. Events from the life of St. James are depicted in Baroque ornamentation over the main entrance.

The lobby is like a small museum with carvings, tapestries, and paintings hung beneath a sixteenth-century vaulted ceiling. The hotel's public rooms are furnished with both antiques and reproductions. Cloisters standing two stories high surround a courtyard garden planted with ivy, shrubs, and trees. The Provincial Archaeological Museum boasts the exquisite eleventh-century carved ivory Crucifix of Carrizo. This museum is part of the still-used Gothic Church of San Marcos, which features a façade adorned with sculpted cockleshells.

The guest rooms are in three different areas: in the main building and towers, "cells" in the old section of the building, and in a newer wing with modern decor. Some rooms have four-poster beds and views of the cloisters; others have views of the parking lot. But any room allows you to relive history in an indulgent manner undreamed of by any pilgrim.

An elegant dining room looks out on the river. The Castilian cuisine includes *sopa Leonesa* (a trout, bread, paprika, and garlic soup) and *cecinas de vaca curada* (a thinly sliced smoked beef dish). A night club provides evening entertainment.

Plaza de San Marcos 7, 24001 León. Tel: 011-34-987-23-73-00. Fax: 011-34-987-23-32-58. Rooms: 200, including 170 twins, 15 doubles, and 15 suites; all with bath. **Rates:** Expensive; doubles from 18,000Ptas; tax not included. **Dates closed:** Open all year. **Dining facilities:** Restaurant; bar. **Children:** Under age 2 free; discounts for age 2 through 14 sharing with parents. **Facilities for disabled:** Yes. **On-site recreation:** None. **Nearby diversions:** Horseback riding; Alpine skiing; tennis; golf; fishing; hunting; the medieval town of León and its cathedral. **Operated as a hotel since:** 1965. **U.S. representative:** Marketing Ahead.

Directions: Located in the northern region of Old Castile, León is served by train and bus. To reach the hotel, go to the town center. Next to the Bernesga River is a roundabout with a fountain in the middle. A signpost marked "San Marcos" directs you north along the river to the hotel.

Parador de Sigüenza

A Twelfth-Century Castle

To spend a night in this imposing stone castle in the heartland of Spain is to pass through nearly fifteen hundred years of Spanish history. Now classified as a Spanish National Monument, Sigüenza has such a peaceful atmosphere that it is difficult to imagine the battles and royal intrigues that went on here for centuries.

THE PAST 🌀 Once called Segontia, the ancient town of Sigüenza was a major center even before the Roman conquest. After a long campaign, the Romans finally subdued Sigüenza, destroying it completely. Later, the Moors recognized the strategic importance of the site and built an *alcazaba*.

During the period of the reconquest the fortress changed hands several times (El Cid once took possession). In 1124 Bishop Bernardo de Agen claimed ownership, and from then on the fortress became the residence of the one hundred bishops of Sigüenza.

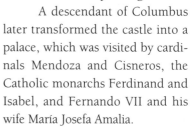

A descendant of Columbus later transformed the castle into a palace, which was visited by cardinals Mendoza and Cisneros, the Catholic monarchs Ferdinand and Isabel, and Fernando VII and his wife María Josefa Amalia.

Through the centuries the castle housed soldiers from various countries, including the troops of Archduke Charles of Austria, the pretender to the Spanish throne during the War of Spanish Succession; Napoleon's troops during the War of Independence; and Carlist troops (supporters of Don Carlos, an unsuccessful pretender to the Spanish throne).

After centuries of abuse, the castle was left in ruins. The prelate of the diocese sold it in 1941 to the Ministry of Education and Science for a little more than two hundred thousand pesetas. Still nothing happened, and the castle seemed doomed to crumble away.

Fortunately, in 1971 the Ministry of Tourism chose the castle for restoration and conversion into a national parador. Reconstruction began under the direction of architect Dr. D. José Luis Picardo, and after three years the huge stone castle faithfully resembled its former glorious self. In 1978 King Juan Carlos and Doña Sofia presided at the parador's inauguration.

THE PRESENT The thick walls of this trapezoidal castle surround a courtyard featuring a well remaining from the Moorish period. Its entrance, flanked by twin towers, faces the town and has remained unchanged for seven centuries. Smaller towers flank the castle's western side, and beneath them is a labyrinth of subterranean rooms, cellars, and dungeons. Decoration inside is in a medieval style, with one public lounge featuring two fireplaces, several enormous chandeliers, suits of armor, tapestries, and bright banners.

Like the rest of the castle, guest rooms are spotlessly clean and simply furnished with carved wooden furniture and handwoven rugs. Some have large canopy beds and balconies looking out over a valley filled with orchards and pine trees.

A wood-beamed ceiling highlights the main dining room. The menu features Castilian dishes such as roast kid, lamb, and succulent pork in wine sauce. An enormous grand dining room used for special events has a series of impressive arches. Called the Comedor de Doña Blanca, its namesake was an ill-fated woman who was imprisoned here by her husband, Pedro the Cruel. King Juan Carlos and his wife, Doña Sofia, once hosted a state banquet here.

Plaza del Castillo s/n, 19250 Sigüenza (Guadalajara). Tel: 011-34-949-39-01-00. Fax: 011-34-949-39-13-64. Rooms: 81, including 3 singles, 68 twins, 6 doubles, and 4 suites; all with bath. **Rates:** Moderate; doubles from 12,500Ptas; tax not included. **Dates closed:** Open all year. **Dining facilities:** Restaurant; bar. **Children:** Under age 2 free; discounts for age 2 through 14 sharing with parents; play area. **Facilites for disabled:** None. **On-site recreation:** Gymnasium; sauna. **Nearby diversions:** Walks through the medieval town; the cathedral (which displays an El Greco painting and the "Doncel"—a fine example of Spanish sepulchral art); Museo Antigua (with a painting by Zurbarán). **Operated as a hotel since:** 1976. **U.S. representative:** Marketing Ahead.

Directions: Sigüenza is 135 kilometers northeast of Madrid. From the main Madrid-Zaragoza highway (National Road II), turn off onto C-204. A sign for the parador shows the way. Sigüenza is a stop on the main Madrid-Zaragoza railway.

Parador de Úbeda

A Sixteenth-Century Palace

Andalusia brings to mind images of the Moorish architecture of Córdoba, Granada, and Seville. Flamenco dancers, sherry, and sun-worshipping towns along the Costa del Sol complete the picture. But there is another, less well-known side of Andalusia. In the northern province of Jaén, you can explore the remarkably well-preserved Spanish Renaissance town of Úbeda. Now a Spanish National Monument, this charming town features narrow cobblestone streets and many aristocratic mansions and churches.

THE PRESENT 🐚 Relics in the town's archaeology museum tell us that Úbeda's origins date back to the Paleolithic era and Roman times. Captured from the Moors in 1234, the town served as a stronghold in the Christian reconquest.

By the sixteenth century, this prosperous town was completely transformed. When the Habsburg emperor Charles V ascended the throne in 1516, Spain enjoyed its golden Renaissance age as Spanish architects and craftsmen accepted the Italian styles in their work. Úbeda reflects this trend. The Plaza Vázquez de Molina is the monumental center of the town. It is surrounded by buildings of this era, one of which is the parador.

Many of the most beautiful buildings were designed by Andrés de Vandelvira and Diego de Siloé, two of the greatest architects of the era. The fine iron grill work on the church of Santa María (and on the royal chapel in Granada) was wrought by Master Bartolomé.

The most famous personage to come out of Úbeda was Francisco de los Cobos, who rose from poverty to become chief secretary to Charles V. It was Cobos who essentially ruled Spain during Charles V's long absences. He laid the foundations of Spanish bureaucracy and presided over the financial demise of Spain as a result of Charles's disastrous foreign adventures. Much of Úbeda's prosperity and glory was due to the influence of Cobos.

THE PRESENT 🐚 Though the parador faces the plaza with a rather plain façade, inside you find a charming courtyard filled with plants and blue tile-work and enclosed by two levels of Moorish arches. To one side of the courtyard are a sitting room and library. Another large room with stone arches and low beams is used for special festivals (three giant barrels filled with wine are on hand for such occasions).

A large stairway leads up to the guest rooms, which feature high ceilings and spacious bathrooms. The period furnishings are mostly tasteful reproductions, but some are antiques. Throughout, attention is given to detail, such as floors inlaid with small hand-painted tiles of animals and Andalusian scenes.

The dining room is a friendly place, with Andalusian cuisine presented by waitresses dressed in traditional costume. The three-course meals often include garlic soup, rabbit, and quail.

Plaza de Vázquez Molin s/n, 23400 Úbeda (Jaén). Tel: 011-34-953-75-03-45. Fax: 011-34-953-75-12-59. Rooms: 31, including 23 twins, 7 doubles, and 1 suite; all with bath. **Rates:** Moderate; doubles from 16,500Ptas; tax not included. **Dates closed:** Open all year. **Dining facilities:** Restaurant; bar. **Children:** Under age 2 free; discounts for age 2 through 14 sharing with parents. **Facilities for disabled:** None. **On-site recreation:** None. **Nearby diversions:** Walking tours of Úbeda; Baeza and its wonderful old plaza. **Operated as a hotel since:** 1930. **U.S. representative:** Marketing Ahead.

Directions: Úbeda is 42 kilometers east of Bailén, which is located on National Road IV (the Madrid-Córdoba highway). Trains and buses connect Úbeda to Jaén, Linares, and Baeza. In town, signs marked "parador" lead the way through the narrow twisting streets.

Parador de Villalba

A Fifteenth-Century Tower

Though the town of Villalba isn't a must-see, what it lacks in breath-taking wonders is more than compensated for by one of the most charming paradores in Spain.

THE PAST 🌀 This fine example of a Galician keep is all that remains of what was once a great fortress. No one is quite sure of the tower's origins, but historians place it somewhere between the eleventh and thirteenth centuries.

The Castro family from Castile owned the castle until the middle of the fourteenth century, when Pedro I transferred the property to the Andrade family. This family did much for the community by building monasteries, churches, and hospitals.

One hundred years later the castle was rebuilt. Though there is no record of the castle's demise, in the twentieth century all that the government could salvage from the rubble was the tower.

THE PRESENT 🌀 After crossing the dry moat on a tiny wooden bridge, you enter the tower through an arched portcullised doorway into a two-story-high entry hall. A medieval atmosphere prevails with arrow-slit windows set in ten-foot-thick walls, wrought-iron light sconces, horseshoe archways, and frescos of medieval scenes decorating the walls (one of these scenes commemorates the victory over the French in Italy by the second count Fernán de Andrade).

Each of the three floors above reception holds two guest rooms. You can either climb a winding stairway past the arrow-slit windows to your room or take an elevator. The surprisingly large rooms have beamed ceilings and hardwood floors and are simply furnished with wooden headboards, writing desks, and wrought-iron reading lamps. To see out of the tiny windows, you must walk into the recesses of eight-foot-thick walls.

In keeping with the baronial atmosphere, the castle's restaurant has wrought-iron chandeliers, and antlers decorate the whitewashed walls. Galician specialties include shoulder of pork with parsnip and *pollo con piñones* (a dish made with chicken, pine nuts, tomatoes, peppers, and onions). The town's famous San Simón cheese (a firm, lightly smoked cream cheese) and *roscón de Villalba* (an almond-flavored cake) are also served.

 Calle Valeriano Valdesuso s/n, 27800 Villalba (Lugo). Tel: 011-34-982-51-00-11. Fax: 011-34-982-51-00-90. Rooms: 6 doubles; all with bath. **Rates:** Moderate; doubles from 10,500Ptas; tax not included. **Dates closed:** Open all year. **Dining facilities:** Restaurant; bar. **Children:** Under age 2 free; discounts for age 2 through 14 sharing with parents. **Facilities for disabled:** None. **On-site recreation:** None. **Nearby diversions:** Tennis; hiking. **Operated as a hotel since:** 1967. **U.S. representative:** Marketing Ahead.

Directions: Villalba is 36 kilometers north of Lugo in Galicia on N-634. The parador is in the center of town and signposted. Local buses stop in town, but there is no train connection.

Parador de Zafra

A Fifteenth-Century Castle

The ruggedly beautiful region in southwest Spain known as Extremadura features bleak mountains and empty plains populated only by sheep. The best time to visit is in spring, when the meadows bloom with daisies and red poppies. Extremadura is also one of the poorer regions of Spain, a fact that spurred many conquistadors to leave the region in search of riches in the New World.

Zafra is a pleasant town and a convenient base for excursions throughout the Extremadura region: to Mérida, famous for its Roman monuments; and Trujillo, the birthplace of Pizarro. It is also a stopping-off point for an easy drive into Portugal.

THE PAST 🦪 Zafra is an ancient site, fortified first by the Celto-Iberians and later by the Romans. The Moors captured the area and built a great *alcázar*. Many of the narrow, twisting streets and whitewashed walls of today's town reflect their influence.

The castle is built on the foundations of the *alcázar* in a square plan, with a round tower at each corner and two more flanking the entryway. In the rear, a massive round keep looks out over the town. This present structure, commissioned by Lorenzo de Figueroa, was begun in 1437 and took six years to finish. His shield and that of his wife, Doña María Manuel, hang over the doorway.

In the sixteenth century Juan de Herrera, the architect of the Escorial, added an inner courtyard surrounded by archways and Doric columns of white marble, as well as some outside terraces and galleries. Two very fine examples of Gothic-*Mudéjar* artistry are the chapel, with an octagonal cupola designed by Don Lorenzo in the sixteenth century, and the Sala Dorada—a noble's room adorned with a carved, gilded ceiling.

Through the centuries the dukes of Feria—members of one of the most noble houses of Spain—held court at the castle. One of their more notable guests was the conquistador Hernán Cortés, who lived here before setting off for the New World.

THE PRESENT 🦪 Rated four stars, this hotel offers every modern convenience, including air conditioning and central heating, yet retains its authentic ancient atmosphere. A lounge has paintings of Cortés on its walls, and well-groomed gardens invite leisurely walks. At night, the great wooden

doors creak open atmospherically, and the white marble columns glow with a luminescence in the dark.

Guest rooms are large and comfortable and furnished in excellent taste.

A charming dining room offers several different varieties of smoked ham (a specialty of Extremadura) as well as lamb, pheasant, and trout.

Plaza Corazón de María 7, 06300 Zafra (Badajoz). Tel: 011-34-924-55-45-40. **Fax:** 011-34-924-55-10-18. **Rooms:** 45, including 37 twins, 7 doubles, and 1 suite; all with bath. **Rates:** Moderate; doubles from 14,500Ptas; tax not included. **Dates closed:** Open all year. **Dining facilities:** Restaurant; bar. **Children:** Under age 2 free; discounts for age 2 through 14 sharing with parents. **Facilities for disabled:** None. **On-site recreation:** Seasonal swimming pool. **Nearby diversions:** Horseback riding; trekking. **Operated as a hotel since:** 1968. **U.S. representative:** Marketing Ahead.

Directions: Zafra is located off N-630 and N-432. It also can be reached by bus or train. Directions to the castle are signposted as you come into town.

Parador de Zamora

A FIFTEENTH-CENTURY PALACE

Conquering princes, powerful kingdoms, and a Spanish folk hero are all part of the former glory of Zamora. Rising from the plains of Old Castile, with protective walls and the Duero River to one side, the city looks impregnable. Zamora is known as the "Museum of Romanesque Art." Here, as in many cities in Spain, the ancient and modern lie side by side.

Though noted for its Romanesque architecture, Zamora is not visited by tourists as often as are the Spanish cities offering more famous cathedrals and Holy Week processions. Still, the city makes a good base for excursions around the region of Old Castile.

THE PAST 🌀 On the way to the parador, travelers pass through a narrow archway flanked by two towers inscribed with *"Afuera! Afuera! Rodrigo el soberbio castellano"* ("Away! Away! Rodrigo the proud Castilian"). More commonly known as El Cid, Rodrigo Díaz de Vivar was born in 1043 to a Castilian family of lesser nobility. As was the custom of the time, he was sent to be educated at the court of the Emperor Ferdinand. Under Ferdinand's son, Sancho II, he soon rose to chief military commander and is thought to have been knighted in the eleventh-century church of Santiago de los Caballeros in Zamora.

Before Ferdinand died, he broke from Leonese tradition and divided his kingdom among his three sons. Two of the sons, Sancho II and Alfonso VI, carried out a long and bitter feud. El Cid, commanding Sancho's armies, defeated Alfonso on two occasions, forcing him to seek refuge at Moorish Toledo. Sancho and Alfonso's sister, Doña Urraca, supported Alfonso's claims. Doña Urraca barricaded herself in the fortress of Zamora, Alfonso's stronghold. A siege was laid on the city by El Cid. (The motto, *"Zamora no se ganó en una hora"*—"Zamora was not won in an hour"—can be seen on carved stone shields in the town.) One Sunday an assassin slipped out from the walls and stabbed Sancho to death. Alfonso promptly returned to take possession, and El Cid, before swearing allegiance to him, requested that Alfonso swear an oath of noncomplicity in the assassination of his brother. Although both men were major figures in the reconquest of Spain, their relationship was never friendly. Eventually banished from Castile, El Cid found fame and fortune in Valencia.

Located in the center of the old city, two blocks from the Plaza Mayor, the parador occupies the site of a former Roman castle. The palace was built in 1459 by the first count of Alba y Aliste, a member of one of Spain's foremost noble families. The building was heavily damaged during the *comunero* rebellion during the time of Carlos V. Rebuilt and embellished by the fourth count, it was converted to a hospice for elderly people in 1798.

THE PRESENT Combining a

feeling of austerity and splendor, this large stone structure opens onto an impressive cloistered courtyard surrounded by glass partitions. A monumental stone staircase with Lombard carvings leads up to glassed-in balconies. Beautiful antique furniture, tapestries, and carpets adorn the hallways and rooms. Old armor, chests, wood paneling, fireplaces, and potted plants complete the picture.

The newly renovated guest rooms are large and comfortable.

The dining room has a view of the swimming pool and the distant countryside. Its menu features roast kid and other Castilian specialties as well as a full-bodied red wine from the nearby vineyards of Toro.

Plaza de Viriato 5, 49001 Zamora. Tel: 011-34-980-51-44-97. Fax: 011-34-980-53-00-63. Rooms 27, including 21 twins, 4 doubles, and 2 suites; all with bath. **Rates:** Moderate; doubles from 13,500Ptas; tax not included. **Dates closed:** Open all year. **Dining facilities:** Restaurant; bar. **Children:** Under age 2 free; discounts for age 2 through 14 sharing with parents. **Facilities for disabled:** None. **On-site recreation:** None. **Nearby diversions:** Walking tour of the old city; street processions during Holy Week. **Operated as a hotel since:** 1968. **U.S. representative:** Marketing Ahead.

Directions: Zamora is 62 kilometers north of Salamanca on N-630. Buses and trains link Salamanca with Zamora.

Adare Manor:
Tel: 800-462-3273. Website: http://www.adaremanor.ie/.

Best Western Hotels:
Tel: 800-528-1234. Website: http://www.bestwestern.com/.

BTH Hotels: Tel: 800-221-1074.

Consort Hotels Ltd.: Tel: 800-552-6676.

Dromoland/Ashford Castles: Tel: 800-346-7007.

E & M Associates: Tel: 800-223-9832.

Euro-Connection:
Tel: 800-645-3876. Website: http://www.euro-connection.com/.

Grand Heritage Hotels International:
Tel: 800-437-4824. Website: http://www.grandheritage.com.

Josephine Barr: Tel: 800-323-5463.

The Leading Hotels of the World:
Tel: 800-223-6800. Website: http://www.interactive.line.com/lead.

The Luxury Collection—ITT Sheraton:
Tel: 800-325-3535. Website: http://www.sheraton.com.

Marketing Ahead: Tel: 800-223-1356.

McFarland Ltd.: Tel: 800-437-2687.

Pinto Basto:
Tel: 800-345-0739. Website: http://www.pousada.com/psada5.htm.

Preferred Hotels and Resorts: Tel: 800-323-7500.
Website: http://www.preferredhotels.com/preferred.html.

Premier World Marketing: Tel: 800-877-3643.

Relais & Châteaux: Tel: 212-856-0115. Fax: 800-860-4930.
Website: http://www.integra.fr/relaischateaux/.

Schlosshotels:
Tel: 800-828-8485. Website: http://www.travelfile.com/get/ddiintl.html.

Scots-American Travel: Tel: 800-247-7268.

Small Luxury Hotels of the World:
Tel: 800-525-4800. Website: http://www.slh.com.

Utell International:
Tel: 800-448-8355. Website: http://www.utell.com/.

Resources

Castles for sale. Website: http://www.dnai.com:80/~ted/castle.html. German castles that are for sale.

Castle hotels on the web.
Website: http://www.bpe.com/travel/europe/castles.

Castles on the web. Website: http://fox.nstn.ca/~tmonk/castle/castle. This top-rated web page devoted to castles has links to castles around the world.

Custom castle tours. Worthy International Travel, London. Tel: 011-44-171-824-8995. Fax: 011-44-171-824-8545. Arranges tours of private British castles that include meeting with the titled owners.

Educational organization. Europa Nostra. Tel: 011-31-0-70-3560333. Fax: 011-31-0-70-3617865. Mail: Lange Voorhout 35, The Hague, The Netherlands, 2514EC.
Now merged with the International Castles Institute, this membership organization publishes a bi-annual magazine and sponsors conferences and study tours.

Packaged castle tours. Leave the planning to someone else.

- **Abercrombie & Kent International.** Tel: 800-323-7308 or 800-98-PRIDE. Website: www.abercrombiekent.com.
  Pride of Britain hotels offer "A Medieval Tour" (with stays in two castles) and "Garden Tours" (with tours of several manor and castle gardens and stays in several manor houses and a castle).

- **Chateaux Bike Tours.** Tel: 800-678-BIKE or 303-393-6910. Fax: 303-393-6801.
  Luxury bicycle tours through France with overnight stays in castles.

- **Ciclismo Classico.** Tel: 800-866-7314.
  Bicycle trip with castle stay in Tuscany.

- **Collette Tours.** Tel: 401-728-3805. Fax: 401-728-1380.
  The "English Castles & Countryside" tour includes several castle tours and a two-night stay in a private castle.

- **In the English Manner.** Tel: 800-422-0799 or 213-629-1811. Fax: 213-689-8784
  All-inclusive tours, or room reservations in privately owned castles.

- **Pinto Basto.** Tel: 800-345-0739.
  Website: http://www.pousada.com/psada5.htm.
  Escorted tours to the Portuguese pousadas.

- **Posh Journeys.** Tel: 702-852-5105.
  All-inclusive tours to Italy, Germany, and Norway that combine day visits to castle museums and overnight stays in castle hotels.

- **Untours.** Tel: 610-565-5242. Fax: 610-565-5142.
  Website: www.untours.com.
  Affordable two- and four-week apartment rentals in a fourteenth-century moated Bavarian castle; includes air and car.

- **The Wayfarers.** Tel: 800-249-4620.
  Walking tours of the border castles of Wales.

Rent a castle. For details, contact:

- **At Home Abroad.** Tel: 212-421-9165.

- **Country Cottages.** Tel: 800-674-8883 or 407-395-5618 (handles Great Britain only)

- **Rentals in Italy.** Tel: 800-726-6702 or 805-987-5278.
  Fax: 805-482-7976.

- **Villas International.** Tel: 800-221-2260. Fax: 415-281-0919.

Study about castles.
The Oxford Berkeley Program, co-sponsored by the Department for Continuing Education of the University of Oxford and University Extension at the University of California at Berkeley, has in the past offered "Castles and Country Houses: A Social, Economic, and Architectural Study."
Tel: 510-642-4111. Fax: 510-642-0374.

Glossary

A

abbatial — pertains to an abbot

alcazaba — a Moorish defensive structure including massive square towers, extensive walls, and labrythine paths

alcázar — a Moorish palace built around a garden; from the Arabic word *qasr*

armory — a storage place for weapons

arrow-slit window — a very narrow window that permits only an arrow to pass through

azulejos — glazed ornamental earthenware tiles of Moorish origins

B

balustrade — a railing with closely spaced supports

barbican — a house or tower that defends a castle's gate

baronial — pertaining to a baron or noble of the landowner class

Baroque — a highly ornamental style of architecture from the seventeenth to the mid-eighteenth centuries

barrel vault — a deeply arched vault having the appearance of a tunnel

bastion — a projection from a wall or tower

battlements — a parapet alternating on the top with crenels and merlons; sometimes called crenellations

Benedictine — from the monastic order founded by St. Benedict in 530

blazon — a coat of arms

blockhouse — a small square fortification

bow — an ancient Norman gateway

burg — a German fortified castle

C

cairn — an ancient burial mound

capitals — the top of a column

caput — a stone installed on a hearth signifying a title

casemate — a chamber in a rampart with openings for arrows

castellan — governor of a castle

catapult — an offensive device for hurling stones over a castle's walls

chevron — zigzag molding or design

Cistercian — a branch of the Benedictine monastic order

coffers — sunken square or octagonal ceiling panels

cornice — decorative projection along the top of a wall

coronet — a title for a junior officer

crenel — the open space between two merlons on a battlement

crenellate — to build a castle

curtain wall — a wall connecting various castle elements

D

doge — an Italian chief magistrate

donjon — a keep

dovecote — shelter for doves

drawbridge — a heavy bridge that could be raised or lowered over a moat

E

Elizabethan — from the period of Queen Elizabeth I of England (1558-1603)

embrasure — a space in a wall or battlement that has a wide opening on the inside tapering to a narrow slit on the exterior used for shooting at the enemy

enceinte — the enclosure or fortified area of a castle

escutcheon — a shield on which a coat of arms is depicted

F

Franciscan — from the monastic order founded by St. Francis of Assisi in the 13th century

free quarry — a quarry open to everyone

frieze — a decorative band of sculture between the top of a wall's projections

G

gallery — a long, covered walkway or corridor

garderobe — a medieval toilet

Georgian — from the period of King George I, II, III, and IV of England (1740-1830)

Gildenmeester — a Dutch consul

Gothic — a style of architecture from the 12th and 16th centuries characterized by pointed arches and ribbed vaults

great hall — a principal building that held the meeting and dining areas

J

Jacobean — from the period of King James I of England, (1603-1625)

K

keep — a castle's main tower

L

lancet — a high, narrow window with an arched top

loophole — a tall, narrow wall slit for looking or shooting

M

machiolation — a projecting gallery on castle or tower's outside, with holes in the floor from where oil is poured or rocks thrown

mangonel — an offensive device with projectile arms that turn and throw rocks

Manueline — from the period of King Manueline I of Portugal (1495-1521)

merlon — the solid stone between two crenels on a battlement

minstrel's gallery — an area where the musicians performed

moat — a protective ditch surrounding a castle, usually filled with water

Moor — a loose term for a Muslim of Berber-Arab blood living in northwest Africa or Spain

motte and bailey — an earth mound with a keep made of wood or stone surrounded by a palisade enclosure

Mudéjar — a Gothic style of Muslim art with a strong

Moorish influence; developed in Spain after the Christian reconquest from the 11th to the 15th centuries

mullion — a vertical piece of stone or wood dividing a window

murder hole — a place between the castle gate and inner portcullis where an attacker was vulnerable to hot oil, rocks, and arrows thrown down from the roof above

oriel window — a bay window

oubliette — a dungeon entered by a trap door; from the French word *oublier,* which means "to forget"

palisade — a defensive fence of wooden stakes set firmly in the ground

parapet — a low wall sometimes placed on the top of a rampart

passant — British expression that describes the lion in official seals, emblems, flags, etc.

pilaster — a rectangular wall projection with capital and base imitating a column

Plateresque — an intricate, lavish style of stonework decorating building façades in Renaissance Spain; from the Spanish word *plata* because the effect resembled fine silverwork

portcullis — a strong grating made of iron or wood that dropped along grooves in a doorway to prevent passage

Portland stone — a type of manufactured stone

postern — a castle's back door or gate

Q

quadrangle — an inner courtyard

quattrocento — an Italian designation referring to the 15th century

R

rampart — a defensive stone or earth wall surrounding a castle or town

refectory — a communal dining hall

Romanesque — a style of architecture from the 9th to the 12th centuries using heavy masonry, round arches, and barrel vaults

S

schloss — a German castle or baronial mansion, usually a little more elegant than a burg

sovereign — a king or ruler

T

tracery — decorative intersecting ribwork in the upper part of a window

turret — a small round tower often used as a lookout

V

vassal — a person granted land in return for military service

vault — an arched ceiling

W

wicket — a small door forming part of a larger one

Select Annotated Bibliography

Castle Cats of Britain & Ireland, by Richard Surman (HarperCollins, ©1995). This utterly charming book features text plus color photos of cats making themselves at home in their castles.

Castles and Fortresses, by Robin S. Oggins (MetroBooks—Friedman/Fairfax Publishers, ©1995). With glorious color photographs of major European castles, this book tells you how castles evolved and what life was really like inside.

Castles of England, Scotland and Wales, by Paul Johnson (HarperPerennial—HarperCollins, ©1989). Beautiful color photographs illustrate an educational text. Operating schedule for each castle is included.

Cathedrals and Castles: Building in the Middle Ages, by Alain Erlande-Brandenburg (Harry N. Abrams, ©1995). Explains the nitty-gritty about castles.

For Children

Castle, by David Macaulay (Sandpiper—Houghton Mifflin, ©1977). Detailed line drawings and text describe how an imaginary typical castle and adjoining town were constructed in thirteenth-century Wales.

Castles of the World Coloring Book, by A.G. Smith (Dover Publications, ©1986). A great introduction to the subject.

Easy-to-Make Playtime Castle, by A.G. Smith (Dover Publications, ©1987). Especially designed for ages 4 through 10, this cut, fold, and glue castle comes complete with a drawbridge and ten armored knights.

Gwendolyn's Gifts, by Patty Sheehan (Pelican Publishing Company, ©1991). Illustrated with nice watercolors, this sweet little story tells of a Queen who finds fulfillment by developing her own abilities.

Knights in Shining Armor, by Gail Gibbons (Little, Brown and Company, ©1995). Describes the skills needed to become a knight and provides detailed illustrations of their armor and weaponry.

Life in a Medieval Castle and Village Coloring Book, by John Green (Dover Publications, ©1990). Realistically depicts daily life in a castle, castle sieges, and other events.

Mystery History of a Medieval Castle, by Jim Pipe (Copper Beech Books, ©1996). Discover what it was like to live in a medieval castle. Clues, puzzles, and mazes help you track down a deadly assassin as he murders his way through feasts, tournaments, and sieges. Fun and educational for adults, too.

Nora's Castle, by Satomi Ichikawa (PaperStar/Putnam & Grosset Group, ©1986). A little girl explores a deserted castle at the edge of her village and makes friends with a variety of animals.

Note: All books can be ordered through Carousel Press.

TOP TENS

(listed in alphabetical order)

MOST ROMANTIC

Domaine de Castel Novel (France)
Château de la Chèvre d'Or (France)
Cliveden (England)
Hotel Danieli (Italy)
Hotel Schloss Dürnstein (Austria)
Château d'Esclimont (France)
Inverlochy Castle (Scotland)
Burg Hotel-Restaurant auf Schönburg
   (Germany)
Château de la Treyne (France)
Villa d'Este (Italy)

WHEN MONEY IS NO OBJECT

Château de la Chèvre d'Or (France)
Cliveden (England)
Hotel Danieli (Italy)
Château d'Esclimont (France)
Hotel Gritti Palace (Italy)
Inverlochy Castle (Scotland)
Schlosshotel Kronberg (Germany)
Hotel im Palais Schwarzenberg
   (Austria)
Thornbury Castle (England)
Villa d'Este (Italy)

STILL OWNED BY NOBILITY

Parkhotel Wasserburg Anholt (Germany)
Hotel Schloss Auel (Germany)
Schloss Ernegg (Austria)
Wald & Schlosshotel Friedrichsruhe
   (Germany)
Kilravock Castle (Scotland)
Jagdschloss Kühtai (Austria)
Leslie Castle (Scotland)
Hotel im Palais Schwarzenberg (Austria)
Thornbury Castle (England)
Schloss Weitenburg (Germany)

FOR THE SPORTSMAN

Adare Manor (Ireland)
Ashford Castle (Ireland)
Cliveden (England)
Inverlochy Castle (Scotland)
Kilkea Castle (Ireland)
Hotel Schloss Leonstain (Austria)
Hotel Schloss Pichlarn (Austria)
Villa d'Este (Italy)
Grand Hotel Villa Serbelloni (Italy)
Waterford Castle (Ireland)

BEST VIEWS

Hotel Cappuccini Convento (Italy)
Château de la Chèvre d'Or (France)
Hotel Danieli (Italy)
Hotel Schloss Fuschl (Austria)
Inverlochy Castle (Scotland)
Hotel Schloss Labers (Italy)
Pousada de São Filipe (Portugal)
Burg Hotel-Restaurant auf Schönburg
   (Germany)
Château de Trigance (France)
Villa d'Este (Italy)

CHEAP SLEEPS

Château de la Caze (France)
Schloss Ernegg (Austria)
Burghotel Götzenburg (Germany)
Burg Hornberg (Germany)
Kilravock Castle (Scotland)
Burghotel Lauenstein (Germany)
Lundy Castle (England)
Castle Matrix (Ireland)
Romantik Hotel Post (Austria)
Hotel Restaurant Burg Reichenstein
   (Germany)

FAMILY-FRIENDLY

Palace Hotel do Buçaco (Portugal)
Château de la Caze (France)
Cliveden (England)
Dornröschenschloss Sababurg
   (Germany)
Hotel Schloss Leonstain (Austria)
Lundy Castle (England)
Markree Castle (Ireland)
Hotel Schloss Pichlarn (Austria)
Saddell Castle (Scotland)
Villa d'Este (Italy)

AUTHOR'S FAVORITES

Parador de Alarcón (Spain)
Palace Hotel do Buçaco (Portugal)
Domaine de Castel Novel (France)
Hotel Schloss Dürnstein (Austria)
Château d'Esclimont (France)
Lundy Castle (England)
Burg Hotel-Restaurant auf Schönburg
   (Germany)
Thornbury Castle (England)
Château de Trigance (France)
Château de la Treyne (France)

MILES OF SMILES:
101 Great Car Games & Activities

Anyone who has ever been trapped in a hot car with bored kids is well aware that the world needs a sure-fire way of easing the resulting tensions. This clever book fills that need. In fact, according to one enthusiastic user it just "may be the ultimate solution for back seat squabbling." The book is filled with games and activities that have travel-related themes. Ninety-seven require just your minds and mouths to play, and the other four need only simple props: a penny, a pencil, and some crayons. A helpful index categorizes each game and activity according to age appropriateness, and humorous illustrations that kids can color add to everyone's enjoyment. *128 pages. $8.95.*

THE ZOO BOOK:
A Guide to America's Best

Detailed descriptions of the top 53 U.S. zoos are included. The author has visited each zoo, and his review includes hours and admission fees, driving and bus directions, don't-miss exhibits, touring tips to make a visit easier and more efficient, and details on the entertainment available. Each zoo's featured exhibits are highlighted—plus other exhibits are described, special attractions for the kids are noted, and what's new at the zoo is discussed. Smaller zoos, aquariums, and other places that display animals are also described, as are noteworthy zoos in Canada, Mexico, Europe, and other areas of the world. An entire chapter is devoted to descriptions and photos of interesting zoo animals. *288 pages. $14.95.*

THE FAMILY TRAVEL GUIDE:
An Inspiring Collection of Family-Friendly Vacations

These meaty tales from the trenches promise to help you avoid some of the pitfalls of traveling with children. Information is included on hot spots of family travel (California, Hawaii, Washington D.C., Europe) as well as on lesser-touted havens (Las Vegas, New York City, Belize, Jamaica), and how-to-do-it details are provided on home exchanging, RVing, selecting souvenirs, and traveling with teens. *The New York Times* says this "is clearly the book for parents who prefer their reading to be more *National Geographic* than 'Hints from Heloise.' " *432 pages. $16.95.*

WEEKEND ADVENTURES
IN NORTHERN CALIFORNIA

The vacation riches of Northern California are detailed—including the Gold Rush country, ski resorts, and family camps. This award-winning book covers where to stay, where to eat, and what to do and also provides appropriate information for families—such as the availability of highchairs, booster seats, and cribs. Don't leave home without it! *416 pages. $17.95.*

TO ORDER DIRECT
call Carousel Press at 510-527-5849